INTERNATIONAL HANDBOOK OF FUNERAL CUSTOMS

INTERNATIONAL HANDBOOK OF FUNERAL CUSTOMS

KODO MATSUNAMI

GREENWOOD PRESS
Westport, Connecticut • London

Library of Congress Cataloging-in-Publication Data

Matsunami, Kōdō, 1933–
    International handbook of funeral customs / Kodo Matsunami.
      p. cm.
    Includes bibliographical references and index.
    ISBN 0–313–30443–2 (alk. paper)
    1. Funeral rites and ceremonies. I. Title.
  GT3150.M27   1998
  393′.9—DC21   97–43929

British Library Cataloguing in Publication Data is available.

Library of Congress Catalog Card Number: 97–43929
ISBN: 0–313–30443–2

First publsihed in 1998

Greenwood Press, 88 Post Road Westport, CT 06881
An imprint of Greenwood Publishing Group, Inc.

Printed in the United States of America

The paper used in this book complies with the
Permanent Paper Standard issued by the National
Information Standards Organization (Z39.48–1984).

10 9 8 7 6 5 4 3 2 1

Even though we pass away

Like the dew drops melting here and there

Our hearts rest on the same calyx of flower.

Pure Land Master Honen (1133-1212)

Contents

Prologue

Most of us probably think of death as a dreadful thing that we would like to avoid. But it is a reality that we have to face sooner or later. There is a saying that someone else's death may be permissible, but our own death is not possible. In his book *La Mort*, Vladimir Jankelevitch, a French philosopher, classified death into three categories, namely, the deaths of the first, second and third persons. The death of the first person is "my death," whereas that of the second person is "my acquaintance's death," and the third person's is "other death." "My death" is the most difficult to confront because it means our own end. The death of the third person, on the other hand, is an everyday occurrence, which may not be an immediate concern and is easily forgettable.

The information on the various funeral customs in the world in this book mainly focuses on the death of the second person. In other words, I examined the way people living in different countries deal with the death of an acquaintance and what kind of post-mortem arrangements are made. Although this kind of study may seem somewhat morbid, I believe that one can get a better understanding of the different ways of life through viewing people's individual and collective behavior in funeral customs.

I first became interested in the various funeral customs in the world when I was asked to hold memorial services for those who had died in major plane crashes. In such cases, I hastened to the crash site with the bereaved families to assist in making arrangements to identify the bodies of the victims and in conducting a memorial service for the dead. I did this at the request of the airline companies in the wake of air disasters, including a crash of a JAL plane in the suburbs of New Delhi, India, in June 1972, a crash at Shermechievo International Airport in Moscow in December of the same year, and an accident involving a Pan Am plane in the mountains in northwest Bali, Indonesia, in April, two years later.

Such accidents produce a great number of casualties at once and the site of the crash presents such an alarming sight that one cannot help but turn one's face from it. Moreover, the collection and identification of the remains and their subsequent conveyance to their home countries and the holding of memorial services for the dead must be done with the utmost sincerity in the midst of the agony and grief of the victims' families. Often a variety of foreign passengers of different nationalities, faiths and beliefs are traveling in the same plane, and the manner, customs, legal procedures and so on, of the place where the accident occurred are not necessarily in accord with those of the deceased and their families. In the situations where I mediated between those who had suffered (the bereaved families) and those who had caused the suffering (the airline company), I could not help but worry about how to deal with the situation in a way that would satisfy all parties. Thus it occurred to me that it is absolutely vital to examine the various funeral customs in the world in order to avoid confusion and misunderstanding. I believe that such information would be useful not only for travelers going abroad but also for those who wish to strengthen their understanding of each other.

The study of the customs of funeral services in various countries has been made mainly by cultural anthropologists and folklorists. Since the 18th century when the voluminous work *Ceremonies et Coutumes Religieuses de Tous les Peuples du Monde* (English translation is available) by Barnard Pickart of the Netherlands was first published, many books have been written on this subject, including a joint work by Habenstein and Lamers entitled *Funeral Customs the World Over* (1972). However, these works present fragmentary analysis dealing only with past practices, and none seems to treat the current funeral customs prevailing throughout the world. Thus, I have briefly introduced the funeral customs now practiced in various parts of the world. Although I firmly believe that someone will have to wrestle with this problem in further depth sooner or later, in order to do this properly it is necessary for a group of scholars to research the subject in cooperation and to look at the problem from various angles. Consequently, it would be impossible to complete the work in a short time. But we cannot wait with folded arms for such a work to be published. Even as I write, many travelers are in fact dying in foreign lands.

At present there are more than 190 independent countries in the world. The funeral practices in each are closely related to the culture, history and geography of the country concerned. Funeral customs differ widely according to the area, racial demographics, social and political structure, religion and so on. Even within a single country, it is therefore difficult to define general characteristics. However, for the sake of convenience, I have broadly classified the countries within the following geographical framework: Asia, Oceania, Africa, Middle East, Europe, Commonwealth of Independent States, North and

Central America and South America.

With the exception of a few underdeveloped countries, regardless of whether one is a citizen or a foreigner, the law requires that after a person dies, his or her death should be certified by a doctor and reported to the nearest public records office.

This book was written with reference to my personal research, documents and various sources that I have consulted over the past 20 years. I would greatly appreciate comments and feedback to make, in the future, any revisions, additions or deletions, based on updated and more accurate information about the funeral customs in the world.

Acknowledgments

I would like to express my deepest appreciation to my English-speaking colleagues and the foreign diplomatic corps in Japan who have kindly helped in checking my manuscripts. I would like particularly to express my gratitude to Peter Bellars, Maya Hara, Yvonne Marsden, Burt G. Mathias, Kimiko Matsunami, Thomas McDonald, Bessie Okada, Paul Robins and Kakuko Shoji. Without their assistance, I could never have accomplished my work. I must also acknowledge the many contributors whom I referred to as sources of information on various funeral customs in the world. Particularly, my deepest appreciation goes to the following publishers who have kindly permitted me to quote: Harper & Row for *Religion and Man*, by W. Richard Comstock (1972), Japanese edition; Pinter Publishers for *Rites of Passage*, edited by Jean Holm with John Bowker (1994); Praeger Publishers for *Death and Afterlife*, edited by Hiroshi Obayashi (1992); Routledge for *Death and Bereavement Across Cultures*, by Colin Murray Parkes (1997); the University of Chicago Press for *The Rites of Passage*, by Arnold van Gennep (1965); Simon & Schuster for *Encyclopedia of World Cultures*, edited by David Levinson (1996); and The English University Press for *The Disposal of the Dead*, by C. P. Polson and T. K. Marshall (1975).

Last but not least, I want to thank Greenwood Press for the care taken in the publication of my manuscript into a book form.

Introduction

In the 1960s, an American anthropologist, Ralph S. Solecki, discovered the remains of eight late Neanderthal men, who were believed to have lived about 50,000 years ago, in the Shanidahal cave in Iraq. Not too far from the remains he found the ancient pollen of thistle, hollyhock and cornflower, which never grew in that area. These men may well have been the first in human history to be buried in solemnity. The discovery of these remains together with the pollen of flowers could possibly be the beginnings of funeral customs as well as religion in the world.

It is natural that, when someone dies, the bereaved family, relatives and friends gather together and perform some kind of ritual in order to mourn the loss of the deceased and to console themselves. A French anthropologist, Arnold van Gennep, aptly noted in his book *The Rites of Passage* as follows:

It is a transitional period for the survivors, and they enter it through rites of separation and emerge from it through rites of reintegration into society (rites of the lifting of mourning). In some cases, the transitional period of the living is a counterpart of the transitional period of the deceased, and the termination of the first sometimes coincides with the termination of the second-that is, with the incorporation of the deceased into the world of the dead.[1]

Religion is believed to have originated from the awe or fear that people felt when confronted with natural or supernatural phenomena of change, and the attempt to overcome such feelings by joining together and performing rites of reconciliation with the supernatural powers they regarded as the cause of their awe or fear and the change. In the beginning, therefore, different kinds of funeral rites were performed widely among different peoples in different places and varied according to the geographical and social environment of the deceased. However, later they gradually amalgamated into institutionalized religions by placing theoretical meanings onto them.

At present, we can see different kinds of funeral customs, which constitute both indigenous and theoretical elements, practiced throughout the world. The former is often characterized as the "popular," "lower" stratum based on people's sentiments and emotions, whereas the latter is considered the "normative," "higher" stratum based on reason and is given the authority of the respective religions. Because of these two strata interacting with each other, various funeral customs have come into being, enriching and developing both their reasoning and practices.

What is important is not that people nowadays deal with supernatural beings or theoretical explanations about death but rather that they provide a powerful way in which people's social solidarity can be expressed. In his book *Religion and Man*, the American sociologist of religion W. Richard Comstock wrote:

Ritual is an element of religion and culture that needs to be emphasized, even at the risk of exaggeration, since the opposite error of understanding its importance is more serious. Yet ritual is the element most likely to be neglected by Western intellectuals, who are inclined to be strongly influenced by the ideational elements in culture and life. Thus, in considering a phenomenon like religion, the tendency is first to stress the thought content of religion and to ask questions concerning the "belief" of a given people or religious group.[2]

Funeral customs are often repetitive, but these factors serve as important means of channeling emotion, guiding cognition and organizing social groups and community. At the time of the funeral, the crucial moment of parting with the deceased, people's intentions are revealed through their behavior and ritual actions. Therefore, a comparative study of funeral customs in the world is perhaps just as important as comparing the social and religious structures in the world.

In this introductory chapter, I present an outline of the general perspective on death held by the major world religions. In the main chapters, I will cover the funeral customs currently practiced in the various regions throughout the world. The chapters are classified by region and the countries are listed in alphabetical order under each region.

BUDDHISM

The Buddha taught that human existence is constantly in a flux of fear and is threatened by death. No one can escape from this reality and avoid an end. His analysis of this condition includes an understanding that human suffering comes from our resistance to accepting this impermanence. We desire to remain forever the same, never to change, much less to die. The remedy he proposed for this spiritual distress was to cease struggling against our impermanent state and to transcend it.

Buddhist monks take part in funerals, but they are not for the benefit of the dead person. A funeral is a reminder of mortality and impermanence, and it is quite appropriate that monks should take the opportunity to preach the teaching of the Buddha out of compassion for the bereaved.

Concerning the Buddhist attitude toward death and bereavement, Christopher Lamb wrote:

One of the chief ways by which the laity gains merit (for an auspicious rebirth from which ideally to reach nirvana) is by offering food to monks either at the daily almsround or by inviting monks for meals. In the case of the dead, the merit gained by the relatives is thought to be transferable to the dead person.[3]

The most important innovation for lay people is their post-mortem tonsuring and ordination as disciples of the Buddha as part of their preparation for deliverance. If possible this is done before death. Then the lineage chart is transmitted, incorporating the dead into the lineage of the Buddha's family. A discourse is preached on impermanence and the coffin is circumambulated around the cremation ground, weaving in and out of four gates set in the four directions.[4]

Regarding the contemporary view that many Buddhist have toward death and bereavement, Frank E. Reynolds described it as follows:

When the death of a Buddhist is properly achieved, the soteriological benefits are not limited only to the person who has died. The deceased is assured a favorable rebirth, and the other members of the community who participate in the process accumulate important soteriological gains as well. All involved are once again confronted in a direct and vivid way with the basic Buddhist truth concerning the impermanence of all composite realities and the ephemeral character of this-worldly values and pleasures. Therefore their soteriological consciousness is sharpened. In addition, all of the participants are engaged in a merit-making process that has given rise to soteriological fruit not only for the deceased to whom the merit has been transferred, but also for the participants themselves. For the act of transferring merit to others (and especially transferring merit to a parent or elder) is, in itself, a selfless act of giving, and as such it is taken to be an act that generates even more merit (hence, better deaths and better rebirths) for one who performs it.[5]

CHRISTIANITY

For Christians, the death of Jesus of Nazareth is the focal point in understanding the destiny of human beings, which has underpinned traditional Christian cultures. It is the foremost example of a "model" of death for them.

Concerning the Christian attitude toward death and bereavement, Douglas Davies wrote as follows:

From the earliest days of their religion Christians have linked the death and funerals of their believers with the death and resurrection of Christ. The ritual of the last rites in the Catholic tradition involves the confession of sin, absolution by the priest, anointing with oil and communion. The idea is to prepare the dying for the journey to God that follows. The communion part of this rite is called *viaticum*, a Latin term meaning the provisions for a journey.[6]

After death comes the preparation of the body for burial, followed in most church traditions by a service marking the movement of the dead from the realm of the living. The Christian doctrine of the resurrection of Jesus deeply influenced the funeral service because the dead are buried or cremated in the hope of a future life brought about through a divine act of resurrection. Just as Jesus was raised from the dead, so the dead Christian will be brought to a new existence through the creative power of God. God is thanked for the life that the person led, the congregation is reminded of the mortal nature of human life, and all are encouraged to lead their own earthly lives in light of this knowledge. The dead person is then given back to the earth or to the fire with the understanding that we come from natural elements and to them we return until the resurrection of Jesus.[7]

In the Catholic tradition the liturgy for the dead refers to the journey the soul undertakes as it moves to God and is welcomed by the saints. Sometimes a special requiem mass is observed for the dead as a means of benefiting them in the afterlife through the offering of the mass and the prayers of the church. The Protestant tradition has been far less ready to talk and assume any knowledge of what awaits any particular individual. The Orthodox tradition stresses fundamental commitment to the resurrection of Jesus, referring to the belief that it is Jesus who keeps the dead alive in the memory of God.[8]

As for the contemporary Christian view of death and bereavement, Hiroshi Obayashi wrote as follows:

To start with "death," Christianity has been convinced from the early part of its history that human beings are mortal. Any attempt to see them as immortal and infinite is rebuffed by the power of God, the Creator. Human beings as creatures possess no "natural" immortality of their own. Natural immortality would be an endless life apart from any relationship with God. A demon's immortality as conceived by the popular belief is a case in point. Though fallen and rejected by God, the demon does not have to die the way human beings do. Such an immortality without God's blessing means no more than a curse. Tatian (c. 160), an early Christian father, unequivocally denied that human beings possessed any immortality of that kind. Living endlessly, in itself, contains no delight or any good. It is living in communion with God that makes immortality delightful and desirable. For this reason Christianity prefers to use the expression "the eternal life" instead of "immortality" to avoid its vicious implication of a meaningless prolongation of life. There is "nothing desirable about living forever." Those who ask for an endless life should realize what they are getting into. The life eternal, not immortality, should be pursued and cherished. In Christianity, "the life eternal" means being alive in God both now and always. Grasping for (natural) immortality on one's own is not only a futile attempt, but even if possible, would never lead to a desirable state. Human beings are mortal, and only by faith in God's power of resurrection and conquering death can they hope to be raised into a new life. Thus the Christian faith does not preach the circumvention of death, rather it teaches the acceptance and the overcoming of death as exemplified by the cross of Jesus himself.[9]

CONFUCIANISM

Confucius, the founder of Confucianism, suggests, "You want to know of Death? Well, I shall save my breath. When you know life, why then, we'll talk of Death again." However, in later years, his idea was diffused widely among the Chinese and the Koreans, and was amalgamated into a folklore.

Xingzhong Yao described the following about the Confucian view of death:

From the viewpoint of the rites of passage, death is the last phase, which signals the completion of a life cycle. Technically, the rites for death have three parts: the effort to recover the "deceased," the mourning, and the funeral.

Death was believed to be caused by the departing of the soul from its body, in the hope that this departure was only temporary, like a dream. Also some action was performed to avoid taking a false death as a real one. When a senior member died, such practices were required immediately to check whether it was final. Someone, usually the deceased's intimate, went up to the roof from the front side of the house in which the dead person used to live, carrying the dead person's clothes, then faced north, which was believed to be the direction of the yin world, and shouted three times, "So and so, return!" Then he or she quickly descended from the back side of the house and carried the clothes, which were believed to be possibly still carrying the wandering soul, to the body. If the "dead person" recovered, this was explained as the soul having wandered out into another world and now having been awakened and brought back. If there was no recovery, the rites for mourning would begin.[10]

When a person died, he or she was believed to change his or her living place from the yang world to the yin. For this change, permission must be obtained from the yin world. A report of the death was made to the proper governing authority in the underworld, through some intermediary such as *Tu-ti* (the god of the land), *Cheng-huang* (the god of the city), or *Wu-tao* (the god of the Five Roads), depending on local tradition, who would report further to the kings of hell. Only with their permission could the soul of the dead enter the spirit world.[11]

The contemporary Confucian view on death and bereavement was treated as follows by Judith A. Berling:

Perhaps the most profound message of Confucianism was that of the interconnectedness of souls. The living were surrounded by and connected to the dead, and the dead influenced and continued to connect with the living. This idea provided ways for the Chinese to maintain the proper relationships among the living, and between the living and the dead.[12]

HINDUISM

For Hindus, there is a common belief in the transmigration of souls. They believe that all physical and mental activity is a reflection of greater universal principles yielding increased benefits and resulting in an improved form of transmigration at its next cycle. A person becomes good through good actions and bad through bad actions.

Concerning the Hindu attitude toward death and bereavement, Gavin Flood wrote as follows:

If a householder does not renounce worldly affairs, then when he dies his body will undergo a funeral. Death, as in most cultures, is inauspicious in Hinduism and a death in the family brings the twofold danger of pollution and a potentially malevolent ghost. The last *samskara* attempts to neutralize this pollution and danger by reintegrating the family back into the social context from which they have been momentarily separated, and allowing the spirit of the dead to travel on its way, leaving the family in peace.

While there are concerns of bereavement, the neutralizing of death pollution and the freeing of the spirit from worldly attachments are pan-Hindu concerns. The actual funerary rites vary to some extent in different regions of India and among different castes. Cremation is not unusual, though among lower castes inhumation takes place, and children and holy men are generally not cremated but buried. Indeed, a holy man, having previously undergone his own symbolic funeral at renunciation, might be simply immersed in a river, having transcended his social identity.[13]

The contemporary Hindu view toward death and bereavement was treated by Thomas J. Hopkins as follows:

All beings that die will be reborn as long as they are still engaged in the karmic process, so that physical remains are only a transient and insignificant reminder of their passing. Moreover, all beings similarly have the possibility of final salvation, although this may be many lifetimes in the future. Any individual death is, therefore, only a transition point in a larger cycle that will present many conditions and opportunities in the course of many lifetimes. How one uses the circumstances of one's earthly life determines one's ultimate afterlife.[14]

ISLAM

For Muslims, Allah is the one who creates people from clay, who sustains them, causes them to die and finally calls them from graves. Therefore, they leave the world as they enter it, accompanied by texts proclaiming the reality of God and His revelation.

Concerning the Islamic view toward death and bereavement, Clinton Bennet wrote as follows:

A Muslim believes in life after death, in the resurrection of the body, and in the Day of Reckoning; the extended doctrinal creed bears witness to these deep convictions. The Qur'an warns that those who rebel against God will be punished, whereas those who live in harmony with His will have no reason to fear. It also provides vivid descriptions of heaven and hell. In heaven, the believers will be reunited with their loved ones. Their most prized reward, though, will be fellowship, harmony, and *tawhid* (union) with God. Pious Muslims know that if they have observed the obligatory duties (Islam's five pillars), lived good and moral lives in conformity with the *Shari'ah* (Islamic law), and repented (*tawbah*, turned back to God) whenever they did wrong, God will show them the same mercy He showed Adam at the beginning of time. They know that mere outward observance, attempting to selfishly accumulate merit for salvation or appearing pious before others, is valueless unless accompanied by a pure *niyyah* (intent) to worship and serve God for His sake alone.[15]

Before the funeral, the mourners recite the *niyyah*: "I have purposed to offer up to God only with a sincere heart this prayer." The funeral prayer may take place in the mosque, after one of the canonical *salah* prayers is given, although here local customs may vary. Sometimes the mosque courtyard is preferred. Relatives and friends should accompany the coffin, reciting the *shahadah* (confession of faith) en route. Walking is recommended unless the distance is too far.[16]

As for the contemporary Islamic view toward death and bereavement, William C. Chittick wrote the following:

Islam distinguishes three major stages of becoming after death. The first is the period from death until the Day of Resurrection, which occurs at the "end of the world," when the possibilities of human existence in this world have been exhausted. For each person, the interworld represents an awakening in relationship to the life in the world, so the soul is more aware of itself and its surroundings than it was when it lived in clay. Because its existence is now totally imaginal, it perceives itself and its surroundings in appropriate bodily form. At this stage the soul does not enter into heaven or hell, since those two abodes will not be populated until after the Day of Resurrection. It receives, however, a foretaste of its ultimate and permanent state. As the Prophet said, death is the "lesser resurrection" and the grave is "either one of the pits of hell or one of the gardens of paradise."[17]

JUDAISM

Judaism has a long history extending back to a thousand years before the beginning of the Christian Era, and some of its major tenets have deeply influenced both Christianity and Islam. In the Talmud, a Jewish theological text produced in the fifth century A.D., the emphasis seems to lie on the resurrection of the body.

Concerning Jewish views toward death, Alan Unterman explained:

This world is described in Rabbinic literature as a corridor leading to the world to come. Humans have to prepare themselves in this corridor before entering the hall which is their destination. Despite this, the message of Judaism does not concentrate on death and the hereafter but on life. Indeed, the most common greeting exchanged between Jews when drinking together is "*Le-haim*" ("to life").

Death has its own associated rituals. Before dying, persons should confess their sins and, if possible, end their life with the declaration of the first line of the Shema on their lips: "Hear, O Israel, the Lord is our God, the Lord is One." It is particularly meritorious to die affirming the oneness of God. In the presence of a dying person, it is prohibited to do anything that will hasten death for active euthanasia is abhorrent in traditional Judaism.

Death is defined as the cessation of breathing, which may be tested for with a feather or a mirror. A dead person should be buried as soon as possible after death, preferably on the same day. Leaving the body without burial is considered a desecration of the dead, as is cutting up the corpse in a post-mortem examination unless this is absolutely necessary.[18] The belief in resurrection had its effect on Jewish funeral practices as well. Rabbis and others compare resurrection to apparently similar processes on nature: the seed disintegrates and gives birth to a new plant, and so too, the old body decomposes but a new one springs forth from its dust. This conception led to the idea that even as the body returns to dust the small bone in the base of the spine called *luz* never completely disappears. [19]

As for the contemporary Jewish view toward death and bereavement, Robert Goldenberg wrote as follows:

The need to preserve the dead body from utter destruction is also one of the roots of the well-known and ancient Jewish abhorrence of cremation. Although there are Jewish people living in countries that widely practice cremation, they themselves have avoided this means of laying their dead to rest. [20]

NOTES

1. Arnold van Gennep, *The Rites of Passage*, translated by Vizedom and Caffee (London: Routledge and Kegan Paul, 1965), p. 147.

2. W. Richard Comstock, *Religion and Man* (New York: Harper & Row, 1972, Japanese edition), p. 66.

3. Christopher Lamb, "Buddhism." In Jean Holm and John Bowker, eds., *Rites of Passage*(London: Pinter Publishers, 1994), p. 31.

4. Ibid. p. 38.

5. Frank E. Reynolds, "Buddhist Perspectives with Particular Reference to the Theravada Tradition." In Hiroshi Obayashi, ed., *Death and Afterlife* (Westport, CT: Praeger Publishers, 1992), p. 165.

6. Douglas Davies, "Christianity." In *Rites of Passage*, p. 54.

7. Ibid. p. 55.

8. Ibid. p. 56.

9. Hiroshi Obayashi, "Death and Eternal Life in Christianity." In *Death and Afterlife*, pp. 110-111.

10. Xinzhong Yao, "Chinese Religion." In *Death and Afterlife*, pp. 165-166.

11. Ibid, p. 166.

12. Judith A. Berling, "Death and Afterlife in Chinese Religions." In *Death and Afterlife*, p. 191.

13. Gavin Flood, "Hinduism." In *Rites of Passage*, p. 154.

14. Thomas J. Hopkins, "Hindu View of Death and Afterlife." In *Death and Afterlife*, p. 154.

15. Clinton Bennet, "Islam." In *Rites of Passage*, pp. 106-107.

16. Ibid, p. 109.

17. William C. Chittick, "The Muslim Understanding of Death and Afterlife." *In Death and Afterlife*, pp. 136-137.

18. Alan Unterman, "Judaism." In *Rites of Passage*, pp. 134-135.

19. Robert Goldenberg, "Death and Afterlife in the Jewish Tradition." In *Death and Afterlife*, p. 101.

20. Ibid, p. 102.

INTERNATIONAL HANDBOOK OF FUNERAL CUSTOMS

CHAPTER 1

Asia

BANGLADESH

The People's Republic of Bangladesh is located on the largest delta in the world at the mouth of the Ganges in the northwestern part of the Indian subcontinent. The land is mostly flat. In the northern part of Bangladesh, there are some minority groups, but the majority of the people are Bengalis. Because of frequent cyclones, the life of the people is difficult and unstable.

Islam is the national religion of Bangladesh, but freedom of religion is ensured, so there are also Hindus and Buddhists.

When a Muslim dies, the body is washed with soap and a disinfectant solution, then wrapped in white cloth. Some perfume is sprayed onto the body as well. After the notice of death is submitted to the district government office, the family, together with the mourners, transports the body to the graveyard. At that time, women usually do not participate, because they are considered to become too emotional. People who are sitting on the roadside as the procession passes never fail to stand up in expression of respect for the deceased.

At the graveyard, the leader stands by the body, and the mourners encircle the leader. When the leader prays, raising his hands to the height of his ears, the people join him, and then recite the beginning section of the Qur'an. After repeating this four times, everyone prays for the last time, and the body is buried in the ground. The deceased's head must face Mecca. Because Allah does not like sorrow and suffering, the mourners recite the following section of the Qur'an: "Surely we belong to God, and to Him we return" (II Cow 151).

The Chkma, a minority group that lives in southeastern Bangladesh, are predominantly of the Buddhist faith. The Hindus and the Buddhists cremate the body at a crematorium and scatter the ashes over a river or bury them in the ground.

BHUTAN

The mysterious land of Bhutan is located in the Himalayas, and for a long period of time it was closed to foreigners. In 1971, however, the Kingdom of Bhutan joined the United Nations and opened the country. The number of tourists visiting the country has increased each year.

The majority of the people are the Drukpa, and Dzongkha is the official language. Bhutan once had a close relationship with Tibet. The *dzon*, which are located in various places around the country, are government offices as well as Lamaist temples. In Bhutan, politics and religion are not separated. The role of Lama monks is very important as they lead the people in all aspects of life including administration, education, weddings and funerals, so the life-style in Bhutan is closely associated with religion.

When someone dies, the family must report it to the Lama monks who live in the *dzon*. The funeral begins and ends with the recitation of the *sutras*, accompanied by music. At the deceased's home, white flags called *darshin* are raised. The number of flags must be the same as the deceased's age. The body is cremated at the outdoor crematorium, and the ashes are scattered in the river. No graves are made except for the Lama monks. Some of the ashes are made into a ball called *tuatua* and enshrined in a *cholten*, a Buddhist pagoda. In the remote areas, there once was the custom of "sky burial" as in Tibet, but it is not common today. In the case of an accidental or abnormal death, the body is buried very deeply in the ground. In Bhutan, all the ceremonies are usually held by the entire community.

Only among the Nepalese immigrants does one find Hinduism or a combination of that tradition with Tibetan Lamaism being followed. However, the idea of ritual cleansing of the body has diffused here from India.

BRUNEI

The Sultanate of Brunei is located to the northwest of Borneo and is divided into two areas. For many years, Brunei was a self-governing territory of Great Britain, but in 1984 it became completely independent. Most people are Malay, and the national religion is Islam. Because Brunei has abundant natural resources, such as crude oil and natural gas, the country has enjoyed rapid economic growth.

In the capital, Bandar Seri Begawan, there are beautiful mosques. The people of Brunei hold their funerals mainly according to Islamic customs. The body is interred as soon as possible.

The Bisaya who live there are primarily Muslims engaged in wet rice cultivation, but their belief is animistic; there are shamans and diviners. Spirits of the dead can be dangerous if not properly mourned. The wealthy give large amounts of food to the mourners at the funeral.

CAMBODIA

Cambodia is located in the southern part of the Indochinese Peninsula. It is an agricultural country where plains spread out from two rivers, the Mekon and the Trensap. The majority of the people are Cambodians, who follow Theravada Buddhism. Political strife is still evident today, so the country is unstable.

A death is first reported to a nearby government office. In some cases, inspection by a medical examiner or the police is required. The body is prepared for the funeral by the family. Then a monk (*bhikhu*) is invited to recite sutras. The family serves food. The funeral is usually held in a Buddhist temple. While the monk is reciting the sutra and funeral music is being played, one end of a thread is tied to the deceased's hand and the other end is tied to the monk's hand. Those who were home on the day of the deceased's birth are not supposed to attend the funeral.

The majority of the people choose cremation. In the case of Buddhists, an auspicious day is chosen after the funeral for cremation. There are even times when the body is cremated six months or a year later. Christians, Muslims, and those who died of unnatural causes, such as suicide, are interred.

Right after the establishment of the Pol Pot regime, great numbers of Buddhist monks and nuns were massacred, and the religion was abolished from the nation's political structure. However, the general funeral customs do not seem to have been affected. Even now one can see long funeral processions passing through rural districts.

The Khmer place importance on foretelling one's death by using a book called *Kampi*. If there is any chance for survival, the *haoporn* ceremony is held; if there is no hope, the *ke ayo* ceremony, which is used to call the soul, is held. When someone dies, the body is dressed in new white clothes, then placed in a casket. Thereafter, a monk is invited to hold the funeral. Three days after the funeral, the body is cremated. At the time of cremation, the body must face west, and thereafter face east. This is called *play ruk*. The ashes are placed in a bone box. The wealthy place the ashes in the *caedy* or the *ruk kamoi*. They use a grave with a roof and a graveyard called *kuk kamoi*.

The Cham, living in the Tonle Sap and Chau Doc areas of Cambodia and in southcentral Vietnam, bury their dead twice; once provisionally right after death and then permanently after a certain period of time has passed. The bones for the permanent resting place are buried along with the deceased person's belongings at the common cemetery. The Hindu Cham, by contrast, cremate the deceased, and the remains are placed in a family sepulcher.

CHINA

The People's Republic of China, after Russia and Canada, is one of the largest countries in the world. Mainland China is bordered by 14 countries; to the east it has a long Pacific coastline. The southwestern mountains include the Tibetan plateau. In the northwest, the Tien Shan mountain separates the Tarim and Dzungarian basins. The low-lying east is home to two-thirds of the population. The Han people account for 94 percent of a population that stands at nearly 1,130,000,000. Minority groups live in the remote areas and have self-governing territories.

After World War II, China became a socialist nation ruled by representatives of the proletariat class. Since then, any religious activity that conflicted with national interests has been forbidden. Religious facilities for prayers and worship such as temples and churches were partly destroyed during the Cultural Revolution, and the religious leaders were suppressed by the changes. Nevertheless, the people preserved their age-old traditions and customs. Eventually, the freedom of both religious followers and non-religious people was allowed. Soon renowned Buddhist temples of historical value were rebuilt and religious activities began to be revived. At present, religious ceremonies are only for the followers of the religion, and the majority of Chinese think the funeral is just a secular custom that has nothing to do with their beliefs.

Because the land of China is vast and there are regional differences in customs and life-styles, it is impossible to generalize. However, in most cases, in the urban areas the family reports the death to a nearby police station (*gong'an*), and the people's commune (*renmin-gongsh*) takes care of the funeral. The body, sans coffin, is carried by micro-bus to the crematorium, which is operated directly by the local government. Whereas before the revolution a Buddhist or Taoist priest was called to officiate at the funeral, now the funeral is quite simple and conducted in the following order: the eulogy, prostration three times, and the farewell message. Family members may weep very loudly at the funeral. When the body is removed from the room by the people in charge of cremation, the mourners go outside and burn flower wreaths and paper money, and set off firecrackers. After the funeral, the body is cremated and the bones are kept in a niche. In the rural areas, the people's commune takes care of the funeral. After the funeral the body is buried in a nearby cemetery.

In some areas outside the cities, the family places the deceased's feet toward the entrance, bathes the body, and dresses it in fresh clothes. The death is announced to the neighbors, and at the wake elderly women from among the relatives cry out very loudly. Some elderly people recite sutras. Some families buy coffins in advance, whereas others order one after a family member has died. The top of the coffin is sometimes painted red or with floral patterns.

The body is placed in the coffin and the lid is tightly fastened. Then the coffin is carried to the cemetery by volunteers. The procession is accompanied by a mourning flag and the sound of firecrackers. Most of the mourners wear black mourning bands. There are no special mourning clothes. When the body is buried, they cover it little by little with earth and continue this process for two or three months until it is completely covered. After the funeral, mourners go to the deceased's house, and the family offers a light meal to the mourners.

In the past, the location and position of the grave were determined by yin-yang geomancy, but later, because such practices interfered with the national policy of modernizing agriculture, industry, national defense and scientific technology, the scattered graves were reorganized, and because of a "reformation of funeral customs," certain basin areas have been designated as cemeteries since 1956. In the remote areas, older people prefer traditional burial in the ground. In the Cho-chan State alone, 470,000 graves were erected recently, taking up 2,000 million square meters of farmland per year.

The funerals of the common people are kept simple, but when social or political leaders who have served the nation or society die, a grand memorial service is held. A large gathering place is used for the funeral, where the deceased's body is placed in view, together with a portrait and flower offerings. To the strain of solemn Chinese music, the head of the funeral committee recites the deceased's personal history and honors. Words of condolence are also read. In the case of former premier Chou En-Lai, after the formal ceremony bidding farewell, he was cremated, and his ashes buried in the Babaoshan Cemetery on the outskirts of Beijing. Prior to this formal ceremony at the cemetery, a farewell ceremony was held in Beijing. At the entrance, the Cabinet ministers lined up and thanked the mourners for coming.

In 1985, the Chinese government divided the land into coastal areas and inland areas where transportation is difficult. For those who live in the coastal areas, cremation was made an official requirement. At present, there are about 1,200 crematoriums, and most city dwellers choose cremation. From 1990 to the present, about 30 percent of the dead have been reported to be cremated in China.

In Beijing, people usually hold funerals at the Babaoshan mortuary (*Binyiguan*) in the city, and after cremation, the bones are kept in locker-style niches with the deceased's pictures. In the Babaoshan mortuary, there is a hall that can accommodate hundreds of mourners. If the deceased is a member of the temple, the family may ask for the prayers of a priest. In Shanghai City, there are 14 crematoriums, 15 public graveyards and 9 niche halls. Recently, more people prefer burial at sea. The Babaoshan Revolution Public Cemetery and Mortuary on the outskirts of Beijing was established in 1949, right after the revolution, as the cemetery for VIPs of the nation and the party. In 1958, a crematorium was added to the cemetery. It takes care of two-thirds of the funerals in the city now. After the funeral, the body is loaded onto a stretcher and transported to the cremation furnace. The family receives the ashes three days after the cremation. If the family does not come to pick up the ashes within one month, the office of the crematorium takes care of the ashes. The Lo-shan Guhuitang is in the vicinity, so many people ask them to keep the urn, a wooden box with carvings on it. The contract period is three years, but if the family wishes, the contract may be renewed. On the locker-style shelves, urns are lined up. Gifts and artificial flowers are not allowed to be placed there. On the west side, outside of Beijing, there are the Futian Public Cemeteries, and the affiliated hall of niches and private graves are lined in rows. There are public cemeteries in most cities, where all the tombstones look alike, and one can see only the graves of people who have recently died.

The memorial services are usually held on the seventh, forty-ninth, one hundredth days or one year after the death and are attended by relatives and friends. If someone other than a relative of the third degree wishes to attend the ceremony of condolence, he must obtain permission from the people's commune or from the people's committee he belongs to. If he is allowed to attend, he will not be paid his day's salary. The immediate family and the relatives go to the graveyard on the anniversary of the death or on the Memorial Day (*Qing ming jie*), which usually falls on April 5. It seems that these types of traditional customs are kept more in the rural areas than in the urban areas, and more often in southern China than in northern China.

Even after China became a socialist country, the Chinese custom of respecting one's ancestors continued to be practiced. It seems that this custom has been properly respected to this very day. In the past, as we can see from the ruins of the Yin Dynasty, dating from 1300 B.C., that were excavated in the vicinity of the village of Shaodon in Henan, and in the tomb of Mawang, dating from 200 B.C. and excavated in the suburbs of Changsha City in Hunan, when a man who held power passed away, his subordinates often practiced self-immolation. Also, the deceased's belongings and gifts were buried together with the body. This kind of practice, however, was limited to people like the former Head of State, Mao Zsetung, or the Father of the Revolution, Sun Yat-sen.

On the south side of Tienanmen Square in the heart of Beijing, there is the magnificent Mao Zsetung Memorial Hall. It is an octagonal marble tower decorated with traditional azure-colored tiles, where Mao's mummy-like body is preserved. In the case of Sun Yat-sen, who died in 1925 in Beijing while he was visiting the city, his remains were buried in a temple on the outskirts of Beijing. But in 1929, the remains were moved to Chung-shan Mausoleum in Nanking. Even now many people visit there to pay their respects to him.

Small graves are scattered in the fields and in the mountainous forests. The tombstones, if any, simply state the deceased's name and the date of death.

The Chinese government set up the Mortuary Regulation in Feburuary 1995, encouraging cremation, instead of burial, for all deceased. Ever since, many have cremated their deceased at a crematorium near the place that the funeral service takes place and deposit the urns in the charnel house. They pay a fee of one yuan per year for three years and thereafter pay an additional fee of twelve yuan annually. Only a third of the bereaved families renew their deposit at the crematorium, and the rest never come to claim the ashes of their deceased family members. After Chinese king-maker Deng Shao Ping's death on February 19, 1997, his ashes were scattered according to his will; thereafter many Chineses have come to prefer scattering their ashes after passing away. According to the recent report of the Administration Office of Shanghai, a total of 2,300 deceased's ashes have been scattered into the East China Sea since 1991.

In the Three Gorges Region near Chong-qing, caskets were displayed on the outside of the caves in the upper part of the cliffs along the Yangzi Long River. It is believed that the higher the casket is enshrined, the more easily the spirits of the dead can ascend to heaven.

Hong Kong

Hong Kong comprises Hong Kong island, lying off the southeastern coast of China, Kowloon and the New Territories on the mainland, and 235 adjacent islets. Its strategic position has made it one of the world's leading trade and financial centers. In 1997, Hong Kong reverted to China, when the 99 year lease to the United Kingdom expired. Most of the people of Hong Kong are Chinese, but there are also Caucasians, Indians and others. The life-style is influenced by both the Chinese and the Europeans, creating a unique atmosphere. The official language is Chinese, and the majority of the people believe in Buddhism, Christianity or the native syncretic religions of China.

When someone dies, a member of the family or a friend or relative goes to the government district office with a medical certificate and registers the death. The family asks a nearby funeral home to arrange the funeral services. On the island of Hong Kong and the peninsula of Kowloon, the funeral is usually held at the funeral home in accord with the family's religion.

Hong Kong is crowded with high rises and houses, and it is very rare that a funeral is held at one's home. A shrewd businessman named Siu Ming, who was once a dealer in coffin materials, paid attention to this fact and began to build funeral homes one after another. In 1951, he bought the Hong Kong Mortuary, which had been operated by a foreigner, at a discount price, and built his fortune in one generation, so people call him "Casket King" (Kwan Wang).

A Chinese funeral in Hong Kong is extravagant. It seems that the people think that the most important thing is to hold the best possible funeral for their parents. They have a custom of displaying the casket in one's home before the person's death. A casket made of material produced in the Dingzhou area of Fujian Province will cost 50,000 to 150,000 dollars (as of 1995). It is not hard to imagine how big the funeral industry is. When the funeral ends, the body is buried in a cemetery often selected through geomancy. Although interment is more conventional, the government recommends cremation, probably because Hong Kong's land is limited. There are six government-owned crematoriums and a private one. In 1976, the ratio of interment to cremation was 65 to 35 percent, but in 1981, the rate of interment stood at only 57 percent, and the rate has continued to decrease since then. Together with the change in the method of disposal, a new custom has arisen of digging up the dead body after a certain amount of time, usually five years, washing the bones, and then reburying them.

In Hong Kong, there are 24 community cemeteries in the city and 12 outside the city. When a family wishes to bury the dead in their homeland in mainland China, or when a cemetery has not been decided on, the body is packed in a box with lime and placed in a niche at Tung Wah Coffin Home, in Tai Hau Wan in the western part of Hong Kong Island. Within the spacious niche area, which is closed off by a heavy iron door, there are 17 cubicles where the caskets are placed. Caskets, urns, baskets, cans and other containers in which remains are preserved are packed into the cubicle. This place is known as the "the Mansion of the Dead" or "the Hotel of the Dead." Even this kind of graveyard has become popular among those who come to visit their ancestors in order to comfort them on April 5, Memorial Day (*Qing ming jie*). When people visit the cemetery, they customarily offer flowers and gifts, but they take food home and share it with everyone.

As for ancient cemeteries, there is one in Li Cheng Uk in Kowloon. It belongs to the early Han period from about 2 B.C. The remains found in the tomb are on display for the public in a nearby museum.

Remote Regions of China

In the remote areas of southern China, there are many smaller ethnic groups who have different beliefs and customs from the Han. For instance, the Archan in the Yunnan call a priest who reads a sutra when someone dies. After it is read, the coffin is carried out of the house. At that time, close family members kneel down on both sides of the door and let the coffin pass over them. This is the gesture of making the bridge, for the deceased to symbolically cross the river to the next world. Then the body is carried to a grave outside of the village, and is buried in the ground.

The Chinko tribe near the border has another set of customs. They fire a gun to announce a death to their neighbors. For the funeral, a cow is killed as an offering to heavenly deities, and the family invites the neighbors to join them in the ceremony. A gravesite is chosen by a fortune-teller, and stones are piled up and bamboo poles are placed around it. The funeral continues for several days, and the mourners enjoy dancing together.

With the Jino tribe, all of the deceased's possessions are buried as accessories to the next world. A grass-thatched shack is built in the graveyard, and a bamboo table is placed in it. For one to three years, meals are placed on the desk three times a day. Also certain people, called "the keepers of the grave," live by the grave for several months. After that, the shack is destroyed, and the remains are thrown into the field.

Sinkiang Uighur Autonomous Region and Inner Mongolia

It is not widely known to the outside world that there are as many as 13,000,000 Muslims in China (as of 1997). These people, called the Huimin of Islam, live mainly in the Sinkiang Uighur Autonomous Region. They have been isolated for a long time, and they preserve their own customs. They worship at a mosque (*qingzhen*) that looks like most Chinese temples, and follow the five Islamic precepts. Funerals are held in the Islamic way and officiated by the *ahon*, their spiritual leader. The body is buried in their communal cemetery.

At the time of the Cultural Revolution, Buddhists and Christians were oppressed by the Chinese government, but the Muslims were not persecuted. Moreover, they were allowed to establish their own self-governing institutions, and to build mosques, food stores and restaurants. They built these establishments because the Muslims do not eat pig and wild boar, which are an indispensable part of Chinese cuisine.

As for the Mongols in the Autonomous Region of Inner Mongolia, interment is the most common way of disposing of the body. Among the nomads, the body used to be left in the wilderness, but that custom is no longer practiced. At the funeral, such things as thin silk and mutton are offered to the mourners, and candles, made from the condensed milk of sheep or cows, are lit. The mourners wear white clothes and white hats, and strike their heads against the ground to pay their respects to the dead. The nomads respect and admire Genghis Khan as their hero, and every year on August 4, they hold a festival in front of his mausoleum.

When someone dies, the tent, called *geru*, where the deceased lived, is removed after the funeral, and the bereaved family mourns for forty-nine days, during which time they refrain from celebrating any happy event.

Tibetan Autonomous Region

Tibet, once called the world's region of mystery, was annexed by the communist government of China in 1965. The supreme religious and political head of Tibet (at that time), the Dalai Lama, was exiled with the people close to him to Dharamsala in northern India. Since then, Tibet has been one of the self-governing territories of the People's Republic of China. Because of the change in government, the privileges of the priest class and the serf system were abolished, but the life-styles and the customs have not changed drastically.

When someone dies, the Lama monks take the initiative in determining how to take care of the deceased. There are various ways of disposing of the dead bodies: the enshrinement of remains in the mausoleums or pagodas for monks, who are always mummified or cremated; sky-burial for the masses; water or simple burial for those who died of contagious diseases or criminals or children; cremation; and abandoning the body of a poor person in a remote place. In the case of cremation, the deceased's brothers must build the fire, and the cremation must start from the head. In Tibet, there is a unique ranking system of the five elements "earth, air, fire, wind and water," which make up the universe. Among these, air is ranked the highest, while earth is ranked lowest. For this reason, the sky burial and cremation are valued more highly than inhumation. At the sky-burial, which takes place in the early morning, only the Lama monks and professional undertakers participate. No one is allowed to touch the deceased's body until a ceremony called *Poa*, in which the soul is transferred from this world to another, is performed.

If the soul is good, it is transferred to heaven, but if it is bad, it goes to hell. Through the prayers of the Lama monks, the family appeals for the soul to be transferred to heaven.

A bowl that the deceased used is kept full of food by his pillows, and the butter oil lamp is left unlit. During the mourning period, the family members do not wash their faces and take off all of their jewelry. Until the deceased is sent out, a *gunpa*, a Lama monk, stays with the family and prays day and night in order to expiate the deceased's sins. The funeral date is determined by divination, and with the help of a *ragyapa* (a Tibetan undertaker), the family bends the deceased's legs and ties them in a sitting position, and wraps them with white cloth. The body is then placed on a stand in a corner of the house, separated by a white curtain, in which offerings are placed.

On the day before the funeral, the mourners visit a nearby temple and dedicate a sword, which serves as a charm, and do not return to the deceased's home. The Lama monk who prayed at the family's home receives some money as a token of gratitude and returns to the temple. On the day of the funeral, at around 4 A.M., which is the hour of the tiger, the funeral procession departs from the house after the body, which sits on the coffin stand, is turned three times to the right and three times to the left in front of an incense stand.

This ends the funeral and the mourners return home. As for the *ragyapa*, they immediately set out to carry the body up to a brick dais at the outcrop of the rocky mountains. After offering prayers, a piece of flesh from the back of the deceased is cut. Then the body is turned on its back, and the stomach and chest area are then cut and chopped apart. The flesh that has been chopped away is then tied to a stone post with a rope. The different parts of the body, such as the skull with the brain, are cracked into small pieces and mixed with *tsam-pa* (roasted barley flour) to make it easier for the vultures, which feed on the carrion, to eat. After the Lama monk has prayed, everyone including the *ragyapa* leaves. Before long vultures fly over and eat the flesh. The *ragyapa* washes his face and hands with water, and then the family treats him to tea and food made from roasted barley powder and cheese. The *ragyapa* must not return to the deceased's home that day. In the capital, Lhasa, there is such a "sky burial" site near the Sera Monastery and in Shigatse near the Tashilhump Monastery.

After a death, a memorial service is held every seven days. On the forty-ninth day, the end of the mourning period, the family invites many people to their home and gives many gifts to the Lama who performed the service. Rice wine and tea are also offered to the people who helped the family. Every year a memorial service is held on this anniversary, and the family expresses their joy and their appreciation that the deceased was able to become a good soul.

In Tibet, there is a sacred book of esoteric Buddhism called *The Book of the Dead* (third edition, Oxford, 1957), which was first translated by a Tibetan scholar, W. Y. Evans-Wentz of Oxford University, in 1927. Here, *samsara*, the transmigration of the soul, is fully explained. It also tells us that if you know how to die, you will know how to live, and if you do not know how to die, you will not know how to live and you will have to wander in *samsara*.

INDIA

Separated from the rest of Asia by the Himalayan mountain range, India forms a subcontinent. Besides the Himalayas, there are two other main geographical regions, the Indo-Gangetic plain, which lies between the foothills of the Himalayas and the Vindhya Mountains, and the central southern plateau. It resembles an upside-down triangle with the southern part jutting out into the Indian Ocean. The climate in India ranges from a frigid to a semi-tropical zone. However, as a whole the country is usually hot and humid. The majority of the people are Indo-Aryans and Dravidian, who are mostly Hindu, but there are also Muslims, Christians, Parsees, Sikhs and Buddhists. Depending on the religion and place, funeral customs differ.

In general, when someone dies, the family simply goes to the crematorium with a doctor's medical report and makes arrangements for the funeral. In the case of foreigners, the death must be reported to the respective embassy. A medical report and a death certificate must be submitted. If the death is accidental, the opinion of the medical examiner must be submitted as well.

Hindu

For the Hindu, the funeral is an important event because the distinction between this life and the next life is determined at the funeral. Thus, the funeral must be performed properly so that the soul may be released from the body and the transmigration of the soul can begin. Where the soul goes depends upon what the deceased did in this world, and on the final judgment of *Yama*, the king of the realm of Death.

When death approaches, the family or relatives call a *Brahmin* (Hindu priest) and ask him to purge the dying man of his sins. In southern India, the people call this *Kavali* or *Samudra Susana*. As a token of appreciation, the family usually gives money, but sometimes such things as a cow are given.

When someone dies, the family members and relatives run out of the house and weep. Then they pray, facing the south, where it is believed that Death resides. The body is wrapped in a white cloth (if the deceased is a woman, the cloth is red) and placed on the funeral bier. While chanting "*Rama nama sathya hai* (God is Truth)," the body is carried to an outdoor crematorium, where all of the relatives and the family members put holy water taken from the Ganges into the deceased's mouth, and while chanting a mantra, they sprinkle holy water all over the body. After this, the body is placed on a funeral pyre, decorated with flowers, and blessed by the Brahmin. The family and relatives then walk around the body five times and set fire to the wood. When a parent dies, the eldest son lights the fire; if a child dies, the father lights the fire. Sometimes butter oil and gasoline are poured over the wood to make the fire stronger or sandalwood is added to give off a nice fragrance. Finally, the ashes are scattered over a nearby river after the cremation. When a young child dies, the body is tied to a rock and placed into a nearby river without being cremated.

In the past, when the husband died, the wife took her own life by lying in the fire with her husband's body. This custom (*sati*) was banned in 1828, when India was under British rule.

The mourning period begins from the day of the cremation. It is said that the soul ascends to heaven 10 days after death. During these 10 days, they hold ceremonies every day. The eleventh day marks the end of the mourning period. Male members of the family who have grown their hair and beards during the mourning period then shave and trim their hair. All the relatives gather together, and a Brahmin holds a ceremony (*pu-ja*) to honor their ancestors and to set the soul free. After the *pu-ja*, a memorial is held every month on the anniversary of the death for one year.

Muslim

When a follower of Islam is in critical condition, the family recites the *Shahadah*, excerpts from the Qur'an, for the sick person to listen. After the person dies, a ceremony of purification is held, and the body is wrapped in white cloth and placed in the casket. In the same manner as with the Hindus, the body is carried to the graveyard. It is said that the deceased's body is led by angels, so no one tries to impede the progress of the procession. The funeral is held in a nearby mosque or open space. The mourners stand in a line and, following the lead of the *imam*, they recite the *Takubir* saying "Allah Akbar" in chorus. Women are not allowed to participate in the ceremony.

After the prayer, the body is taken out of the casket and is buried in the community cemetery, the head facing Mecca. The grave is about a meter and a half deep. Three days after the burial, the family and relatives go to visit the grave. After that, the family goes to the cemetery 40 days after the burial or on the next Friday after the 40th day. This ends one round of the funeral service.

Christian

In the case of Catholics, the priest gives the last unction at the deathbed. After the death, the body is placed in a casket, and candle stands and a cross are set on a table by the deceased's head. On the day following the wake, the funeral is held in a church, and then the body is buried.

Parsee

The funeral customs of those who live near Mumbai (former Bombay) are a little unusual. At first the body is bathed and every part of the body, except the face, is covered with a white cloth. Then a prayer of purification is read. After that, the body is placed on a dirt floor because the corpse is considered to be the most defiled thing that can be encountered. The body is then carried to the Silent Tower of Dakhma to be eaten by vultures. For the Parsee, cremation profanes the fire, whereas interment profanes the earth. Therefore, they cannot cremate the body as the Hindus do nor can they bury the body as the Muslims do. Because they want the soul to ascend directly to the kingdom of the gods or heaven, "sky burial" is the ideal method of disposing the body.

When the body is placed on the platform, the head should face north, and pictures are drawn around the body with an iron stick. Then the *nesasusara*, who is to carry the body to the platform, arrives, but he cannot step into the pattern that has been drawn around the body. The body is placed on an iron coffin platform and carried in a procession led by the priest to Dakhma. The mourners, who are dressed in white clothes, follow the procession. When they reach Dakhma, only the *nesasusara* goes into the tower. There he takes off the white cloth, places the body on the platform, gives a prayer, then leaves. After everyone has left, the body is eaten by vultures.

At the family's home, the people who attended the ceremony wash the exposed parts of their bodies. Then a "holy fire" is kept lit for three days where the dead body had been kept. The bereaved family does not cook during this period and are fed by other people.

Sikh

The Indians who wear turbans are Sikhs, who have different customs from the Hindus. When someone dies in a Sikh family, they must see to five "K"s: (1) the hair and beard must be kept in their natural state, (2) a comb for the hair, (3) a ring for the right hand, (4) a dagger and (5) a shirt.

The funeral customs of the Sikhs are flexible, either cremation or interment is acceptable. According to their founder Nanak's teaching, God is the only one who knows whether cremation or interment is better.

Buddhist

For the Tibetan Buddhists in the Ladakh area of northern India, right before the moment of death, a *ngappa*, an ascetic devotee, is invited to the home, and he recites the *Bar-do Thos grol* (The Book of the Dead) for 49 days after the death. In so doing, the *ngappa* forecasts the best day for the funeral. After death the corpse is placed in the living room, and all the family members leave the house, except the women who spend the mourning period wailing in the kitchen. On the day of the funeral many people from the neighborhood come to join the ceremony. The funeral procession is led by the *Limpoche* (a high monk), and only male mourners join the procession. The body, which is wrapped in a five-color flag called *Dharcho,* is carried to the outdoor crematorium, where the monk lights the holy fire. Three days after the cremation, the ashes are scattered by the family at a remote place in the mountains. The Tibetan Buddhists never make graves. All of the deceased's possessions is auctioned off, and the proceeds are donated to a temple. On the forty-ninth day, the soul of the deceased returns to nature, and the mourning period comes to an end. From that day on, the family life returns to normal.

There are outdoor crematoriums by rivers or in remote fields near residential areas. In the capital, New Delhi, there is one by the Jamuna River, and in Mumbai, there is an electric crematorium at Chanda Wadi.

As a rule, the body is carried to the crematorium in the daytime, but in the case of a death caused by an epidemic disease or the death of a poor man or woman, there are no restrictions concerning the time of cremation. The ashes after cremation are collected on the day of the cremation (in south India they do it on the following day), and scattered over the holy river within 10 days. In the case of the members of the nobility, the body is carried to a place that is considered to be holy, such as Benares, Narba or Allahabad, and then the ashes are placed in the middle of the river. The Hindus believe that the body is reincarnated into another human being or living creature. Therefore, graves are not needed.

At the *ghaat* (river bank) of the Ganges River in Benares City, many pilgrims come early in the morning to pray toward the rising sun. Then they bathe in the river. They believe that by doing so they are purged of their sins and will be rewarded by ascending to heaven when they die.

On the holy ground, there are not only young pilgrims who wish to live better lives but also many very old pilgrims who hope to be reborn after death. The old pilgrims facing death enter a building called the *Shanti* or *Muktivawan*, a kind of hospice, where family members take care of an elderly relative until he or she dies. The building is dark and damp with a bare concrete floor but it is not at all gloomy, for the people there have confidence that they will be reborn.

When someone dies, the body is carried to the outdoor crematorium, the

Manikanica ghaat. The body is placed on firewood and covered with oil, then it is cremated. Where the shades of night fall, the ashes are placed in the river together with floral wreathes in an unglazed dish filled with ignited kerosene. The people watch the fire on the dish as it floats away and pray for the deceased's happiness in the next life. This scene reminds us of the Japanese custom of placing lanterns on the water as offerings. The people believe that the deceased's body is purified by the fire and water.

Some guidebooks say that the grave of Mahatma Gandhi is located in New Delhi, but it is actually only a cenotaph. Gandhi's ashes, following Hindu custom, were scattered over the Himalaya mountains. Except for the Muslims and Christians, the people of India do not make graves.

The largest grave in India is the Taj Mahal, a white marble mausoleum by the River Jamuna in Agra. The fifth ruler of the Mughal Empire, Shah Jahaan, spent a fortune building the Taj Mahal in the early half of the 17th century for his beloved wife Mumtaz-i-mahall. According to the people of India, the Taj Mahal looks most beautiful in October on the night before a full moon with the light reflecting off the pond in the front.

Next to the Taj Mahal is the huge grave of the second ruler of the Mughal Empire in New Delhi. There are some large mausoleums for Muslim saints, but none of those mausoleums can compare to these two. There are many varieties of Muslim graves from the very simple mound type to elaborate tombstones and mausoleums. They seem to testify that money matters even after death.

On the outskirts of the city of Imphal in central Assam, there is a cemetery where tombstones are arranged neatly in rows, for Indian veterans who died during World War II. This is unusual for India.

INDONESIA

The world's largest archipelago, the Republic of Indonesia's myriad islands stretch 5000 kilometers eastwards across the Pacific from the Malay peninsula to New Guinea. The main islands of Sumatra, Java, Kalimantan, Irian Jaya and Sulawesi are mountainous, volcanic and densely forested. Formerly the Dutch East Indies, Indonesia achieved independence in 1949. About half of the population is Muslim, and the country is proud to have the largest number of followers in Islam in the world. There are also those who follow Christianity, Hinduism, Buddhism and the native religions.

In the case of the Muslims, the family first notifies the *imam* and their relatives of the death. The body is buried at the earliest possible time within 24 hours. For instance, if someone dies at ten o'clock in the morning, the body is buried in the afternoon; if someone dies at four o'clock in the afternoon, the body is buried by ten o'clock the next morning. The body is interred as quickly as possible, because the corpse quickly decays in the tropical heat. But this is also because the Muslims are fearful of the dead soul that may wander from the body and harm those who are still alive.

The women in the neighborhood who have heard the sad news gather together bringing rice, while the men bring things that are necessary for the funeral. The elders tie the deceased's jaw closed with a piece of string and cross the arms. The body is laid on a bamboo mat, the head facing north. After a final bath, the body is wrapped in muslin cloth, and the head, chest and feet are tied with string. During this time, others stand beside them and recite the Qur'an. Finally, the coffin is carried out of the house. The children of the family are not to see the deceased, so that they will not be harmed by its curse. Also, the women do not go to the graveyard.

The funeral procession is led by the person who carries the gravepost on which the deceased's name and date of death are written (the gravepost for men has a pointed end, while the one for women is rounded). After the man, who carries the post, follow people, who carry containers with rice, flowers and other offerings. They scatter the rice and flowers along the road as they go. The deceased's coffin and the mourners follow. At the graveyard, the *imam* whispers the confession of faith three times into the ear which faces Mecca and then recites passages of the Qur'an to the deceased in either Arabic or Javanese. After the burial ceremony, bricks or rocks are placed on the grave, the gravepost placed at the head of the grave, then flowers such as roses, jasmine and gardenias are offered to the deceased.

After the funeral, the family offers some food to the mourners at their home. On the third day, seventh day, fortieth day, hundredth day, after the first two years and on the thousandth day, memorial services are held. Then the temporary grave mound is replaced with a tombstone. Such a memorial service may be done in place of the funeral. The rich usually hold their funerals at a mosque. Every year before and after Ramadan are the times when one visits the grave. All the family members join in cleaning the area by pulling weeds and polishing the tombstone at this time.

Although Islam is the national religion, the majority of the people have customs that are mixed with the native religion. Therefore, the funeral customs differ depending on the place.

On the island of Borneo, a distinction is made between natural and abnormal death. Death at birth, death in battle and death by accident are considered abnormal deaths. It is believed that the soul of one who dies abnormally does harm to those who are alive, unless a special ceremony is performed. Therefore, the graves of those who died abnormal deaths are separated from the other graves. They do not fear the souls of those who died natural deaths, which are considered to be guardian spirits. Especially when the chief of a tribe or a shaman dies, the death is favorably accepted by the people and remembered through memorial services. The world of death is completely separated from the world of the living, and by having a traditional funeral, the deceased can live peacefully and comfortably.

On the island of Sulawesi live the Sadan Toraja tribe. When a tribe member of high social rank dies, a large party is held to show respect to the dignity and social rank of the deceased. The traditional customs, interwoven with liturgies that have been memorized and are passed on by generations of priests, are followed.

For the Sadan Toraja tribe, the funeral is a large event, though services vary in length and complexity, depending on the deceased's wealth and status. Funerals consist of a provisional part and a permanent part. The first part is called *dipalambi'i*, which takes place in the *tongkonan* house just after death. The second takes place months, even years, after the death, depending on how long it takes the bereaved family to save for the expense of the ceremonies. If the deceased was of high status and rich, the second ceremony may go on for over a week, drawing thousands of mourners, and even involving entertaining activities such as buffalo fights, kick fights, chanting and dancing. At this time, water buffaloes, regarded the most sacred of animals, are sacrificed and the liturgy called *Passamba Tedong* is read as the priests cut the carotid artery of the buffalo with a long knife. Later, the bones of the deceased are wrapped in ikat textiles and placed in rock-cut tombs on rock walls near the village.

In the eastern part of Indonesia, and on the smaller islands west of Sumatra, the body is buried in a remote place and no formal grave is made. Platform burial (where the corpse is left for the wild animals) is also common.

The religion of Bali is usually said to be Hinduism, but it is quite different from the Hinduism of India. For instance, there is no caste system in Bali and the various Hindu icons are not worshiped. The gods do not rest in one's home, but they come down into the space below the blue sky. The custom of cremation is, without doubt, due to Hinduism, but it is not as simple in form as it is in India. The funeral procession is extraordinarily gorgeous, and the people attach a lot of importance to it. The people of Bali respect their ancestors more than the people of India do. It is believed that if they neglect their customs, they will be cursed by their ancestors. Many taboos concern directions and dates, and it is believed that if one violates the customs, one will later face disaster.

When someone is dying, he or she is moved to the eastern wing of the house, the favorable direction. When the person dies, the body is moved to the center of the yard on the western side of the house and placed on an *asagan* (stand for the coffin). Then the people of the neighborhood wash the body and place flowers behind its ears. The body is wrapped in white cloth and tied with rope. It is carried to building to the west and laid down. The head must face the west. After that, the leader (*pu mank*) is invited to give the ceremony of purification. During this time, other people prepare for the burial.

When the body is carried on the shoulders of the mourners, coconut milk is poured in front of the house. As the procession proceeds to the graveyard, which is usually in the southern end of the village, it must pass in front of temples and shrines. The family purifies the house with holy water. Sometimes the funeral ends there, but usually the remains are cremated later. In the case of a rich family, a coffin in the shape of an ox is carried by many people from the house to the graveyard. The coffin is set on an elaborately decorated stand at the crematory. The fire for the cremation is set in the late afternoon. When the cremation ends, the ashes are placed in a coconut shell and after the leader's prayer, they place the coconut in the sea or river. Families with long histories often observe a memorial service called *mukul*, on the forty-second day after the cremation. Usually, however, it is believed that the soul rises to heaven and the soul returns on a day set by the calendar into the *sanga* in the northeastern part of the deceased's home. The family places offerings in front of the shrine and prays.

Among the Chinese immigrants to Indonesia, many are Buddhists, who live mostly in the urban areas. The funeral, however, is somewhat mixed with the style of the native religion. For them, Pali is the language used for ritual. There is also a new religion, Kebatinan, which became popular after World War II.

In the remote areas, such as Western New Guinea and the Sulawesi district, where the Melanesians live, traditional funeral customs used to be common. The areas were gold mines for anthropological studies. Many scholars did their research there, the results of which are presently available. The book *Primitive Concepts of Death* by Joji Tanase (Tonan Asia Kenkyu Sosho) has detailed records of fieldwork done in the area.

The Dani, living along the Balim River in the central highlands of Irian Jaya, still retain the century-old tradition, and stay almost naked all year round. Death itself is considered to be caused by magic or witchcraft, and the funeral service takes place in the village yard, led by the chief of the village. However, such traditional customs have gradually changed since World War II, because of the influence of modern civilization.

JAPAN

A constitutional monarchy, with the emperor as the symbolic head of state, Japan is located off the East Asian coast in the North Pacific. It consists of four principal islands, Honshu, Shikoku, Kyushu and Hokkaido, which are connected either by bridge or by underground tunnel, and more than 3,000 smaller islands. The terrain is mostly mountainous with fertile coastal plains; more than two-thirds is woodland.

When someone dies, it must be reported to the Health Department of a nearby municipality, and the death certificate issued by an attending doctor submitted. An affiliated temple or mortuary is also necessary for funeral arrangements. The Health Department then issues a permit for the disposal of the body by either cremation or burial 24 hours after the death. Presently, most local government by-laws and regulations prohibit interment of whole bodies, so almost all corpses are cremated at crematoriums in Japan (98.9% of the corpses are cremated as of 1996). Remains are mostly interred in family tombs or repositories either at temples' affiliated cemeteries, public cemeteries or incorporated memorial parks.

The majority of the people follow the Buddhist tradition, and a wake (*tsuya*) is held the night before the funeral service either at the bereaved family's home or at a temple or mortuary. Relatives and close friends spend the last night with the corpse, praying for the repose of the departed. The body is laid out with its head to the north. A picture of the deceased and a bowl of heaped rice with the chopsticks stuck vertically into it are set on the altar. A Buddhist priest is invited to officiate at the service; and the deceased is given a posthumous name (*kaimyo*), which is written on a wooden tablet.

At the funeral service the next day, mourners gather wearing subdued clothes. Traditionally they bring monetary offerings (*koden*) to the funeral service. In the temple, they proceed to the altar to offer incense and put their hands together in prayer. After the service and the last viewing of the deceased, the nails in the coffin lid are pounded in with a stone and the coffin is loaded into the hearse. There is also a Shinto funeral service, in which instead of the offering of incense at the cemetery, sakaki sprigs are offered. At a Christian funeral service, flowers are offered instead of incense or sakaki sprigs.

At present, there are more than 1,600 public and semi-public crematoriums throughout the country, which are open every day of the week except on the day of *tomobiki* (tailing friends). On this day, it is said to be inviting another death so that the people used to avoid funerals on this day. This custom, called *Rokuyo* (six-days calendar of fortune) was imported from China in the 14th century and has been practiced in Japan ever since.

At the crematorium, friends and relatives gather the bone fragments with chopsticks and put them in an urn that is later buried in a graveyard. Afterward they are treated to drinks and food, which is referred to as a refreshment feast, called *otoki*. Sometimes before leaving, salt is sprinkled on their shoulder to cleanse the impurity of death so that they do not carry impurities into their daily lives.

Besides the memorial services for the deceased, people usually hold annual events during the *Obon* and *Higan* festivals. The *Obon* festival, which is held in honor of the deceased, was originally held on July 15 according to the lunar calendar, but nowadays it is generally held between August 13 and 16. The *Higan*, the equinox festivals, fall twice, once in spring and once in fall. During these days, people pay respectful visits to the deceased at their family graves, offering candles, flowers and incense sticks. They also sit at the family altar and recite the sutra. In old times, ancestral spirits and departed souls were believed to return to their families during this period.

In both Buddhist and Shinto funeral services in Japan there are cases where people send flowers or goods to the bereaved family. It is also customary to read the condolence telegrams at the funeral service. If a condolence gift is sent, something is always received in return later. This is called *koden gaeshi*, an appreciation gift consisting of tea, soap, towels or something practical. These are often sent directly from the department store with the thank-you note written on the front. Newspaper obituaries are usually reserved for well-known people or people in high positions, so many immediately know about their deaths. These days, it is not uncommon that their families to ask others to refrain from sending gifts of any kind, and instead to contribute to charity.

Those who are not affiliated with any religious organization, yet wish to have their funeral services according to such an organization, may proceed as follows:

Buddhist Temples

Most temples grant the bereaved's wishes and conduct funeral services after the ordination (*motsugo saso*) and posthumous name as the Buddha's disciple are given by a full-fledged priest.

Shinto Shrines

Most denominations to which a shrine belongs accept the bereaved's wishes and conduct their funeral services as they will eventually become a *kami* (Shinto god) after they pass away.

Christian Churches

If they so wish, funeral services may be acceptable, but no mass will be held for non-Catholic members who are not baptized.

Islamic Mosques

Unless the deceased has confessed that Allah is the only one God, a funeral service cannot be held. There is an Islam cemetery at Enzan City, Yamanashi Prefecture, 70 kilometers west of Tokyo, where the bodies are buried.

According to the Buddhist tradition, it is believed that by the forty-ninth day after death, the karma of the deceased takes a certain form. Thereafter, 49 days of mourning are usually observed by the bereaved family after death, during which time they refrain from merry-making, and go to visit the graveyard where the deceased's ashes are interred. After that, the one-hundredth day, the first, third, seventh, thirteenth, seventeenth and twenty-third year memorial services are observed, ending with the thirty-third-year memorial, from which time the individual soul is believed to be assimilated into the collective ancestral soul. At the memorial services, incense, flowers and food are offered at the family altar and the grave, usually with the Buddhist priest officiating. During the spring and autumn equinoxes (*Higan*) or the *Obon* season in July and August, people usually visit the grave, where they offer incense, flowers and the deceased's favorite food.

The cemeteries are owned by municipalities, temples or corporate organizations, from whom the bereaved family purchases the perpetual right of use as long as they pay the annual management fee. At the request of the bereaved family, sometimes the urn may be kept in the temple or the posthumous name (*kaimyo*) of a deceased may be kept on file in the temple records, so that perpetual memorial services can be held for the deceased even though the family may move away or die.

In the past years, the cost of funerary services in Japan has skyrocketed. Despite the economic recession, which is evident in almost all areas of business in Japan in recent years, according to a report released in 1997 by the Japanese Ministry of Social Welfare, the funeral business is the one of the few that continues to flourish. Moreover, deluxe funeral homes and memorial parks, with elaborate, colorful funeral rites, have mushroomed all over Japan.

In Okinawa, the southern tip of Japan, the islanders, who are frequently confronted with natural disasters, observe the memorial services and the visitation of the graves more often as the occasion of tightening a family's solidarity, and erect ornate graves or mausoleums. In the past, they would take out the buried remains after a year and cleanse them before reburial. These customs and manners must have been greatly influenced by those of neighboring China and Taiwan. When people meet misfortune, particularly as a result of transgressing taboos, they usually ask a shaman, called *yuta*, for guidance.

Among the Ainu who live on Hokkaido at the northern tip of Japan the mourners use different words of condolence in honor of the deceased, depending on the degree of contribution to their community. At the wake, the village elders used to recite an epic called *yukara*, but this custom has been gradually diminishing as the elders pass away.

At the end of World War II, atomic bombs were dropped on Hiroshima and Nagasaki, and some 140,000 people died in Hiroshima and 70,000 died in Nagasaki. In both cities the death rate within a kilometer from each hypocenter was close to 100 percent, which led Japan to a total surrender to the Allied Powers on August 15, 1945. Both cities have held memorial services for victims every year since 1946. At Hiroshima Peace Park, there stands a cenotaph on which is inscribed the phrase, "*Let all the souls here rest in peace; for we shall not repeat the evil.*"

In case of a foreigner's death, people are not authorized to move a corpse for any reason, until after examination by the Japanese medical doctor and issuance of release. (This applies only if a doctor is not present at the time of death.) If a private doctor is not available, it is required to call another doctor, or call the nearest police box or station, and also inform their embassy or consulate. The options available are embalming of the corpse with burial either in Japan or elsewhere, burial in Japan without embalming or cremation with interment of the ashes in Japan or elsewhere. The embassy or consulate can provide further details.

NORTH KOREA

The Democratic People's Republic of Korea (North Korea) comprises the northern half of the Korean peninsula and is separated from South Korea at the 38th parallel. Much of the country is mountainous; the Chaeryong and Pylongyang plains in the southwest are the most fertile regions. Established as an independent communist republic in 1948, North Korea remains largely isolated from the outside world. In the past, religious activities were conducted by professional clergy from the respective faiths—Buddhism, Christianity and Confucianism. However, because such religious activities are undesirable according to national policy, there are now restrictions on them.

It might be natural that the concerns and interests of young people in religion have declined because they are educated with the *chuche* thinking, which values subjectivity toward the people in general. However, traditional funeral customs are not likely to disappear in a short period of time. When someone dies, a very respectful funeral is held in the local community or in the people's commune.

When someone dies, the family or the relatives report the death to the government district office, and the name of the deceased is deleted from the public records. The family also sends a death notice to his work place. In this way, from among the 40 vacation days with pay, 3 days off are officially given to the family. If they submit a medical report, 10 *won* and 1 *to* of rice are given to the family as a funeral subsidy.

Although there are considerable funeral expenses, the bereaved family does not have to bear all the costs. Sometimes the money comes from a budget of their community organization; for those who have contributed to the country or to public organizations, the costs are covered by public funds. Funeral expenses stem from such things as the tombstone, which is often very luxurious. Sometimes those who are wealthy have tombstones made of cement. A truck, not a hearse, is used to transport the body. Customs such as decorating the deceased's picture with flowers and a black frame have been discarded. Also the bereaved family and mourners wear casual clothes with black belts.

In the rural areas, interment is still common, and the body is buried in a community cemetery. Public cemeteries can be found everywhere, on the southern slope of sunny hills or farmlands, which have now been converted into farms. In the cities, however, cremation has gradually become more popular. The funeral usually continues for three days and the mourning continues for a year. However, in the case of a Communist Party officer, like the Revolutionists, a funeral committee is organized, and everyone helps to prepare for the funeral, and the body is buried in the mausoleum of the Revolutionists.

After a death, on the fifteenth day of the eighth month in the lunar calendar, the people go back to their hometowns. Especially in the rural areas, traditional food is offered at the grave. Once this kind of custom was labeled a feudalistic event, but recently the controls and restrictions have been eased, so such customs have been gradually returning.

A memorial ceremony to mark the one hundredth day of the mourning period for the late President Kim Il Sung was held on October 16, 1994, in Pyongyang, according to the Confucian tradition.

SOUTH KOREA

The Republic of Korea (South Korea) occupies the southern half of the Korean peninsula in East Asia. It is separated from North Korea by a wide demilitarized zone which roughly divides the country along the 38th parallel. Over 80 percent of its terrain is mountainous and two-thirds is forested. Rice is the major agricultural product, grown by over 85 percent of South Korea's three million farmers. Most of the urban population lives along the coastal plains. The people of South Korea are mainly Koreans, and the official language is Korean.

In South Korea, politics and religion are officially separated and freedom of religion is recognized, so there are various religions like Buddhism and Protestant Christianity. Confucianism used to have a strong influence, so when someone died, the body was buried in the family grave on the slope of a hill. Recently, however, because of a shortage of land, cremation has become more common. According to a recent government survey, the rate of cremation was at 8 percent, but it has increased to as much as 20 to 30 percent in recent years. Previously, only monks, followers of Buddhism, unmarried people or those not able to buy houses were the majority of those who were cremated.

In most local areas there are traditional groups called *taesang*, which are organized to assist people with funerals. In most cases, the funeral proceeds according to a set order: *moree, rosae, sosung, taesung, kisae* and *bosae*. The *moree* is the funeral, at which time the body is buried. The soul is believed to be separated from the body and stays within the mourning house. Only after the *rosae*, three days after the funeral, the *sosung*, a year after the funeral and the *taesung*, the second year after the funeral, does the soul finally leave the mourning house. After that, the souls of the past three generations will be welcomed at the *kisae* by the bereaved family, who will pray for them. Other souls of the following generation are cared for at the *bosae* ceremony, which takes place in October every year.

The *taesang* takes care of the arrangements for the first funeral. The role of the *taesang* is to go to the mourning house and pray, offer some money and gifts, send out the notice of death and also to prepare the area where the funeral is held, to bury the body, and finally to transport the mourning carriage which carries the casket to the cemetery.

The legs and arms of the deceased are straightened and burial clothes are placed on the body. The head must point north and the face is covered with a white cloth. Then the relatives and friends are notified of the death. A note concerning the death is placed at the gate of the mourning house, which reads "in the midst of mourning" or "mourning family." Some dried meat and sweet rice wine are offered to the deceased until the body is placed in the casket. This is called *cheon*. Incense is provided and a photograph of the deceased is displayed for the mourners. The body is placed in a wooden lacquer box 24 hours after the death, and the deceased's official title and family name are inscribed on the cover of the box. Then the box is wrapped in special paper and tied with a rope.

At the wake, called *pamseum*, the head of the mourning family, relatives and friends get together and pray for the deceased with deep bows. All through the night, the mourners discuss the life of the deceased while burning incense. Sometimes they play mahjong as well. The funeral is held on the third, fifth or the seventh day after the death. The head of the mourning family is the eldest son of the deceased. The husband is never the head of the funeral for his wife or children. In the past, one's mourning clothes were selected strictly according to one's relationship with the deceased. Now, however, things have been simplified. In the case of Korean clothes, they wear white or black, while in the case of western clothes they wear black with a mourning badge or white flower.

In the Buddhist funeral, the priest goes to the family's home, but this is different from the farewell service, and regular mourners do not attend. The farewell service is held in front of the house. The casket is placed on the hearse or palanquin. On the floor, offerings are lined up, incense is burned and rice wine is offered. After the head of the funeral finishes the ceremonial matters, mourning messages and songs are recited. Finally, relatives and mourners burn incense. If it is a famous person, they sometimes use a special hall, and if the deceased is a Christian, the funeral and farewell service are held in a church.

The funeral procession to the cemetery proceeds in the following order: the deceased's picture, the casket, the bereaved family and the mourners. On the way, relatives or friends may have prepared offerings and burn incense in order to comfort the soul. This is called the "road ceremony." When the casket arrives at the cemetery, the mourners stand on both sides of it and bow. The body is buried in the ground and covered with lime. In front of the grave, holy food, incense and incantations are prepared, and everyone raises wine cups and participates in comforting the soul of the deceased until the completion of the service. When the people return from the cemetery, everyone laments very loudly in front of the house. Then the picture and memorial tablet are placed in the holy place outside the house, and everybody begins wailing again.

Three days after the funeral, the family goes to the graveyard, but there are no offerings at this time. Instead, on the first and fifteenth of each month, the family members go to the grave and offer food. In the third month, there is the Ceremony of the Ending of Mourning Period. They prepare ceremonial objects and food, and hold a ceremony with a priest. After this, even if something very sad happens, there is to be no wailing.

The mourning period for parents, grandparents and spouses is 100 days from the day of the death. The mourning period for others is until the day of the funeral. The family invites friends and holds a ceremony for the memorial services. This is considered to be the completion of the funeral. The location of the graveyard used to be decided by a fortune teller according to *param mul seol* (geomancy). Recently, however, more families make use of the nearby public or church cemetery. There are also some people who place the remains in a niche. In front of the grave, the people build all kinds of things like stone statues and lanterns.

The deceased's name is inscribed on the front side of the tombstone, and the epitaph on the back. Among the graves of the rich, there are many which are made into the mound-type graves. The body is placed in a casket, and a mound is made over it. The tombstone is placed in front of the mound.

In Korea, in order to assist each other, there is a custom of giving monetary offerings to the family, just as in Japan. The money is placed in an envelope with a piece of paper on which the donor's name and the amount of money are written. Burning incense is very common. For Christians, flowers are offered. The stem of the flower must face the deceased. If the deceased is well-known, a special hall may be used. Both the funeral and the farewell service are usually held in a church.

Because of the influence of Confucianism, ancestors are cherished. Going back four generations, each person's memorial day is remembered and a service is held. For an ancestor who dates back more than five generations, an auspicious day is chosen in the first year and 10 months of the lunar calendar. On that day, all of the family members gather together in front of the grave and hold a ceremony called *Sije*. At that time, a lacquer memorial tablet is placed in the altar. If the deceased had any rank or title, the title is inscribed on the tablet. If he does not have any title or rank, the tablet is inscribed with "student." There are also simplified tablets on which pieces of paper are pasted. The eldest son, even if he is young, must lead the ceremony of removing the deity from the altar and recite the prayer. Then all of the participants bow twice to the deity and, from the oldest person of the family to the younger members, a cup of rice wine is offered in the order of age. At the end, they offer rice wine three times to the ancestors. Garlic and red peppers, which are later given to the mourners, are not used as offerings.

When a parent dies, the eldest son, who is the head of the mourners, must continue mourning for three years. The first two years are, respectively, called *shosung* and *taesung*; the third year is called *sannenso*. In the Yi Dynasty, a shack by the grave was built and the chief mourner confined himself there for two years. During that period, he would offer food to the soul of the deceased twice a day in front of the Buddhist altar, in which the memorial tablet was placed. He also placed meals on a table covered with a white cloth in the corner of the room and poured rice wine or water into a box containing soil from the graveyard. The whole family would get together to hold a memorial service every month on the first and fifteenth.

On the outskirts of Pusan, there is a United Nations military cemetery where 2,267 remains of soldiers from 21 countries who died during the Korean War were buried.

LAOS

The People's Democratic Republic of Laos is a land-locked country surrounded by Vietnam, Cambodia, Thailand, Myanmar and China. The Mekong River forms its main thoroughfare and feeds the fertile lowlands of the Mekong Valley. In 1953, it became independent of France, but because of continuous civil war in the Indochinese peninsula, Laos had suffered for many years. However, the country is now enjoying a respite from war. About half of the population is Laotian, while the rest of the population is multi-ethnic. Many follow Theravada Buddhism or the native religions.

When someone dies, the family or relatives wash the body. In the case of a local wealthy person, it is the custom to place coins or gold between the deceased's teeth. The body is wrapped in a white shroud, and after being encoffined, it is placed on a banana tree log. Then a monk recites sutras.

For the Laotians, death is not a sorrow or misfortune. It means entering into *nirvana*, where all earthly desires are extinguished, and it proves that all living things must perish. Therefore, rather than grieve, the mourners seem to approach the funeral as an auspicious event, in which festivities continue for seven days. After that, the body is transported to a shack built in the corner of the rice fields. The family never fails to bring food to the shack in order to comfort the deceased. In the open field, firewood is placed in a pile for the cremation. They select an auspicious day and carry the body to the site of the cremation. Then the monk recites a sutra, and with many people watching, the fire is set and the body is cremated. The ashes are gathered together and placed in an urn to be buried in a temple.

The funeral of the mountainous Lame is a little different. The family wails for three days and three nights. A bonfire is kept lit in front of the house until the funeral ends to keep the dead soul from possessing others. All the villagers join the funeral, and then the body is buried on the mountain. The soul is believed to reside in the head and feet, so heavy stones are placed on the head and feet.

Among the Moi, when someone dies, the body is transferred to a hut called "the house of souls" (a mausoleum), which serves as the grave for the dead.

In the capital, Vientiane, the funeral is held at the family home in the presence of monks, and then the body is moved to the temple and cremated. However, aside from the Savan Temple, no temples have crematory equipment. In most cases, when it is necessary, temples build a temporary crematorium with concrete blocks.

When a foreigner dies, the death must be reported to the city hall and to the police to obtain approval for burial, after reporting it to the Central National Hospital and receiving a medical certificate. In the rural areas, these matters are taken up with the military office or the police, and the body is cremated in a nearby temple. If the remains are to be moved out of the country, permission must be obtained from the Ministry of Foreign Affairs and (as of 1988) an airline ticket must be provided for the deceased.

MACAO

Macao is located in the southern part of Kanton Province in China. It consists of the Macao Peninsula, Taiba Isle and Coloane Isle, and is an autonomous region of Portugal. It has a total area of 16 square kilometers and a population of about a quarter million. Despite a veneer of Portuguese architecture and custom, it has retained its Chinese character, and during the twentieth century the province has been much affected by events in China. Most people are Chinese, but Portuguese is the official language, although Chinese is also used. On December 20, 1999, Macao will be returned to China. As in Hong Kong, a Special Administrative Council is to be established, and for a period of 50 years after its return to China, the Macao government is to be given the right to self-govern, except in its diplomacy and national defense. Most people follow Buddhism, but there are also Catholics. When someone dies, the family asks a nearby funeral home to make the arrangements for a wake and the funeral to be held there, and then the body is buried in a public cemetery. Recently, cremation has become more popular; in the case of interment, they now dig up the bones and rebury them, because of the shortage of land.

MALAYSIA

Comprising the three separate territories of Malay, Sarawak and Sabah, the State of Malaysia stretches over 2,000 kilometers from the Malay Peninsula to the northeastern end of the island of Borneo. It shares borders with Thailand, Indonesia and the enclave states of Singapore and Brunei. The territory is mainly mountainous, and most of the developed areas are used for the cultivation of gum trees. Aside from the Malay, many people are of Chinese or Indian origin. Article Three of Malaysia's constitution states that Islam is the national religion, but it also ensures freedom of religion. In general, the Chinese are Buddhists and the Indians are Hindu, and there are also Christians.

Funeral customs differ depending on the religion and the ethnic background of the people involved, but in all cases a death must be reported to the government office with a doctor's medical certificate, and the funeral is held according to the religious customs of the family.

Islamic funeral customs are rather simple. When someone dies, the family informs their mosque leader as well as their relatives and friends. The body is laid in the middle of the living room of the deceased's home. The family or relatives bathe the deceased with water. Then the body is wrapped in a seamless shroud of white cloth and placed in a coffin with holy verses from the Qur'an inscribed on the cover. The family or relatives do the prayer for the deceased's home.

Then the coffin is carried to the mosque for prayer before the funeral. At the graveyard, the body is placed in the grave with white cloth partly removed to enable the head to face Mecca. The leader, sitting on a mat, says a prayer, and sandalwood perfume is sprayed on the coffin from head to foot. After the prayer, soil is shoveled over the coffin, and a gravepost is placed at the head of the grave. Sometimes flowers are placed on it.

In any case, the body is buried as soon as possible. If a death occurs in the morning, the body is buried that afternoon; if the death occurs in the afternoon or night, the burial takes place on the following morning. Also, the Muslims in Malaysia hold a service after the burial in order to comfort the soul of the deceased. The people pray that the deceased may be blessed by God. This is not an authentic Islamic custom but is unique to Malaysia. However, all Muslims are buried in the ground, and the tombstones, which may be made of brick or stone, come in various shapes such as a star or the moon.

The Chinese Buddhists hold elaborate funerals, with processions to musical accompaniment. The Chinese usually hold the funeral at a temple-style gathering place called the "Social Hall." Recently, because it is difficult to obtain a grave site, more people have been keeping the remains, usually cremated, in temple niches.

On the island of Borneo, there are tribes such as the Iban, the Kayan and the Kenyah who hold simple funerals, but there are also other tribes, such as the Balito and the Berawan in the Sarawak District, who still perform complex funerals. These people remove the buried bones and wash them. Then they hold another funeral. The deceased is given a bath at a place specially set out for the funeral, and is wrapped in a death robe so that it can be observed by those who wish to say farewell to the deceased. Finally, the body is buried in the ground. In the case of a complex funeral, the body may be placed in a coffin or temporarily kept in the resting place. When the corpse decomposes, rituals are performed, and then the bones are placed in an urn and buried in the graveyard. This type of complex funeral is quite popular among the rich and famous.

In Sava, Northern Borneo, stands Mt. Kinabaru (4,101 meters), the highest mountain in Southeast Asia. In the Kadazan language, it is called *Aki Nabalu,* meaning the dwelling place of the ancestral spirits. The local people used to go up to the mountain-top and offer seven sacrificed chickens and eggs.

MALDIVES

The Republic of Maldives is an archipelago of 1,190 small coral islands set in the Indian Ocean southwest of Sri Lanka. The islands, of which only 200 are inhabited, rise no more than 1.8 meters above sea level and are protected by encircling reefs. Tourism has grown in recent years, though the holiday islands are separate from the settled islands. In 1965, the Maldives became independent. The majority of the people are Sri Lankan Sinhalese, but there are also Indians and Arabs.

The Sinhalese used to be Buddhist, but now they follow Sunni Islam, which is by law the national religion. The religious customs, which are very strict about violations of Islamic law, penetrate deep into the people's life-styles. Punishment for those who violate the precepts is often quite serious.

On each island, there is a mosque in the charge of a *katibu*, who is paid by the goverment. The ethos of Islam appears to be very strong in Maldives and many pray five times a day and read the scripture. Because of the importance placed on religion, death rituals also hold great significance. When someone dies, the *katibu* is informed and a conch shell is blown. Then the deceased is washed, tied and shrouded as specified in Islamic tradition and put into a coffin or a leaf box, and family members and friends dig the grave and lay the corpse in it with the face toward Mecca while reading passages from the Qur'an.

MONGOLIA

Land-locked between Russia and China, Mongolia rises from the semi-arid Gobi Desert to mountainous steppe. Mongolia was unified by Genghis Khan in 1206 and became part of Manchu China in 1697. In 1924, Mongolia became an independent communist state, but in 1990 it became the first Asian nation to abandon communism. The majority of the people are Mongolian, but there are some Kazaks in the remote areas. The official language is Mongolian. After 1946, they adopted the Russian writing system, but recently they have started to use their own ethnic writing system again.

In the past, Tibetan Buddhism was widely followed in Mongolia, and there were many temples and monasteries. However, since 1921, when the People's Revolutionary Party overthrew the Lamaist government, it has become a socialist country. As a result, temple property became nationalized, and the Lama monks were forced to give up their religious life and become laymen. Due to the spread of materialistic education, young people, who make up the majority of the country's population, do not depend on the magical prayers of the Lama monks. However, traces of the old life style which predates the revolution still remain.

When someone dies, the family reports the death to the nearby government district office called *holoholin*. The body is buried after the funeral. The date of the funeral used to be decided by a Lama, and the day of the funeral was either Monday, Wednesday, or Friday. On the chosen day, the body would be carried to the graveyard to be buried. Before the revolution, the body was carried to a burial place where it was left for the wolves, foxes and vultures to eat. If the body was completely devoured by the animals within three days, it meant the deceased was a good person. The Russian adventurer Przhevalsky, who visited Mongolia in the latter half of the 19th century, wrote that during a funeral in a graveyard by the Ulga River they did not bury the body but left it on the ground so that dogs, vultures, and eagles could eat it. It was a shocking scene. The area was covered with piles of bones, dogs slinking among them.

Today, there is a public cemetery on the southern slope of a hill in the suburbs of cities. The body is placed in the ground so that the head points south, and the mourners walk around the body three times while they pour *ailag* (fermented horse milk) on the ground. When the mourners leave the grave, they do not look back. At the bereaved family's home, rice with raisins in it is served. The 49 days after the death are the mourning period for the family. During that period, women do not use make-up or wear ornaments. Also, celebratory events such as weddings are not held. They use individual graves to bury their dead. There are tombstones in the Russian style with the sign of a star over an obelisk to be seen there. Every year the people visit the graveyard at the beginning of April. There is no custom of offering flowers at that time.

At present, the Lama monks practice in such monasteries as Gandan Temple in Ulan Bator, the capital of Mongolia. However, they are not very active in missionary work. There were more than 500 temples before the revolution, but most of them have since been destroyed or have become dilapidated over time. Today, not very many remain standing. However, since perestroika in 1990, the Mongolians, who value tradition and respect the elderly, are now looking for an identity with which they can rebuild the country on the Lamaist model.

MYANMAR

Forming the eastern shores of the Bay of Bengal and the Andaman Sea in South East Asia, the Union of Myanmar is mountainous in the north, while the once-forested, fertile Irrawaddy Basin occupies most of the country. Then called Burma, it gained independence from British colonial control in 1948. In 1989 the Saw Maung regime changed its name to Myanmar and the country under the socialist Ne Win regime has recently experienced widespread political repression and ethnic conflict. About 70 percent of the population are Mongolian Burmese, who are different from the people of India and Bangladesh. There are also the Karen, the Mon, the Arakhan and the Chin. The majority of the people follow Theravada Buddhism, but freedom of religion is ensured.

When someone dies, the body is thoroughly washed, and the lower half of the body is wrapped in a white cloth. Then the deceased's best clothes are put on the body inside-out. The body is then placed on an altar in front of the house.

The wake may continue for two or three days. Wailing women may also be hired from the neighborhood. In general, the body is placed in the coffin in the afternoon of the day of death or on the following day and is carried to the graveyard on a stretcher. A monk is invited to accompany the funeral party. The procession is led by the chief mourner, followed by the *bhikhu* (monk), a band, the family, relatives, and acquaintances. At the graveyard, the monk gives the last rites to the soul of the deceased (strictly speaking, the monk recites the *paritta*). Then the coffin is shaken three times back and forth in the grave before it is buried.

If the deceased was wealthy, the body is cremated in a special crematorium, and the ashes are placed in an urn, which is then buried in a small obelisk by a pagoda. However, most are buried in the ground with no tombstones. In the capital, Yangon, there are two crematoriums, but only 36 bodies can be cremated a day, so in other areas the body is cremated in a field which is designated as the cremation spot. When the deceased is poor, the body is simply wrapped in a straw mat and buried in the ground.

When the funeral ends, the family calls the monk and offers *Teppiausun*, and on the seventh day, the *Ietsuresun* (the first seventh-day memorial service) is held. There is also a periodic memorial service called *fneresun*, which is seldom held. The people of Myanmar do not visit the grave very often, but the family invites the monk to their home and holds a memorial service, or they visit a nearby pagoda.

The minority Shan and Mon, who live in the north-eastern part of Myanmar, also follow Buddhism. Most Burmese have oblong tombstones built, while the Shan Kun have pyramid-shaped, perpendicular tombstones.

NEPAL

On the shoulder of the southern Himalayas, the tallest mountains in the world, the Kingdom of Nepal is surrounded by India and China. In 1991, democratic elections were held for the first time since 1959, marking the end of a period of absolute rule by the king. In the valleys, there is a multi-ethnic population that includes the Gurkhas, the Newars and the Gurung. The official language is Nepali.

According to Nepal's constitution, Hinduism is the national religion. There are also Lamaists and Buddhists, but proselytizing of their religious groups is not allowed. However, freedom of religion is ensured, so this multi-ethnic population coexists peacefully. There are also a small number of Muslims and Christians, who follow their own customs by interring their dead.

In the case of Hindus in Nepal, a death is customarily reported to the temple. In Katmandu, the doctor asks the dying patient if he wishes to die by the holy river Pakmati, which flows through the city. If the answer is yes, the doctor transfers the patient to Pashupati Nath Temple, where the god Shiva is enshrined. It is a kind of hospice with meager rooms and beds, with no medical facilities, and is a temple in name only. At the moment of death, the patient's lips are moistened with water from the Pakmati River, and the patient's feet are soaked in the river water. Then the unclothed body is covered with firewood. The eldest son of the deceased inserts a small ignited piece of the firewood into the deceased's mouth, whereupon the relatives set fire to the firewood around the body. At this time, a priest is invited to pray. No oil or gasoline is used to fuel the fire, so it takes several hours to cremate the body. All of the ashes are scattered over the river. During the mourning period, only one meal is allowed. When the mourning period ends on the thirteenth day after the death, the family members are allowed to shave, and a priest is called to say a prayer. It is believed that giving *puja* (offerings) is an act of charity.

When Buddhists die, the funeral is held in a temple such as the Swannabnath Temple. On a small stage by the temple entrance, amateur musicians chant religious pieces to the accompaniment of the accordion, flute, drum and the like. While the music goes on, the body is cremated. The ashes are kept in an obelisk called *panso*. On the anniversary of the death, the family invites the priest to pray for the deceased.

Tibetan Buddhists go to Lama monks to inquire about the date of the funeral, which is determined by a special calendar called *Tuigorze*. In general, poor people prefer burial in the water, because it is less expensive and does not require firewood, while the rich prefer cremation. The family prays every seven days after the day of the funeral, and on the forty-ninth day, they invite a monk to comfort the soul of the deceased.

In the past, at Badi in the Dolbo District, "sky burial" were performed. Today, however, it is prohibited by law. Not long ago, there was an article about a funeral in Nepal. It included the picture taken at Kingal Village in the northwestern part of Nepal of a corpse of an elderly woman. The caption stated that after one elderly Lama monk gave the final recitation of the sutras, another young monk carefully cut the body into small pieces so that the vultures could easily eat it. It is believed that by being eaten by the vultures, she can ascend to heaven. When the monks finished chopping up the body, one of the monks played a conch-shell flute toward the mountain peaks. Then more than 50 vultures flew down and ate the body. This "ceremony of the the birds" takes only four or five minutes, after which nothing remains.

PHILIPPINES

Lying in the western Pacific Ocean, the Philippines is the world's second largest archipelago after Indonesia. It comprises 7,107 islands, of which 4,600 are named and 1,000 are inhabited. There are three main islands groupings: the Luzon group; the Visayan group; and the Mindanao and Sulu islands. Located on the Pacific "Ring of Fire," the Philippines is subject to frequent earthquakes and volcanic activity. The climate is tropical and the humidity is high. The population is Malay-Indonesian, but there are some who are of Spanish descent. The national language is English, but there are many languages such as Tagalog and Ilokano.

When someone dies in town, the family obtains a medical certificate and requests the mortuary to take care of the funeral, burial and other matters. In the rural areas, however, the family or relatives do all the arrangements. In general, the funeral is held at the family home, the church or the mortuary within three days to one week after the death, and a minister from the family church officiates at the funeral. There are various kinds of funeral homes that provide different services. For instance, in the capital, Manila, some have a hearse, chapel, mortuary and morgue and take care various logistical matters, while some homes handle details such as financing the funeral.

At a Catholic church, the funeral is very dignified and the atomosphere is solemn, while at a Protestant church the funeral is not as elaborate and is often accompanied by hymns. Poor family members sometimes raise funds for the funeral by gambling. Recently, many families prefer a simple funeral in the chapel of the funeral home.

After the funeral, the mourners follow the hearse by car to the graveyard. If the family is rich, a band leads the procession. All the hearses in Manila are luxurious American models. Such a procession brings traffic to a stop. People watch quietly and wait until it passes. Among the hearses, there are some that have stereo systems in the car so that they can play funeral hymns along the way. The ministers usually do not attend the burial.

There are private and public cemeteries and private memorial parks. The Catholics and Muslims prefer burial in the ground, while cremation is more common among the Protestants and the rich. Underground graves are not common due to frequent rainfall. Nine days after the burial, the relatives and friends gather at the home of the deceased and pray for the deceased and eat together. On November 1, All Saints' Day, people visit the cemeteries. Some even stay overnight by the grave.

In the past, when the Spanish occupied the Philippines, Catholicism was the only religion officially recognized. The cemeteries of other religions seem to have been segregated, but such discrimination does not exist today. Nevertheless, Chinese, who immigrated here, more commonly bury their dead in Chinese cemeteries. Among them, there are even air-conditioned mausoleums in downtown Manila for wealthy Chinese.

In Makati, in the outskirts of Manila, there is a huge cemetery for American soldiers who died in World War II. White crosses make neat rows across the green grass of the lawn. In Mindanao, where the majority of people are Muslim, funerals are often conducted in Arabic.

In Cabanatuan on Luzon island, there is a Cabanatuan memorial monument, that marks the spot of the Japanese Cabanatuan Prisoner of War Camp where approximately 75,000 American and Philippino servicemen and civilians were held captive from 1942 to 1945, and where approximately 3,000 Americans lost their lives while being held captive.

SINGAPORE

Though it was largely uninhabited between the fourteenth and eighteenth centuries, Stamford Raffles, an official of the British East India Company, recognized the island's strategic position on key trade routes in 1819 and established Singapore as a trading settlement. Today it continues to be a very important port as a crossroads for international trade. Seventy-five percent of the population is Chinese, but there are also Malays, Indians and others. Malay, English, Chinese and Tamil are used as official languages. Moreover, this multi-ethnic population has preserved their own traditional customs. The Chinese tend to follow Buddhism; the Malay, Islam; the Indians, Hinduism and Sikhism. There are also Christians.

When someone dies, the death is reported to the government district office with a doctor's certificate. In the case of an accidental death, the medical examiner from the police station must examine the body. The arrangements for the funeral are usually taken care of by a private mortician, and the funeral is held at a place chosen according to the family's religion.

For the Chinese Buddhists, death is considered impure. When someone dies, the person's soul clings to the family and invites misfortune, so all religious items, mirrors and glass are covered with white cloth. This is to avoid the anger of the deities in the house. Also, at the front, white sheets of paper are put up to indicate that there has been a death in the family.

It is expected that the funeral brings benefits for the dead as well as the living. Therefore, respect and courtesy toward the deceased is expressed, and in return the people ask for protection and help from the deceased's soul. Chinese geomancy is used in the selection of a suitable resting place. It is believed that if the site of the grave is not selected properly, it will bring bad luck to the family.

Instead of bathing the body, the family sprays the body with stream water. Well water, which is called "dead water," or piped water is not used. A white cloth is placed over the face. Pearls and copper coins are placed in the mouth. The burial clothing is made of seamless white cloth, which consists of an odd number of layers. The legs are placed toward the doorway, so that it will be easier for the caretakers to remove the body. It is said that if the corpse touches any part of the entrance, the deceased's soul will return to the house. Therefore, the body is very carefully removed.

In the same way as in Japan, a bowl filled with cooked rice is placed by the pillow of the deceased, and a pair of chopsticks is stuck into the rice. Sometimes a cooked egg is placed under the rice, and some food is prepared before the body is put into the coffin. The mourners pretend to put this food into the deceased's mouth and then they say something for good luck. The mourners also light two sticks of incense apiece to offer to the deceased. Although the wake continues all night long, the people often spend their time playing cards or *mahjong*. Then the body is placed in a thick coffin, which is lacquered on the inside, so that the smell does not escape as the body decays from the heat. Silver threads and gold paper are also packed between the body and the coffin.

Traditionally, when the body is placed in the casket, everyone cries very loudly. At this time, the eldest son wears a white linen shirt and the female members of the family also wear linen shirts, while the sons-in-law wear long white clothes. Everyone must wear a sash. After the casket is carried out of the house, a charcoal fire is made in a portable cooking stove, and the family prays for the prosperity of the children and their descendants. The procession is led by a hearse, and followed by other mourners in their cars. Those who are older or higher in social status do not join the procession. When the procession arrives at the graveyard, everyone goes to the crematorium in the graveyard, holding paper money, flower wreathes and sticks of incense.

The Malay people also consider death an impurity and are afraid of it. The highest concern of a ceremony or a worship service is "purity." This concept is associated with ideas, such as *nasis* and *najasa*, referring to the impurity or stain associated with eating, excretion and filth. Washing the corpse before placing it into the coffin is based on the same concept. The body is rubbed with a mixture of camphor and sandalwood in order to keep dust and dirt away from the body. Then the body is wrapped in white cloth and a pair of scissors is placed on the stomach of the deceased to prevent evil spirits from possession. Incense is burned to comfort the soul of the deceased and to chase away evil spirits. This usually continues for three days.

In connection with the burial, memorial parties called *kundori aruwa* are still held on the third day, seventh day, fourteenth day, fortieth day and hundredth day. After those dates, the *kundori aruwa* is held once a year.

In Singapore, the Muslims and Christians bury their dead in the ground, while the Buddhists and Hindus usually cremate the body. The public cemetery at Mount Vernon is located on the wide hillside of Changi district and is divided according to religion. There are various types of tombstones. Among the Chinese graves, the traditional stones are in the omega shape. The caskets may be bought through the funeral house, but it is possible to directly order them from the Municipal Coffin Company (located on upper Selangon Avenue) and the Singapore Coffin Company (on Lavender Avenue).

When a corpse is to be transported out of the country, the death certificate, certifying that the body was properly treated, and the transport permit from the Health Office are required for permission to remove the body from the country. A transportation tax must also be paid. If it is just the bones that are being transported, the procedure is much easier. The scattering of ashes over a river or the sea is prohibited.

Because Singapore is a multi-ethnic and multi-religious country, each of the religiously or ethnically important days have become holidays. For instance, in May, there is Vesak Day (the Buddha's Birthday), and in November, there is the Islamic Hari Raya Haj (the Festival of the Saints). The Muslims do not eat pork, while the Hindus do not eat beef, so when one eats with them, one must keep this in mind.

SRI LANKA

Separated from India by the Palk Strait, the Democratic Socialist Republic of Sri Lanka comprises one large island and several coral islets to the northwest known as Adam's Bridge. The main island is dominated by rugged central uplands. Sri Lanka, formerly Ceylon, is called "the pearl of the Indian Ocean." It was famous for the production of black tea. The majority of the people are Sinhalese, but there are also Tamils from the south of India.

In general, the Sinhalese are Buddhists and the Tamils are Hindus, but there are also Christians. When someone dies, the family must report it to the government district office with a medical certificate. In the case of an abnormal death, the body must be examined by medical examiners and the cause of death must be ascertained.

Buddhist funerals are held at the deceased's home or at the crematorium, and a Buddhist monk is invited to the ceremony. Hindu funerals are held at the crematorium, while Christian funerals are held at a church. Well-equipped crematoriums are found only in the capital of Colombo and in Dehiwala, Mount Lavinia. In other areas, the body is cremated in a field by burning it on a funeral pyre in a designated area. Cremation costs quite a lot, so the poor prefer interment. Caskets cost from 450 to 4,000 Sri Lankan rupees (as of 1990), and the funeral expenses differ depending upon the scale of the funeral. The more elaborate funerals have processions with drums.

In the urban areas, there are private funeral homes, and usually the family and relatives prepare everything for the funeral. After the funeral, the body is buried in the local community graveyard or the church graveyard. The grave is purchased by the family. Christians wear black mourning clothes, while the Hindus wear white clothes.

On the day of death, the body is given a bath and wrapped in white cloth. It is then laid on a bed under a white canopy, the deceased's head facing west. The corpse is adorned with precious stones and jewelry. Beside the bed, coconut oil lamps are kept lit throughout the night. All the photos on the wall must be turned around or placed upside-down. This custom reflects the influence of the Portuguese when Sri Lanka was a colony of Portugal.

The female members of the family untie their hair and wail to express their lamentation. It is said that this used to continue for as long as four days.

Although they lament over the death, death itself is considered impure. The people believe that an impure spirit remains in the house for three months, so the family refrains from cooking during that period. They eat food others provide for them.

The following afternoon before sunset the burial is usually held, but normally the funeral is not scheduled for Tuesday or Wednesday, which are considered unlucky days. If those days cannot be avoided, an egg is placed in the casket in order to drive away the evil of death before removing the casket from the house. Prior to the cremation, the procession turns three times to the right. Then there is a funeral ceremony led by a monk, who prays that the deceased's soul will ascend to heaven. At that time, the monk recites the *paritta*, and the family pours water into glasses and prays for the deceased saying: "As this water overflows and fills the ocean, may charity and benevolence come to the deceased." Then the monk recites, "May this benevolence be for the family. May the family be happy."

The ashes are either buried in the graveyard or scattered over a river. The family purifies the house by burning herbs with a strong fragrance, and then ends the mourning period. Seven days, three months and one year after the death, the family invites a monk to their home and holds a memorial service. A monetary offering is made to the monk.

The Tamils, who mainly live in the northern part of the island, are Hindu. They also cremate the body and scatter the ashes over a river or the sea, but they do not make graves. Whereas, for Christians and Muslims, burials are taken place where a simple tombstone is built on the grave.

TAIWAN

The Republic of Taiwan lies 130 kilometers off the southeast coast of mainland China. Formerly known as Formosa, the Republic of China was established in 1949 by Chang Kai-shek's Kuomintang, who were expelled from goverment in Beijing by the communists under Mao. The Republic of China still claims to be the sole legitimate ruler of all China, and Beijing considers Taiwan to be one of its provinces. The island is dominated by a mountain region which runs north to south and covers two-thirds of the island. The Taiwanese are mostly Kaoshan highland people or Chinese, who follow a religion that is a mixture of Buddhism and Taoism. One unique funeral customs in Taiwan is that when the deceased is over 80 years old, the death is taken as a happy event rather than a tragic accident, because the deceased had completed his natural span of life. Also the color red is used instead of black for the announcements.

The funeral is considered to be a once-in-a-lifetime event, so it is very large in scale. Even the funeral procession is very impressive. A band leads the procession, and mourners' cars decorated with flowers follow it. It is like an event to entertain the viewers on the roadsides. In Chinshan city, dancers were once hired for rich people's funerals and performed strip shows on the way as entertainment, but this was discontinued by legal order because it carried the idea of entertainment to the extreme.

When someone dies, the family obtains a medical certificate from a doctor and reports the death to the government district office. In the urban areas, the family often asks the mortuary's help in preparing for the funeral. The body is bathed and is dressed in a burial suit. Then the body is placed in a strong lacquer casket that was prepared either while the deceased was still alive or at the time of death. After that, a priest recites a sutra to get rid of the demon, namely, the evil soul of the deceased.

The body is temporarily buried in a public cemetery, and after a certain amount of time, the bones are removed from the ground and washed. The family asks a fortune teller to choose the site of the burial on the mid-slope of the mountain according to the law of "*yin-yang*" geomancy. It is customary to bury the bones in a mountain graveyard in a grave made from concrete or stone in the shape of a horseshoe. The home where they have spent their lives is called the "House of Light" (*Yang-chai*), while the grave which is their final resting place is called the "House of Shade" (*Ying-chai*). The Taiwanese have a tendency to spend a lot of money for graves that lie in the shade. The burial date used to be decided by fortune-telling, but recently cremation has become more popular, especially in the urban areas, there has been an increase in the number of people who wish to be cremated and placed in a niche of a temple. In the capital of Taiwan, Taipei, there is a crematory on Baoshan, and paper markers, pasted on the telephone poles along the way, read "*Namo Amituofo*" (Complete reliance on Amitabha Buddha). The funeral is sometimes held at the family's home, but in general people ask the mortuary to arrange the funeral for them. The body is carried to one of the funeral homes that are scattered here and there around the city. The mourners wear black coats and pin black ribbons on their chest. The family calls either Buddhist or Taoist priests depending on the family's religion. In the hall, fresh or artificial flowers are put out for decoration. After the funeral, the mourners either go to the crematorium directly or go to the public cemetery for temporary burial of the dead. The mourners go in decorated cars that follow the hearse. If they go on foot, mourning flags and a band lead the procession.

In Taiwan, there is a unique custom of burning paper money, clothes and a model house at the funeral, so that the deceased may use them in the land of death. For this purpose, there is a special cremation chamber in the crematorium.

Memorial services are held every seven days during the mourning period, which lasts from the seventh day to the forty-ninth day after the death. Then on the first, third, seventh and the thirteenth year, memorial services are usually held with a priest at the family's home or a temple. The family gives food to the the famished demons that are said to come around to look for food on July 15 of the lunar calendar, which is the Chung-yuan festival (also called the Festival of Demons), and on April 5, Memorial Day. It is said that on this day the *preta*, hungry ghosts, go around in search of food. On that day, the family also burn paper money and pray for peace for the deceased's soul.

In Taiwan, there are many who follow Zhaijia, which is a group of lay Buddhists. They place the dead on a chair and recite sutras, then the body is laid on the floor. Every ninth day, they hold a memorial service, and on this occasion, 33 lines (of 33 characters each) that explain the ceremony are read. After the lines are read, they are burned. As a result of this ceremony, the deceased is believed to ascend to the 33 heavens.

Impressive mausoleums, erected by nouveau-riche Taiwanese, stand on the hill of Hon-chi San-tzan in Tau Yuen Country near the New Taipei International Airport.

At the Lake of Mercy (*Ci-hu*), which is located in the south of Taipei City, is the mausoleum of Chiang Kai-shek. The mausoleum was built there because the area looks like Chiang's hometown in mainland China.

Graveyards for soldiers who have recently died have been built in each of the provinces. For instance, a memorial cemetery for soldiers has been built in Kaohsiung City, in the reclaimed area near the Lake of Mercy. It is neatly divided like a grid, and the graves are regularly arranged. Since 1967, after World War II, thanks to the efforts of Venerable Master Hsing Yung, the biggest temple in Taiwan, Fo Kuang Shan Temple, was built in the suburbs of Kaohsiung City. In this temple, there are many niches to hold the remains of followers. This type of burial is a new trend, resulting from the fact that graveyards are never placed inside the temple grounds.

THAILAND

The Kingdom of Thailand is located in the heart of the Indochinese Peninsula and the northern part of the Malay Peninsula; Siam Bay lies to the north. Thailand has been an independent kingdom for most of its history and, since 1932, a constitutional monarchy with an alternating military and civilian government. Rapid industrialization has resulted in massive traffic congestion in Bangkok and a serious depletion of natural resources. It is a productive granary zone, and high temperatures and humidity are common all year round. The population is mainly made up of Thais, but there are also Malays, Khmers, Chinese and other highland people. The majority follow Theravada Buddhism, although there are Christians and Muslims as well.

Because the majority of the people are Buddhists, the funeral is usually held in a Buddhist temple, and the corpse is cremated in an indoor pagoda-style crematorium on the temple grounds or in an outdoor crematorium called a *furamane*. The casket is placed on a funeral pyre and cremated. The ashes are scattered on the ground or placed into an urn and kept in a pagoda-style building. The funeral date is selected and set after a period of time. Funerals for royal family members or high-ranking monks are not held immediately.

No one makes graves (*bacher*) except the Chinese people. The minorities in the northern mountainous region especially seem to have little interest in graves. This is probably because they are nomadic. The body is buried in a remote area or is just left in a tree for birds to eat. The Miao, for example, leave the corpse on a platform made of wooden sticks.

In Thailand, a death must be reported to the government district office. The body is given a hot bath by the family and relatives and then is placed in a casket. The wake, called *bangsa koon*, is held in the family's home or in a temple between 4 P.M. and 6 P.M. A casket can be obtained easily if the family requests the help of a temple.

The funeral is usually held in the crematorium of the temple. When the casket is removed from the home, a curry bowl that the deceased used and a tea cup are customarily broken by the chief mourner. In the crematorium of the temple, the mourners turn around the casketed corpse three times to the right, then, in the order of their rank, they go up to the platform and light the fire. After the cremation, the chief mourner thanks the others and concludes the funeral. The family members go to the crematorium the next morning with candles, incense, a container of perfumed water and the urn. The monk is invited to hold a *Sambab* (the ceremony of picking the bones). The remains are either placed in a niche or scattered over a river or the sea. However, the bodies of prominent or wealthy persons are often kept for a year or more in a special building at a temple. Cremations are deferred in this way to show love and respect for the deceased and to perform religious services that will benefit the bereaved family as well as the deceased. This meritorious act is called *Tampun*.

The Chinese Buddhists have their own cemetery. The deceased's name is written both in Chinese and Thai on the tombstone, which also records the date of death. On April 5, Tomb Sweeping Day, the family goes to the grave and makes offerings.

In Bangkok, there is an overseas Chinese Mutual Aid Association, called the *Pao du tang*, which helps people who are victims of accidents or natural disasters, regardless of whether they are foreigners or not.

In Kanchanaburi, 200 kilometers northwest of Bankok, there is a military cemetery for the Allied forces who died during World War II, where the remains of British and Australian servicemen numbering 6,982, who lost their lives while being held captive by the Japanese army, were buried. It is located on Saeng Chuto Road between the Kanchanaburi Railroad Station and the Kwae River bridge.

VIETNAM

The Socialist Republic of Vietnam is located on the east coast of the

Indonesian peninsula, stretching from south to north. It was once a French colony, and after World War II, it split into two parts South Vietnam and North Vietnam. In a show of protest against the violence of the reactionary President Ngo Dim Dien government which had driven much of the population to starvation and degradation, the Buddhist monk, Thick Quang Duc set himself on fire and died on the main boulevard of Saigon (Ho Chi Minh) on June 11, 1963. Subsequently, several other monks similarly immolated themselves in a show of their concern for the future of a divided Vietnam. Thus in Vietnam, there was an unforgettable example of Buddhists who sacrificed their lives in order to appeal for racial unity, reverence of Buddhism and the promotion of the people's welfare. A war between the two opposing sides continued for an extended period of time, but after the U.S. troops retreated, the country became unified in 1975. More than half of Vietnam is dominated by the heavily forested mountain range. The most populated areas, which are also the most intensively cultivated, are along the Red and Mekong rivers. The population consists mainly of Vietnamese. It now claims to be a socialist nation and the people have been working very hard to rebuild their devastated land.

In the northern area, probably because of the proliferation of anti-religious education, the life-style and customs of the people are not very religious. In the south, however, many people still follow a form of Mahayana Buddhism which is mixed somewhat with native beliefs and customs. In Vietnam, religious mendicancy is accepted, and as long as it does not conflict with national policy, the people enjoy freedom of religion. Although missionary work by the religionists is allowed, such activities are not promoted.

When someone dies, the family is obliged to report the death to a government office with a doctor's medical report. The funeral is usually held in the local community hall, and the body is normally buried in the ground. In the outskirts of Ho Chi Minh City, one finds the Futo Crematorium, but not many people are cremated. Because Vietnam is located in the tropics, it is desirable to bury the body as soon as possible at a public graveyard in the suburbs of cities.

At the northern end of Dien Bien Phu Avenue is Badin Square, which is the busiest section of Hanoi. This square is the place where Ho Chi Minh declared independence on November 2, 1945. The mausoleum of Ho Chi Minh, who died at the age of 79, was built in the square in 1975. The mausoleum is a marble building in a pantheon style. At the front central entrance there is an inscription in Vietnamese that says, "*There is nothing more valuable than freedom and independence.*" In the mausoleum, the mummified body of Ho Chi Minh is preserved and displayed in a glass case. Even now, an endless stream of people go to the mausoleum to pay their respects to him.

Among the Hmong tribe, living in the mountain regions of Northern Vietnam, Laos and Thailand, Nicholas Tapp reported:

The ritual specialist at death is not necessarily a shaman, whose business is to preserve life. The purpose of the funeral and mortuary rites is to ensure the safe dispatch of the reincarnating soul to the otherworld. Funerals last a minimum of three days, attended by all local male kin within the household of the deceased. The reed pipes are played each day and a special song is sung to guide the reincarnating soul on its journey. Cattle must be slaughtered. The corpse of the deceased is inhumed in a geomantically selected site. On the third day after burial the grave is renovated, and a special propitiatory ritual is performed thirteen days after death for the ancestral soul, which will protect the household. A final memorial service to release the reincarnating soul, held some years after death, in the case of severe illness or misfortune, a special propitiatory ritual may be performed for the same spirit. (Quoted from David Levinson, ed., *The Encyclopedia of World Cultures,* vol. 5, Boston: G. K. Hall, 1993, p. 95.)

Among the minority Muong tribe, living in North Vietnam, the members are provided with boat-shaped wooden coffins when they turn 60 years old. At the funeral, a priest *mo* is invited, and after the burial, a hut is erected on top of the burial ground.

CHAPTER 2

Oceania

AMERICAN SAMOA

American Samoa consists of five volcanic islands and two atolls and is an incorporated territory of the United States. The majority of the islanders are regarded as the last remaining true Polynesians, retaining the extended family system, with chiefs still holding a central role in government and social life.

When someone dies, the relatives and neighbors are informed of the death in person or by telephone or radio. The funeral service is usually held in the yard of the bereaved family. Thereafter, the corpse is buried in a village cemetery or in a grave next to the house.

AUSTRALIA

Australia is an island continent located between the Indian and Pacific Oceans. Its six states and the Northern Territory have a variety of landscape, including tropical rainforests, an arid red-soil desert, snow-capped mountains, rolling tracts of pastoral land and magnificient beaches.

Australia, in which most people are British Australian, used to go by the policy of "White Australia." After World War II, because of a labor shortage, the government allowed immigration of non-British people from Europe and Asia. Most of the people live in areas located on the East coast, such as Sydney and Melbourne, where the climate is more mild. Approximately 35 percent of the people belong to the Anglican Church. However, there are also many Catholics and Protestants. Religion is mostly considered a matter of formality.

When a person dies, the family, relatives or friends must contact a funeral home for assistance in obtaining a death certificate from a doctor, taking care of the corpse, arranging the funeral and burial, informing relatives and friends about the wake and funeral services, and publishing the obituary in the newspaper. When someone dies in a hospital, the body is transported to a mortuary within eight hours. In the case of an accidental death, however, a legal autopsy is required.

Most Australian cities have mortuaries, which are usually privately operated, with facilities like those in America, but they must operate under the direction of the Planning Bureau of the local government. They differ from their American counterparts in that embalming is uncommon. In most cases, the funeral is held within 48 hours of death, and the body is transported to the cemetery by a hearse. The cemeteries are mostly operated by a semi-public cemetery trustee association, with crematoriums. The cremation rate is 50 percent, and that proportion is increasing. However, most Roman Catholics and Jews, who wish to honor their traditions, usually bury the corpse.

For the most part, funeral customs in recent years have been simplified in all religious groups. In the past, the traditions and practices were much more rigid and formal. For example, men often wore derby hats and suits and women wore black mourning dresses. Recently, however, people dress more casually. Also, the flowers used for wreaths or offerings used to be only white, but nowadays colorful flowers have become acceptable.

Another example can be seen in tombstones which were once quite elaborate, such as at Crowery Cemetery on a hill near Bondi beach is a typical cemetery in Sydney which features ornate standing tombstones. Today, however, simple flat tombstones are more common in newly built cemeteries.

In the central plains and in northern Australia, there are aborigines, the native people of Australia. Although their funeral customs and rites differ depending on the tribe, the majority of them bury the corpse, which is later exhumed and placed in a cave. The bones are wrapped in tree bark.

FIJI

Fiji, which gained its independence from England in 1970, consists of 322 islands scattered over the South Pacific Ocean. The main islands are Viti Levu and Vanua Levu. The majority of the people are Fijians and Indian immigrants. The official language is English. Many people are followers of the Methodist Church, Hinduism or Islam. Even this paradise in the South Pacific has been affected by the modern world.

When someone dies in Fiji, a doctor examines the body. In the case of an accidental death, as in many other countries, a coroner from the police station examines the body. The people seldom use public or private mortuaries, and for the most part hold the funeral at a church or cathedral. On occasion flowers are offered, but white flowers are never used. After the funeral, if the deceased is a Christian, the body is buried in a cemetery. In the case of a Hindu, the body is cremated before burial. It seems, however, that on the remote islands the body is sometimes buried at sea. Suva on Viti Levu, which has a terminal for international flights, is a modern British-style city. In other areas, however, the political power of the local chief is still strong, and the funeral rites take place according to the chief's orders. The Fijian people usually wear special skirts made of coconut leaves at funerals.

FRENCH OCEANIA

New Caledonia is the largest island among the French Oceania Islands. The people of New Caledonia are Melanesian or European. Recently, the island has been trying hard to become independent from France. The main city, Noumea, is regarded as a very important crossroad in the Pacific and is called "Small Paris" because of its atmosphere. The islanders were westernized and Christianized before World War II.

When someone dies, the family must report the death to the government district office. In general, the wake is held in the bereaved home and the funeral is held in a church. In Noumea, there are funeral homes, and the body is buried in the public cemetery in the "4-kilo District" of the city. This cemetery has been there since World War II, though recently a new cemetery was built in the "5-kilo District," which is one kilometer from the old one.

The native society was divided into several tribes, and many relatives and friends used to gather at a funeral, but today funerals have been simplified to large extent. In most cases, the body is buried in the ground, and if the family wants to have the body cremated, it must be sent to Australia or New Zealand by air.

In remote islands that are not yet tourist attractions, traditional customs survive. For instance, setting the funeral date is done by a magician. Also, at a gathering place called *piro*, a big funeral is held in the presence of the head chief. At that time, a dance called *birlir* is performed in his presence, and music is played with native instruments made from bamboo pipes and compressed bark and grass. This is a social ceremony, where mercy is asked from the dead and ancestors. After the funeral, the body is buried in the backyard of the family's home.

GUAM

During World War II, the Territory of Guam was used as an airbase for American bombers attacking Japan. Today, however, it is a resort island. Of the islanders, U.S. citizens, about half are native Chamorro, or a mixture of Chamorro and Spanish, Mexicans or Philipinos, who follow Roman Catholic tradition.

When someone dies in Guam, a funeral home takes care of the funeral, just as in the mainland United States. The funeral is usually held at the church or the chapel of the funeral home, and the body is buried afterward in the cemetery. Burial in the ground is most common; probably because it is an island of "everlasting summer," colorful tropical flowers are always given as offerings at the graves.

On September 3, 1982, at Jigo, where was a bloody battlefield during World War II, a memorial tower for peace was unveiled to honor both the American and the Japanese soldiers who died there during the war.

In former times, the Chamorro, who lived on the island of Guam and the surrounding Southern Mariana Islands, believed the deceased ancestors inhabited an underworld paradise. These personages were also worshipped in an ancestor cult for, as the people's guardians, the ancestors were feared and venerated.

KIRIBATU

The Republic of Kiribatu (Gilbert Islands) is a nation consisting of 33 islands in the central West Pacific Ocean. It became independent as one of the republics in the British Commonwealth of Nations. The capital is Bairiki of the Tarawa atolls. Most of the islanders are Micronesian Kiribatese, who are mainly Roman Catholic or Protestant.

When someone dies, the relatives and neighbors are informed, and the funeral service is held at the church of the bereaved family. In the past, the corpse was kept in the family house for three to nine days. If the deceased had been prominent, the corpose would remain in the home for even a longer period. Some months after burial, the skull was removed from the grave and oiled and food and tobacco were offered to it. Nowadays, this custom has declined rapidly because of Christian influence. However, the wake is attended by a large number of mourners, who bring cyrtosperma corns and monetary gifts to the bereaved family and eulogize the departed. Then the corpse is buried in the village cemetery or in a grave next to the house. Moreover, many who live at the north end of the Gilberts still remember the local legends of *Nakaa*, the god who welcomes souls.

The Kanaks on the islands practiced the custom of binding the corpses in the fetal position. Also, mothers who died in labor were buried with a wooden stick in their arms, which symbolized their child, so that their spirits would not come looking for their offspring.

THE MARSHALL ISLANDS

The Marshall Islands are a nation consisting of more than 1,200 islands scattered over the West Pacific Ocean in Micronesia. The islands became independent from the United States in October 1986. Their capital is Majuro. The Marshallese are mainly Micronesians, who are mostly Protestants. This society was traditionally matrilineal.

When a person dies, the death is reported to the neighbors and friends in person. The funeral service usually takes place at the church of the bereaved family. It was believed that the deceased used to carry many of their belongings with them after death, and continued to interact with the living though their physical features desiccated.

MICRONESIA

The Federated States of Micronesia consist of four states; the islands of Ponape (presently, Pohnpei), Yap, Truk and Kasrae in the West Pacific Ocean, which became independent in November 1986 under an agreement made with the United States. Starting with the Caroline Islands, 930 islands belong to this nation whose capital is Palikir. Most of the people are Micronesian, who are predominantly Protestant or Roman Catholic.

As soon as a person dies, female kin wail and other relatives come bringing gifts of woven fabrics, turmeric or food. Burial might be in a church ground or an ancestoral plot. After burial, the grave is watched by close kin for four nights to see if the good soul will possess one of them as its future medium. On the fourth day after burial, the immediate effects are burned and the good soul is believed to ascend to heaven in the smoke.

NAURU

The Republic of Nauru is the third smallest country in the world, following the Vatican City and Monaco. Nauru, which was once a trusteeship of the United Nations, is now an independent nation, where most of the inhabitants are Micronesian, Melanesian and Chinese. English is the official language, and many of the country's citizens are Christians, holding their funerals in most cases in churches.

When someone dies, the relatives and neighbors are informed of the death in person or by telephone or radio. The funeral service is held in the yard of the bereaved family or their church.

The age-old tradition of belief in spirits and gods such as *Tabuarik* is still retained. The family ancestors are also honored with food offerings on an altar outside each family's yard.

NEW ZEALAND

New Zealand consists of two islands, named South and North Islands. It abounds with such scenic beauty that it deserves the name "the Switzerland of the South Pacific." The majority of the people are descendants of immigrants from Great Britain. There are also the native Maori people. Most residents are Anglican, Presbyterian or Roman Catholic. New Zealand still bears a resemblance to the "good old days of England."

When someone dies at home or in the hospital, the family members must report it to a mortuary to arrange for the funeral. In the case of an accidental death, it must be reported to the police, and the corpse must be inspected.

The funeral is normally held at the church where the deceased was a member or in the chapel of the mortuary. After that, the people go to the crematory chamber or to the cemetery to bury the body. Funerals usually are held from 8:00 A.M. to 4:30 P.M., from Monday to Friday. No funerals are scheduled on the weekend or holidays. In Catholic churches, rosaries are held in the evening and a mass for the dead is held the next morning. The family of the deceased will decide whether the body is cremated or buried. Recently, because more people have requested cremation, each city has a crematorium. There are two kinds of cemeteries: public and church-operated. However, most gravesites are sold as private plots. There are also cinerariums and graveyards for joint burials. Roses are commonly planted in the cemetery, so when the flowers are in full bloom, it resembles a rose garden. As for the coffin, there are "boat-shaped" coffins made of rimu or tawa wood. Metal coffins are rare. Probably because the corpse is buried within 36 to 48 hours after death, embalming is rarely done.

Nowadays, the native Maoris are very much Europeanized and hence have lost their unique traditions. Even so, in the rural areas, the Maoris will order a large coffin in which the body is placed with its possessions. Customarily, female mourners are expected to sob and weep loudly as soon as the body is placed in the coffin. Also before and after the burial rituals, the Maori people have a feast called *tangi*, which includes roasted wild pig.

NORTHERN MARIANA ISLANDS

These islands are located in the North Pacific Ocean, and have become a self-governing U.S. Commonwealth Territory. The majority of the people are Chamorro, who follow the Roman Catholic tradition.

In honor of the war dead, a memorial monument was erected near the beach overlooking Tanapag Harbor on the island of Saipan, Commonwealth of the Northern Mariana Islands. It is part of an American memorial park commemorating the Americans and Marianas, who died in the Marianas campaign during World War II. Beside this, there is also a memorial for the Japanese war dead.

PALAU

The Republic of Palau consists of more than 200 small islands that lie between the Philippines and Guam. It was once put under a U.S. Trusteeship, but in 1994 it became independent. The majority of the people are Roman Catholic. Funerals here are costly and elaborate, particularly when the deceased's status was high, reflecting the importance of traditional beliefs. In general, the women maintain the mourning period, while the men handle the financial aspects of the funeral and the family fortune thereafter.

When someone dies, the relatives and neighbors are informed of the death in person. The funeral service is usually held at the family church and the burial takes place in the village cemetery, although in the past burial was under the house platform. A week after the burial, close relatives gather around the grave and send the spirit to its final resting place, believed to be in the south.

PAPUA NEW GUINEA

The Dominion of Papua New Guinea lies to the north of Australia and includes about ten thousand islands of various sizes, such as the islands of New Guinea, New Britain, New Ireland and Bougainville. The temperature and humidity are high, and the islands are mountainous. The population consists of Melanesians, but there are about 1,000 different tribes who live in Papua New Guinea as well. The common language is English, but each tribe has its own language, unique customs and manners, so communication is quite difficult.

Perhaps because the villages are isolated from one another, the funeral customs have not been standardized. Usually, the chief leads the people of the tribe, and the land and other property are owned jointly by all the members of the community. They value the idea of mutual assistance among members of the same community. The funeral and the preparations for it are considered to be a communal event.

Around cities like Port Moresby or in the coastal areas, there are many Christians, but in the remote areas the native beliefs and the worship of the soul still remain. However, the Christian missionary work in New Guinea has been remarkable. Missionaries from the Church of England, the Catholic Church and the Lutheran Gospel Church have gone to remote corners of the country helping the native tribes.

Except for the urban areas, the body is usually buried, but there are also some places where they perform burials at sea or in trees. Also, among the descendants of cannibals, there are people who mummify the corpse as a sign of respect to their ancestors.

Among the studies on the funeral customs of the native people of the Trobriand Isles, *The Sexual Life of Savages in Northwest Melanesia* by Bronislav Malinowski (1884-1942) is a classic, containing detailed descriptions of the native customs. When someone dies, relatives and locals gather at the home of the bereaved family and cry very loudly. After crying, they wash the deceased's body and close the orifices with the fibers of coconut husks. Both legs are tied with string and the arms are tied to the sides of the body, which is decorated with ornaments. After the wake, the body is buried. The following year it is taken out of the ground, and the bones are collected and washed, to serve as a reminder of the deceased. The widow uses the skull as a lime pot and the jaws as a necklace. The other bones, called *hera*, are also preserved. This may sound strange to foreigners, but it is a very serious custom and an obligation for those who wish to receive the favor of the deceased. Recently, however, due to modernization, some of the customs are beginning to disappear.

The Motu, living on the shore of Port Moresby, the capital, were the first to receive Christian missionaries. Now most Motu are church members. However, to gain ancestral support, they traditionally held private ceremonies in a sacred place (*irutahuna*) of the house. Then a feast with dancing was held, during which the bones were disinterred.

SOCIETY ISLANDS

Tahiti, the paradise of the South Pacific, became known world-wide through the paintings of Gauguin. Tahiti is the main island of the Society Islands and is in the center of the Polynesian Triangle, which connects Hawaii, Easter Island and New Zealand. This island was once the most important port in the South Pacific. The people of Tahiti are mainly Polynesian. Tahiti used to be ruled by a chief who refused to allow other people to land on the islands, but Europeans began to come, and when the last chief, Pomare II, became Christian in 1812, he abandoned the native beliefs and westernized the islands.

When someone dies in the islands, the death is verbally reported to neighbors. The funeral is usually held at the family home. In the capital, Papeete, there are funeral homes, which take care of all the funeral arrangements, but in the remote areas and islands, relatives help the family. The deceased is placed in the living room of the family's home with many flowers. Relatives and friends gather around the deceased and pray, and some of the women cry loudly.

The body in the coffin is carried to the graveyard at the corner of the family's yard and buried. Also the body is covered with flowers offered by the mourners. After that, food and drinks are served to the mourners. The mourning period lasts for two to three weeks. After that period, the family's life returns to normal.

There are also descendants of Chinese immigrants in Tahiti who went there as laborers and who have preserved their own culture and traditions. When someone in a Chinese family dies, the body is buried in the Chinese cemetery on the hill of Pilea near Papeete. Recently, a public cemetery was built in Haumi on the neighboring island, Moorea, where they used to bury the dead in the family yard. When cremation is preferred to burial, the body must be sent to Hawaii.

Islands such as Tahiti, Moorea and Bora Bora have recently become commercialized because of tourism. Traditional customs can be observed only in the Tuamotu Islands. For Tahitians, the traditional ceremony associated with death was extremely elaborate, particularly when the deceased's status was high (reflecting its importance in traditional belief). Rank determined the extent of expression in mourning and the length of time the corpse was exposed on a platform before burial. In former times, human relics were preserved among the upper classes.

SOLOMON ISLANDS

The Solomon Islands, which were once called the British Solomon Island Protectorate, became independent in 1978. The country consists of about a hundred islands scattered over the South Pacific Ocean. Today the country is a member of the United Nations. The majority of the islanders are Melanesians and they speak English, the country's official language. Most of the people are Christians, but there are some who follow the traditional religion.

The funeral or burial customs vary according to the area. In any case, however, because the Solomon Islands are in the tropics, the dead must be taken care of as quickly as possible. Upon the announcement of a death, neighbors gather at the deceased's home, and lament and weep loudly, wearing a special type of skirt. In general, the corpse is buried or placed in a cave, but burials in the sea are also done. The funeral is held in an open field, and the mourners dance to music. Then there is a party. At the party people sit on their own tapa mats made of tree bark. Except for the Christians of Guadalcanal Island, where the capital Honiara is located, it is rare to have individual tombstones placed over graves. The graveyard usually consists of communal graves. The islanders avoid the graveyard because they believe that it is occupied by spirits. The island of Kundo is known as the island where dead bodies are buried. In fact, bones of the dead are scattered throughout the island.

When someone dies, a conch shell is blown, and the people stop working. A mourning house called *Balas* is built near where the corpse lay, and the bereaved family stay overnight in it. After three or four days, the funeral service is held at the church, and a boat-shaped coffin is carried to the graveyard to be buried. About one year later, a headstone is placed on it.

TONGA

Tonga, a constitutional monarchy in the South Pacific Ocean, consists of 169 islands made of coral reefs. The majority of the islanders are Polynesians.

When someone dies, the body is washed and then rubbed with candelnut oil, which is made from chewed nuts. Then the body is covered with a cloth made of tree bark and placed in the middle of the house on a bed wrapped with a woven pandanus mat. On the day of the funeral, family members and relatives sit around the bed, and a priest from the church, called *sutewata*, prays for the dead. The mourners place gifts such as flowers and cloth around the dead. They kiss the dead and then leave.

During this time, those who are waiting outside continue to sing hymns.

After the funeral, *kava* drinks are offered to the mourners. The next morning, the body is rewrapped in a new bark cloth, and then the men carry it on their shoulders to the cemetery. After a sermon by the priest, the body is lowered into the grave and the mourners scatter sand over the body. After the burial, the people are usually treated to a feast with *kava* drinks at the family's home. In the past, family members cut their hair, but this custom is no longer practiced. Today, instead of having it cut, the family members leave their hair uncombed. Those who are close to the deceased go to the graveyard for about 10 days. Most graves are decorated with colorful cloth, encircling the grave site.

TUVALU

Tuvalu is one of the smallest countries in the world, as it has a land area of just over 25 square kilometers. Around 95 percent of Tuvaluans are Polynesians whose ancestors came from nearby Tongan and Samoan islands some 2,000 years ago. It became an independent constitutional monarchy within the Commonwealth in 1978. The majority of the people follow the Protestant tradition.

VANUATU

Vanuatu is an island nation in the South Pacific, consisting of the islands around Melanesia. The capital is the port town Vila. Over 100 languages are used, but Bislama, a mixture of Melanesian and English, is most commonly spoken. Most of the islanders are Protestants but native beliefs are also strongly rooted.

The Malekula and other inhabitants in Vanuatu believe that the spirits of the dead are cursing on the living for a year after the deceased's funeral. The Mewun mourn for 12 hours after a death and then take pains not to anger the deceased's troublesome spirit presence.

WESTERN SAMOA

Western Samoa, which consists of nine islands, is a volcanic country approximately 2,900 kilometers northeast of New Zealand. The majority of the islanders are Polynesian. They use both Samoan and English as their official languages. Most of the land is owned by the chiefs who have great political power and a substantial amount of influence over the lives of their people. Nevertheless, the people have freedom of belief, and many of them are Christians belonging to the Congregational or Roman Catholic churches.

Normally all the people in the area participate in a funeral and help to bury the body. They keep a stone coffin with a roof placed over it to protect the body and its property from sunlight. In the remote areas, burials at sea and in caves are still performed, but they are now uncommon.

CHAPTER 3

Africa

ALGERIA

Africa's second largest country, the People's Democratic Republic of Algeria shares borders with Morocco, Mauritania, Mali, Niger, Libya and Tunisia. Algeria, which is located in North Africa, faces the Mediterranean Sea. It was under French rule for 130 years, but after a long struggle, Algeria became independent in 1962. The majority of the people are Arabs and Berbers, and the official language is Arabic. The national religion is Islam, but freedom of religion is guaranteed by the Constitution.

Except for inner Algeria, the climate is quite mild. The people used to work on farms, but since the discovery of oil fields in the Sahara Desert, the pace of industrialization has increased. As a result, the modernization of the urban areas is especially notable. In the capital, Algiers, there is a maze in an old town. It was made famous the French movie "Pepe le Moco" which lies on one of its hills. Recently, the construction of new towns has begun.

In the urban areas, there are professional morticians, who assist the bereaved family in arranging the funeral. Muslims usually hold their funerals at the mosque and bury the body in the community graveyard. The largest Islamic cemetery in Algiers is at El Kettal. There are Christian cemeteries for foreigners at Verkur and St. Eugene. There is no custom of cremation here, so there are no crematoriums.

In the desert, white *kuppa* (onion-shaped mosques) can be seen near residential areas. These are mosques where the religious leader of the Berber, Maragut, is enshrined. These *kuppa* can be seen throughout the Maghreb countries. The bodies of ordinary citizens are buried in community graveyards or in the desert and tend to be ignored in later years.

The funeral customs of the Bedouin and the Tuareg living in the desert generally conform closely to those of Islam tradition.

ANGOLA

The Republic of Angola was the first Portuguese colony in Africa. In 1975, Angola became independent as a result of the People's Liberation Movement, but the country is still suffering from the after-effects of the civil war. The official language is Portuguese. The majority of the people are the Bantus, who believe in the native religion. The capital, Luanda, the country's oldest city, was built by the Europeans and has a Mediterranean atmosphere. However, because the people of European descent are gradually leaving Luanda, the city has become unstable politically and socially.

Angola has a multi-ethnic population with almost no sense of national unity. Because of this, the policy to promote education is not very effective and the illiteracy rate is high. The primitive Bushmen especially have, strictly speaking, no sense of tribal ties. The people depend on collecting plants or hunting to support their lives, and they live in semicircular huts made by female members of the family. It seems that they do not hold funerals as the other tribes do.

In the past, Christian missionaries were very active, but after becoming independent, the government seized all church property. Therefore, it is only in the city areas where the influence of Christian customs is still felt.

The Kongo, numbering three to four million, live in west-central Africa, particularly in Angola. For them, funerals are important occasions of social gathering and family expenditure. They are taken care of by the elders, because their accumulated knowledge and experiences form the collective information in a society without written records.

BENIN

The Republic of Benin is located in West Africa on the coast of the Atlantic Ocean. Once the center of the slave trade, known as Dahomey, it was an underdeveloped country between Togo and Nigeria. Later, it was a French colony for many years, so the people use French as their official language. The illiteracy rate is very high, and most of the people follow the native religious traditions. The population includes many tribes, such as the Fon, the Erve and the Yoruba. Each one preserves its own life style and customs. The anthropologist Melville Haaskovitz and his wife did fieldwork there, and although their studies are not exhaustive, their work has provided much information concerning this country.

The people in general believe in the souls of their ancestors, and believe that when someone dies, the deceased leaves this world by crossing rivers and mountains until he or she reaches the other world. By receiving an appropriate funeral, the soul may become an ancestral soul. In Mina, there is a saying that the necklace of death does not refuse anyone's neck.

Moreover, people still believe that the spirits of the dead have power over certain actions of the living, for example, lack of filial piety or bad relations between kin. These spirits are believed to live in villages and quarters similar to those in the world of the living. From there, they watch over the behavior of their relatives, punishing transgressions such as incest.

When someone dies, many cry out very loudly at the home of the deceased. The body is washed in hot water and wrapped in white cloth, and then usually buried in the yard or in a hut. The dates for the funeral and the burial are set by a fortune teller, and there are several rehearsals before the real funeral, which is considered a merry occasion. Everyone joins in the dancing and shouting. The night of the funeral as well is a festive one as the mourners get drunk and enjoy themselves. The gathering ends with visiting the graveyard on the following morning. The mourning period itself is said to last for three months.

BOTSWANA

The name of the Republic of Botswana in the Kalahari Desert means "the country of Tswana." The capital is Gaborone. Although Botswana received Christian missionaries in the early 19th century and most belong to a church today, precolonial beliefs remain strong among many of the people.

When someone dies, the relatives and neighbors are informed in person. In general, death is believed to have both natural and supernatural causes. Funerals are highly elaborate and expensive, and sometimes prolonged for as long as a week. During the funeral, livestock are slaughtered to feed mourners.

Traditionally, men were buried in their cattle kraals; women in the compounds; and small children under houses. However, village cemeteries are now becoming more common. It is believed that those who die with regrets become ghosts, who remain in the grave by day and haunt the living by night.

BURKINA FASO (FORMERLY UPPER VOLTA)

Burkina Faso is located in the savanna. The majority of the land is covered by bush. Until it became independent in 1960, there were disputes with neighboring countries. The people of Burkina Faso are the Mossi, the Bobo, the Grusi and others. Many of them follow the native religious traditions. However, in the 18th century Islam was introduced, and mosques were built. The mosques here are made of dirt and soil placed on a wooden structure and allowed to dry in the sun.

The people's sense of unity is very strong, so for the funerals, which are elaborate, ethnic dances are performed for several days. Mourners also usually bring food or monetary offerings. The body is for the most part buried in a designated community graveyard.

The Mossi are the most prominent ethnic group in Burkina Faso. Traditionally men were buried to the west of a cleared area of their compounds. Women were buried in household fields; the funeral was performed by members of their patrilineages. Ideally, the bodies of the dead should be taken back to their native villages if the death occurs in town. Upon death, they become part of the generalized community of ancestors who watch over their living descendants. Cemeteries are considered to be dangerous places, not to be visited casually.

BURUNDI

Most of the land in the Republic of Burundi is composed of highlands. Its capital is Bujumbara. In July 1962, Burundi became independent. However, the agricultural Hutu tribe and the nomadic Tutsi tribe have been constant adversaries, and in October 1993, the Tutsi-dominated army mounted a violent coup that resulted in the assassination of the country's first-ever Hutu president. Subsequent suppressions of the Hutu people by the Tutsi-dominated army have sent millions into exile in neighboring countries.

The majority of the people are the Bantu Hutus, who follow Catholicism or the native religion. When someone dies, the relatives and neighbors are informed of the death in person. As in other African countries, funerals are elaborate and expensive affairs, particularly when elders die, since they are highly respected. Livestock is slaughtered during the funeral to provide food for the mourners. Many are still buried in the traditional manner, in which men are buried in their kraals, women in the compounds, and small children under houses. However, village cemeteries are also increasingly used.

CAMEROON

The United Republic of Cameroon is in western Africa by the Bay of Guinea. Cameroon became independent in 1960. Until World War I, it was a protectorate of Germany and after that of France and England. Tribes such as the Bantu and the Semi-Bantu make up the majority of the people. The Pygmies are said to be the native people of Cameroon, but they now only live in the woodlands in the south, and their numbers have dwindled to no more than several thousand. The official languages are French and English. The religion is a mixture of Islam, Christianity and native religions. There are many festivals. For whatever occasion they can find, the people dress up and gather in an open square to celebrate with music and dance.

The funeral is held according to local customs. In remote areas, the funeral continues for as long as one week, and during that time, the male members of the community dance with masks covering their faces. There is no family register, so there is no need to report a death to the government office.

The family informs the neighbors of the death by the beating of a drum. In some areas, the wailing of female kin announces the death to the neighborhood. The body is dressed in black clothes and blindfolded. The chief mourner wraps a white piece of cloth around his hip and accepts the mourners' words of condolence. The people gather in the front yard and dance while crying out "Ai, ya, a," holding a sword or large sticks and stones. Among the female members, there are some who even roll around on the ground, shouting "Ah-a" or "Aha-aba." The burial generally occurs within 24 hours of the death, and the body is buried in a mound-shaped grave. After several years the grave site will have disappeared. However, the deceased's skull is buried in a deep place under the family's home, and sometimes the family digs it up and food is offered to it. Close relatives of the deceased shave their heads and don blue or black mourning clothes. About a year later, lavish death celebrations are performed.

In the capital, Yaounde, and the harbor city Douala, Europeans, Indians and Chinese retain their own life styles and customs. There is no custom of cremation, so there is no crematorium in Cameroon. In the case of the Hindus, they cremate the body in a field far from the city.

CAPE VERDE

The Republic of Cape Verde lies in the Atlantic 560 kilometers off Dakar. It was owned by the Portuguese since the 15th century and used chiefly as a provisioning station for ships and as an assembly point for the slave trade in West Africa. It became independent in 1975. The official language is Portuguese, and the majority of the people are Roman Catholic.

When someone dies, the funeral takes place at the church of the bereaved family, and the corpe is taken to the nearby cemetery to be buried. Thereafter, the mourners attend a party at the bereaved house. The female kin observe a period of mourning for a few weeks.

CENTRAL AFRICA

The Central African Republic is located in the center of the African conti- nent. Most of the land is either plateau or highlands. It is said that the average altitude is 600 meters. The population consists of various tribes such as the Pygmy and the Banda. The official language is French, but for the most part the Sango language is used.

The majority of the people follow the native religion, but Christian missionaries are also very active. The Roman Catholic Church and the Brethren Church have both educational and medical facilities there. Among the immigrants in the capital, Bangui, there are also followers of Islam.

When someone dies, the death is reported to the relatives and neighbors in person. As it is very hot all year round, the body of the deceased is immediately buried in the ground. Funerals are expensive and elaborate, particularly when an elderly person dies. Livestock are slaughtered to feed the mourners.

The Zande fear all deaths, except those of very small children, which are attributed to witchcraft or magic and call for magical vengeance. Therefore, sorcerers are asked to chase away the evil spirits.

CHAD

The Republic of Chad is an inland country. The Sahara Desert lies to the north, so the northern part of Chad is very dry. The southern part of Chad is, however, hot and humid because of its forests. The population is multi-ethnic.

In general, the people of Chad follow Islam or the native religions. Funeral customs vary depending on the tribe. The funeral is designed strictly according to the social status and age of the deceased. In the Lake Chad area, it is a general practice for the corpse to be wrapped in animal skin and buried in places such as the floor of the room where the person died, by a door, within an animal enclosure, in the bush, at an intersection, or in a hole in a tree.

In the case of the nomadic people of the north, the body is buried in the desert without leaving behind any evidence of the fact that they had been at that place. In the agricultural zone of southern Niger, all of the people from the community join together and play instrumental music or dance. The body is buried in a corner of the village or under the floor of the deceased's home.

It is believed among the Sara who live in southern Chad that each person has a *ndil* (something like a soul). At death, the *ndil* separates from the body and becomes a ghost if the proper ritual is performed. Cemeteries are considered dangerous places not to be casually visited.

COMORO

The Republic of the Comoro includes three volcanic islands and numerous coral reefs in the Mozambique Channel between the African continent and the island of Madagascar. Comoro became independent from France in July 1975. Its capital is Moroni. Comoro has been known as a port of call for Islamic merchants and is famous for its spices, such as cinnamon and vanilla. Some years ago, Comoro came into the spotlight with the discovery of coelacanth, a rare fish species, in its waters. The people of Comoro are a mixture of Africans, Arabs and Malayans, the majority of whom follow Sunni Islam.

At death, a Muslim's body must be washed, dressed and wrapped in white cloth. Funerals are conducted by the family and the entire neighborhood. Thereafter, the corpse is taken to the nearby graveyard to be buried. The funeral and burial take place before sunset. Long periods of mourning are observed by the bereaved family.

CONGO

The Republic of the Congo, a newly developed country, is located in Central Africa. Half of the land is covered with jungle. The native Congo and Bantu tribes live here. The official language is French, but in practice the people use their own languages like Lingala.

As a result of the 1978 revolution, about 30 religious groups were suppressed by the government. Those that were accepted by the government were the Roman Catholic Church, the Congo Evangelical Church, the Salvation Army, the Islamic Religious Body, the followers of Simon Kimbangu Prophet, the Lassy Zephirin Prophet Church and the Tenri Temple. Among these, the Roman Catholic Church is the most dominant and powerful, but the Tenri mission also has been active since 1966 in the capital, Brazzaville. Through medical activities and services, they have been successful in capturing the people's hearts. Some members of the Pygmy tribe follow the native religions.

Because it is hot and humid year-round, the dead must be buried quickly. The body is buried in the ground following the funeral. There are specially designated cemeteries in the cities, but there are no such cemeteries in the rural areas. The funeral and the burial take place in the middle of the night, because Congolese people consider the world of death completely opposed to the world of life, and for the dead, their world is the night. The funeral is held under the leadership of the tribe's chief. The ceremony of *Pindookila* is officiated at by the chief, who prays that the evil soul that captured the soul of the deceased may not cause any harm to the village.

Depending on the tribe, different funeral customs are practiced, but in general the people believe in the existence of the god *Nzambi*, the righteous spirit *Binyumba*, and the curse of the ancestral souls called *Bakuyu*. Because they are afraid of the ancestral souls, they present offerings to them. Animism has also started to revive.

When someone dies, the death is announced to the relatives and neighbors in person. The funeral service is held at the bereaved family home. Funerals are important occasions of social gathering and family expenditure. Ideally, the bodies of the dead should be taken back to their native villages if the death occurs in town. Also cemeteries are considered to be dangerous places.

When someone dies among the Azande, the women of the neighborhood form a circle around the deceased; the men remain for the most part in an outer ring, whispering about the distressing event. All burials devolve upon the kinfolk of the dead. The body is wrapped by the relatives of the bereaved family in a cloth made of bark. When death occurs in the morning, the burial takes place in the afternoon; when it occurs in the afternoon, the burial takes place the next morning. Also, when a body remains unburied overnight, an all-night vigil is observed.

DJIBOUTI

The Republic of Djibouti is located at the mouth of the Red Sea and is known to be one of the hottest places on earth. In June of 1977, Djibouti became independent from France. The capital is Jibuti. The population is composed mainly of the Somali-Issa and the Kusi-Afari. Most people are followers of Sunni Islam.

When someone dies, the death is reported to the relatives and neighbors in person. Funerals are elaborate and expensive, particularly when elderly people die. For Muslims, funerals serve as a reminder to the living of the return of the Prophet and the approaching of the Day of Judgment.

EGYPT

The Republic of Egypt is known as the land where the ancient Nile civilization originated. The area was very important port for trade between East and West. Egypt is bordered by the Mediterranean Sea and the Suez Canal. Ninety-eight percent of the population are devout followers of the Sunni Islamic faith, who adhere to the strict commandments of their religion. The people, without fail, pray toward Mecca five times a day. During Ramadan, they do not eat or drink from dawn to sunset. In fact, they must not even swallow their saliva. Also, all worldly pleasures, such as smoking, using perfume, and sex, are prohibited during Ramadan. The sick, the pregnant, the elderly, and tourists are excluded, but those who miss these days must fast at another time to make up for the days they missed.

When a Muslim dies, the family bathes the deceased and sprinkles fragrant oil over the body. After that, the body is wrapped in a white or green cotton cloth. In the case of rich people, silk or cashmere is used instead of cotton. For the procession to the grave, wailing women are often hired. After the funeral at the mosque, the body is taken to the community cemetery and buried in either the men's or women's section.

The body of an *ullama* (instructor) may be buried in the cemetery, but there are certain exceptional cases. One is the grave of the former king, Riza Shah Pahlevi, who was exiled from Iran, at the Rifai Mosque in the capital, Cairo. In the case of the great national hero and former president of Egypt, Nasser, the Jamal Abdul Nasser Mosque was built, and on September 29, which is the anniversary of Nasser's death, an elaborate memorial service is held.

Near the Muqattam Dune, there is a vast town of the dead, Necropolis, throughout which various kinds of mausoleums and tombstones, both large and small, stand. Among the mausoleums in the town, some are equipped with kitchens, toilets, and living rooms, which are not much different from ordinary houses. The graves are generally encircled with a brick wall or an iron fence. The grave room is made underground, about 1.5 meters deep, and is connected to ground level rooms by stairs. After the body is buried, all of the doors are closed and covered with soil. Recently, as an indication of today's difficult economic situation, in the big cities where there are housing problems, refugees and escapees from the prisons have moved here and live alongside the grave keepers.

In the desert area outside the cities, graves are very simple; the people bury the body and leave a round stone on the grave.

Usually after the burial, relatives and friends are given some food at the deceased's home. In the local areas, dishes with mutton may be offered to the mourners. The mourning period lasts from four days to a week.

For Muslims, funerals serve as a way to comfort the bereaved family and as a way to challenge the community to live lives of integrity and responsibility. Therefore, participation in funerals is an important way of validating one's faithful fellowship in the community.

The Coptic Christians, who are separate from the Roman Catholics, have preserved their traditional beliefs. The funeral procession of the Coptic Christians is grand. The St. Katharina Greek Orthodox Church is located at the foot of Mount Sinai, where Moses is believed to have given his followers the Ten Commandments. In a separate building from the church, there are piles of thousands of bones of priests, waiting for the second coming of Jesus Christ.

EQUATORIAL GUINEA

Located in west-central Africa and compising the mainland area and several islands in the Gulf of Guinea, Equatorial Guinea became independent in 1968. However, there is considerable political unrest with guerrilla activity. The majority of the people in this country follow the Roman Catholic tradition.

ERITREA

The Republic of Eritrea was formerly a part of Ethiopia, facing the Red Sea. It became independent from Ethiopia in 1993 as the result of a 28-year guerrilla war. Today, Eritrea is the most stable corner of Africa. The capital is Asmara. The majority of the people are nomads or farmers who are either Muslims or Coptic Christians. When someone dies, the funeral is held in a nearby mosque or a church. The women do not join the burial rituals at the graveyard.

At death, a Muslim's body must be washed, dressed, and wrapped in white cloth. Thereafter, the body is taken to the mosque for the funeral rite, then to the graveyard to be buried. After death, people are judged in a setting much like a secular court, where it is decided if they will proceed to heaven or hell.

ETHIOPIA

The People's Republic of the Ethiopian Federation in the northeast of Africa is bordered by the Red Sea. Most of its land, however, rests on plateaus. The majority of the people are of mixed blood from the Ham and Shem tribes; there are also those who are a mixture of Ham and Negroid ancestry. The official language is Amharic, although those in the middle class also speak English.

After World War II, members of the Ethiopian Orthodox Church, a part of

Coptic Christianity, held power, establishing what seemed to be a national religion. But after the 1974 revolution, brought about by criticism from the Muslim population, government-mandated religion was overturned, and as a result the freedom of religious choice was returned to the individual. The present revolutionary government is now calling for the confiscation and nationalization of church property, stirring up strong anti-religious sentiment.

The Ethiopian Orthodox Church especially is not concerned with salvation in terms of social welfare, so funeral customs have become quite secularized. When someone dies, the body is washed at the home of the deceased and wrapped in muslin or calico, and then wrapped in woven coconut leaves. The mourners wail beside the deceased. How much they wail depends on how close they were to the deceased. The closer they were, the harder they wail. When death occurs in the morning, the body must be buried within the day, while if it is in the afternoon, the body is buried the next day.

The funeral procession starts from the deceased's home, and in the case of the Ethiopian Orthodox Church, an acolyte who carries the cross leads the procession, followed by the minister, the incense bearer, the coffin, the male mourners and finally the female mourners. Sometimes the acolyte carries a bag of flour, which is used to make bread for the Holy Communion, instead of the cross. The procession stops along the way, and the coffin is placed on the ground. The crying women sing a song and the mourners join in the singing. The procession continues on to the church, where an ox is sacrificed, and then passes through the blood-stained churchyard to the cathedral. A funeral mass is held there, after which the body is buried.

Among the Amhara, when an elder is near death, a sharman is called in. He gives last rites, and after death, assigns a burial ground in the churchyard. The body of the deceased is washed, wrapped in a *shama*, carried to the church for the mass and buried at the nearest cemetery. A memorial feast (*tazkar*) is held 40 days after the death, when it is thought that the soul has the earliest opportunity to be freed from purgatory.

In the case of the Oromo tribe in the south, they pile up stones on the grave, which is never the site of rituals or a monument. In the rural areas, stone monuments are erected in forests of acacia trees. If a human figure is carved on the monument, it is the grave of a man of influence in the community. Ordinarily, people are buried in communal cemeteries without any graveposts.

The Dolze, in the Ethiopian central highlands, about 500 kilometers from Addis Ababa, build a bamboo hut near their living quarters where they bury the corpse. They believe that the spirits of the dead will protect the survivors as long as they are treated with respect.

GABON

The Gabonese Republic is an equatorial country on the west coast of Africa, so it is very hot and humid. The abundant forests allow forestry to be one of the largest industries in Gabon.

Most of the people are of the various Bantu tribes and the Fang. Catholicism is the dominant religion, but it is mixed somewhat with the native religion. The people believe in the Catholic doctrines, as well as the native god *Anambye* or the ancestral soul *Malumbi*. The constitution which was issued in 1967 includes a section about the freedom of religion.

Probably because Gabon was a French colony, in places such as the capital, Libreville, and Port-Gentil where crude oil is exported, even now the French life style remains, and the official language is French as well. There is also the Schweitzer Hospital, which Dr. Albert Schweitzer founded, in Lambarene. In the urban areas, there are community and church graveyards. In the rural areas, however, the body is buried in a graveyard designated by their tribe.

Roughly speaking there are seven tribes, but it is said that there are actually over sixty tribes in Gabon. Each of the tribes has a very strong sense of tribal unity. They have their own languages and customs as well. Therefore, it is impossible to generalize about their funeral customs, but the wake seems to be held at the family's home, and the funeral is held at their home, in a church or in a mosque.

For example, the Bongo are the forest foragers whose music is distinct from that of the farmers of Central Africa. At their funerals, they exhibit complex vocal polyphony, incorporating harmonious yodeling, though there are very few musical instruments.

GAMBIA

The Republic of Gambia on the Atlantic coast became the first colony in Africa in the 17th century. Many Gambians were taken to the American continent from here as slaves as related in Alex Haley's epic *Roots*. About half of the population are Malinkes. English and the native languages are official languages.

In the rural areas, animism is strong, and sorcerers who appease the curses of the gods are very active. At a funeral, it is the custom among the mourners to dress up and sing and dance. For the most part, the body is buried in the ground. In the past, members of the praise-singer group were buried in hollow baobab trees, so as not to contaminate the earth, but nowadays this custom of segregation is rapidly diminishing.

There are also many Muslims in Gambia. After the death of a Muslim, the usual Islamic funeral ceremonies are followed. Burial is within a few hours unless the death occurs at night.

GHANA

The Republic of Ghana, which was called the "Gold Coast," is located in the tropical zone on the coast of the South Atlantic Ocean. The dry season is from October until March of the next year, and the rainy season is from April to September. Lakes and the Volta River, which flows through the center of the country, provide the country with water.

In the 19th century, Ghana was one of the British colonies, but in 1957 it became the first independent country among the colonies in Africa. Since then, the government has changed repeatedly.

Ghana is a community consisting of many different tribes, such as the Akan and the Elbe. The chief of each tribe holds actual power over the life of the tribe. Each group uses its own language and preserves its life styles. English is commonly used. Half of the population are Catholics or Protestants, but there are also Muslims and those who follow the native religions.

In the urban areas like the capital, Accra, a death must be reported to the government district office. In the rural areas, however, this is not required. There is no crematorium; everyone is buried in the ground.

Among the native people, the biggest tribe is the Akan, among whom the corpse is bathed right away by the family and close relatives. Customarily, the female members of the family cry very loudly near the body of the deceased. The family and close relatives mourn for at least nine days, and during the mourning period, everyone must fast.

Ghana is different from other countries in that the day of the funeral is separate from the day of the burial. The tribe decides on a funeral day, which is held several days or weeks after the burial. There was even a case when the funeral was held five years after the day of the burial.

The funeral expenses are paid with money donated from the family, mourners and the tribe as a whole. The settling of the debt ends about one week after the funeral. In general, funerals have become bigger and more expensive. Notice of a death is placed in the local newspaper, and they say that this expense amounts to the cost of a student's board in a dormitory for one semester. Four out of a total of sixteen pages of the leading newspaper, *The Daily Graphic*, are filled with death notices, so it is jokingly called "*The Daily Ghosts*."

Traditionally, Monday or Thursday is the day when the people seek reconciliation with God. Saturdays may be included. On the morning of the funeral, drums are played and eulogies are sung. Female mourners and male relatives go around the village three times, and then the funeral party starts. The family must put orange-colored clay on their forehead and shoulders. The widow places palm leaves on her elbow signifying her deep relationship with the deceased. The others wear red or black clothes. The family and the close relatives shave off their hair after the funeral and place it at the burial site. Mourners come from other villages as well.

Some unique customs prevail among Ghana's coastal people such as the colorful fantasy coffins created by the wood-carvers on request and modeled after objects of special importance to the departed, such as a fish-shaped coffin for a fishing chief.

Among the Lobi-Dagarti, funerals for the elderly are expensive and elaborate, because they involve the participation of many people. The funeral takes three to four days, depending on whether the deceased is male or female. Livestock are slaughtered during the funeral to feed the mourners. However, the death of an infant is usually not mourned except by the infant's mother. Dead infants are considered to be wandering spirits rather than human beings, so precautions are taken against their return to this world.

For the Ashanti tribe, the funeral is one of the important events. The village chief is notified immediately of the death. and to commence burial preparations without him is an insult and is punishable by a fine of money and a sheep. The relatives and friends are informed in person. When the dead body is ready for the funeral, the wailing begins and men fire guns. Mourners smear red clay on their foreheads and upper arms, or white clay over their entire bodies if they are of the family of a dead priest. The next step is the offering of food to be eaten by the dead in his journey into the afterlife. Burial takes place on the third day.

The belief persists among the Fanti tribe that the matrilineal clan "owns" its member. So strong is the belief that when a man dies, unless they have the permission of the matrilineal clan head, the widow and children may not participate in his funeral or even be present at it. The body is carried quickly to a nearby graveyard of the matrilineal clan and there placed in a new grave.

GUINEA

The Republic of Guinea, which is located on the Atlantic coast of Africa, became independent from France in October 1958. Since that time, Guinea has clearly expressed an attitude of anti-imperialism, anti-colonialism and anti-racial discrimination. The government has adopted socialistic policies, both economically and politically.

The population of Guinea is divided into 15 tribal groups such as the Malinke, the Tulani and the Susu. About three-quarters of the population follow Islam, but there are also those who follow Christianity or the native religious beliefs.

The sense of unity among the tribal members is very strong in some areas, and they try to avoid contact with foreigners. The people are for the most part illiterate, and usually use their own native language. Among the literate, French is often used. In the local areas, as in the neighboring countries, there are many people who believe in shamanism, ancestor-worship and holy spirits, while in the capital, Conakry, the great majority of the people follow Islam. There are many Muslims, especially among the Dialonke, the Sarakole and the Susu.

Because it is hot and humid in Guinea, it is customary that the deceased be buried on the day of death at the family's home. All the burials are interments.

GUINEA BISAU

The Republic of Guinea Bisau is situated between Senegal and Guinea in West Africa. It is largely composed of swamps and riverine estuaries, and about 85 percent of the population are subsistence farmers. It gained independence from Portugal in 1974. The majority of the people follow traditional religions, and the rest are Muslims.

When someone dies, the death is reported to the relatives and neighbors in person. Funerals are rather simple among commoners. Immediately after death, the body of the deceased is carried to a nearby graveyard and buried. The wandering spirits of the dead are feared, so often religious practitioners who have curative powers and supernatural abilities are employed.

IVORY COAST

The Republic of the Ivory Coast was for many years a colony of France. As the name indicates, this West African country on the Atlantic Coast was known for its ivory trade. The majority of the people are the Akan. Since the country became independent in 1960, the people have been working hard, but they are still far from reaching their economic and cultural goals. The illiteracy rate in the Ivory Coast is high.

In the 1963 constitution, individual freedom of religious belief was permitted, but the government has been trying as a policy to discourage the superstitious elements of the traditional beliefs and is advising the people to convert to Islam or Christianity. Also, the church schools are assisted by national funds. The giant Christian basilica in Yamoussoukro, the capital, is "the must to see" for visitors.

In the Ivory Coast, there is a church called the Harris Church. The unique beliefs of this church combine elements of Christianity with traditional beliefs. The Harris Church is powerful and successful in the rural areas, but in the capital, Abidjan, the church has been losing influence. Such churches now have begun to be taken over by other Christian churches. The Ivory Coast, whose population consists of about sixty tribes, has various ceremonies and funeral styles. Because the life styles and customs of each of the tribes are different, it is hard to generalize, but the people are fond of festivals and dances, and funerals in general are considered to be big events.

When someone dies, the relatives and neighbors are told about the death in person or by telephone or radio. The wake usually continues for four days at the family home, and the funeral service is held on the eighth day after death at a church or mosque, where the people bring offerings of money or kintie clothes.

In Abidjan, there is only one private mortuary, called *Ivosep*, on Boulevard Giscard d' Estaing, that handles funeral procedures. Other activities are handled by relatives or friends. There is a public cemetery on the hill of Williamville where Catholic, Protestant, Muslim and traditional graveyards coexist. There are public cemeteries in the vicinity of towns and villages where the dead are buried free of charge. In the rural areas, the chief of the villagers officiates at the service.

KENYA

The Republic of Kenya is located on the coast of the Indian Ocean at the equator. The landscape is made up mostly of plateaus and mountains, and Kenya is said to be a treasure chest of wild animals. Mount Kenya, located in the center of the country, is 5,199 meters high, and its summit is always covered with snow.

The population consists of various tribes such as the Kikuyu, the Luhya, the Luo and the Kamba. Each tribe believes in its own native religions, but Christianity is the main religion in the inland regions of Kenya, while Islam is the most dominate religion in the coastal areas.

Tribal unity is strong. When someone dies, all the people under the chief help to arrange the funeral. Because Kenya is in the equatorial zone, the body is buried quickly in the ground, and a gravesite is assigned. When someone from out of town dies in Nairobi, the capital, the body is embalmed and then sent back to the hometown by truck for the burial.

Among the people in the rural or remote areas, the concept of "the future" is not strong. They have the attitude of "whatever will be, will be." Only God knows the future, so death is the end of life, and it is something that should be accepted. Death is one's natural fate. At the funeral, the people sing, dance and pray. The Kalenjin tribes do not even hold a funeral. The body until recent times was just left in the bushes or placed in a river to float away. The Teso tribe celebrates the end of the mourning period, so that the deceased will be completely forgotten. The people of Kenya are critical of the revelational religion which has been brought in by Westerners. They sarcastically say, "the Westerners came to Africa with their Bible. At that time, the Africans had the land. Now the Westerners have the land, and the Africans have the Bible."

In the urban areas, there are many immigrants from India. The Indians have economic power in Kenya, and they are not very friendly to the natives. These immigrants have kept their own religions, such as Hinduism, and have kept their own customs. When someone dies, the Indians cremate the body in an outdoor crematorium.

In Kenya, there is a great disparity between rich and poor. The wealthy in the urban areas are usually Christians and hold elaborate funerals in the local churches. They also build gorgeous stone monuments in the community cemeteries. The poor people, who make up the majority of Kenya's population, simply place the body in a meager coffin and bury it in a corner of the deceased's home. The family and friends participate in the burial by placing soil over the body and offering flowers. After the body is buried, a grave marker is erected at the site. After that, the family treats the mourners to a simple meal. Even such a simple funeral is expensive, so relatives and friends often help to defray the costs. Some are forced to borrow money to cover the costs.

LESOTHO

The Kingdom of Lesotho is surrounded on all sides by South Africa, and its economy and politics rely entirely on South Africa. Sethoto and English are the official languages. Most people follow Roman Catholicism or Protestantism.

However, traditional belief of ancestor worship is also practiced. Divination was the means of discovering the wishes of the ancestors, and sacrifice of cattle was the means of propitiation. In Maseru, the capital, a company called the Undertakers (PTY) Ltd. handles funeral and shipment services for the death of foreigners.

LIBERIA

The Republic of Liberia is on the south Atlantic coast of Africa. Because Liberia's tax on ships is low, many foreign owners have their ships registered in Liberia. Liberia is a leading country in the number of ships it has registered.

The majority of the people are the native blacks. The people are followers of the tribal religious tradition. Among the tribes living in the inner part of Liberia, ancestor worship and animism are common. The people are very fearful of the souls of the dead; therefore, they practice various kinds of sacrificial offerings and ceremonies to drive away evil spirits. However, American missionaries once spread the Christian gospel and also tried to establish a place of peace for those liberated in the United States. As a result, there are many Christians and Muslims in Monrovia, the capital.

When someone dies in the urban areas, the family invites a priest of their own religion to hold the funeral. The body is buried at the earliest convenience. There are almost no professional morticians. The coffin can be obtained at a joiner's shop. In the case of a rich or well-known person, the funeral is held at a church or mosque, and the body is buried either in a public or church graveyard.

In the case of the foreigners living in Liberia, the body is either cremated at an outdoor crematorium near the beach, created especially for the Indian population, or shipped to the deceased's country. Prior to cremation, one is required to obtain a medical report from a doctor of the national JFK Hospital or the police. In case of cremation, the ashes may be taken back to the respective country.

LIBYA

The Great Socialist People's Libyan Arab Jamahiriya is located on the coast of the Mediterranean Sea. After Italy, which ruled Libya, surrendered in World War II, the country was placed under the control of the United States, England

and France, but in 1951 it became independent. Libya is mostly desert, but it has produced high-quality oil, which has meant instant economic success for the country. It has also been successful in shutting out foreign capital and nationalizing its oil fields and is aiming at becoming a self-supporting country.

The majority of the people are Arabs and Berbers, and Sunni Islam is the national religion. The official language is Arabic, and the country has even adopted an ultra-nationalistic policy of excluding all other writing systems. Due to the shortage of labor and field experts, the country has been forced to use temporary laborers from neighboring countries, such as Egypt and Tunisia. Foreign laborers make up approximately 10 percent of the total population, and their life style and customs are quite similar to those of the Libyans.

When someone dies, the family washes the body of the deceased with soap and water at the home of the deceased, and then wraps it in white cloth. The funeral is held either at the deceased's home or at a mosque. The body is transported in the coffin in a procession to the graveyard on the shoulders of close relatives. Then it is taken out of the coffin at the graveyard and buried in the ground. The head must face Mecca. Cement tiles or flat stones are placed on the grave, and a mound is made or a gravepost is placed over the grave. If the bereaved family is very devout or wealthy, several days after the burial a leader is invited to the family home, where the Qur'an is recited in unison by the mourners.

Libya, like Saudi Arabia, is very strict about the Islamic commandments, so guests are not entertained with alcoholic beverages.

The Bedouin also follow Islamic practices associated with death. Among some of them, the dead are buried in one place, although it is often difficult to reach this place within the prescribed time according to Islamic law. The funeral rites are very simple and the graves tend to be unmarked or undifferentiated.

MADAGASCAR

The Republic of Madagascar is an island lying in the Indian Ocean about 400 kilometers from the east coast of Africa. It is the fourth largest island in the world. Madagascar became independent from France in 1960; there are many immigrants from Southeast Asia and Africa, some of whom are a mixture of Indonesian and black or Arab. The official languages are Malagasy and French.

Eighteen tribes make up this country, each of them having their own native beliefs, but in the cities there are many Christians (especially Catholics) and Muslims. In the capital, Antananarivo, the family reports the death with a medical report to the government office. The body is wrapped in silk cloth after a bath by the family and close relatives. If the deceased was Christian, the body is placed in a coffin.

Funerals differ depending on the religion and customs. In general, however, the people prefer a big funeral ceremony. Not only relatives but also all of the neighbors come to the cemetery. They eat, drink and sing to comfort the deceased. However, since such elaborate ceremonies can be extremely costly, the younger generation nowadays is critical of them.

When someone dies, the body is placed not in an individual grave, but in a stone room that is shared with other family members. The body is wrapped with silk cloth and strings. In July or August every year, there is a gathering, called *famadiana*, meaning the resurrection of the dead. On that day, family members and relatives get together and open the door to the stone room. The body is taken out of the room, and a party is held in front of the body. The mummy-like body is rewrapped in a new white cloth and is returned to the room after the party. When there are many dead family members, the bodies are put together at the time of the burial, so that the stone room never becomes full.

In the graveyard of the Sakalaba tribe near Molondava, there are remains from an ancient megalithic culture marked by a magnificent square tombstone encircled with a wooden fence. On it is an epitaph with interesting geometric patterns of animals set in relief.

Most of the foreigners residing in Madagascar are employed in the deep-sea fishing business and live in towns such as Tamatawe, Majunga, Nossi-Be and Ambilope. When a foreigner dies, the people who are related to the deceased gather and hold a wake. Then, with legal and official permission, they cremate the deceased at a remote beach or ship the body to his or her home country. Sanchulal Crematorium, which the resident Indians use, is in Antananarivo, where no ready-made urns are available, so they must be specially ordered.

For the Sakalava, as with all Malagasy, it is essential that the bodies be properly entombed and in their rightful place. Funerals for elders are elaborate and expensive and sometimes last for a week. However, the graves for the commoners are simple structures generally void of decoration, found in the forest, in rock grottos by the sea, or in Catholic or Muslim cemeteries.

MALAWI

The Republic of Malawi is an inland country on the west side of Malawi Lake near Mozambique. Most of its commercial activity is based on agriculture. The official languages are Chichewa and English, and the majority of the people are Roman Catholic.

When someone dies, relatives and neighbors are informed in person. Funerals are usually observed according to the matrilineal basis of the society. However, Bemba, the original household religion, was radically altered during the centralization of chiefly authority and the imposition of Bemba paramountcy, in which the chiefs manipulated the religion to enhance their own power. Therefore, the worship of the spirits of dead chiefs has since become an essential element in this society.

MALI

The Republic of Mali is located in Central Africa on the plains of the Niger River. Most of the people are of the Bambara tribe. The people follow Islam or their native religions, so various funeral customs can be seen in this country.

Mali is an important connection in the trade routes between southern and northern Africa. Timbuktu on the Niger River is especially well known as the center of trade in the Sahara Desert. Even today caravans using camels come from northern Africa to sell food, salt and daily supplies. Because the caravan merchants were Muslims, the native people were converted to Islam. Mosques made of mud are seen throughout Mali. In the capital, Bamako, an especially majestic mosque was built as a present from Saudi Arabia.

When someone dies, the relatives and neighbors are informed in person. When an infant dies, there is no funeral service. When an adult dies, the funeral service is held at the bereaved family's house for four days. The neighbors gather at the funeral service with food and money offerings. The dead body is buried right after death at a nearby graveyard. The grave is simply made up of a mound of soil with dead branches or stones on it, and is often deserted. Muslims invite the *imam* to the bereaved family's house on the third, seventh and fortieth days afterward. Sorcerers are also asked to prevent the souls of the dead from placing a curse on the family, because the people are afraid of them.

The worship of spirits is also popular, and each tribal group holds its own traditional festivities. The minority Tuareg tribe are a nomadic people known as the "Heroes of the Desert." They use blue cloth to wrap their dead, who are then buried in the desert. They mourn for the dead for three days.

The funerals of the Dogon tribe are noted for the colorful mask dances that are presented to the mourners. This dance is meant to save the soul of the deceased. It is believed that the soul and spirit of the deceased are very unstable. Therefore, it is necessary to confine them in the family home. Men from the village arm themselves and gather to put on a mock battle. Then, when the mourning period ends, a big masquerade party is held. The purpose of the party is to reunite the soul and the spirit of the deceased and send them on to the next world. It must be noted here that the funeral has two stages. The first is to mourn the death, to separate it from the community of the living, and to send it to the other world. The second stage is to transform the dead into its ancestral soul and to establish a social relationship with the dead.

MAURITANIA

Much of the Islamic Republic of Mauritania lies in the Sahara Desert near the Atlantic Ocean. The majority of the people are Moors, who are a mixture of Arabs and Berbers. They wear blue robes and are called "the People of the Blue Robes." It is their custom to entertain guests from faraway places, and they hospitably let travelers stay in their homes for at least three days. Except for those living in the capital, Nouakchott, and near the South Senegal River, the people are nomadic and live in tents.

Death may be attributed to natural or supernatural causes, and every community has a cemetery. If the deceased is a man, his body is washed and enshrouded by the *faqih*; if a woman, by another woman. If death occurs in the morning, the burial is done that afternoon; if at night, the following morning.

After the funeral, the family digs a very shallow hole, which is only a spread handspan plus an extra half-thumb length in the sand and buries the body. They leave nothing there to mark the grave.

MAURITIUS

Mauritius is a volcanic island to the east of Madagascar in the Indian Ocean. Most of the islanders are immigrants from India, but there are also people from Africa and Madagascar. In 1968, Mauritius became independent from England and is now working toward development, but overpopulation and occasional cyclones that develop from tropical depressions make this difficult.

Many Mauritians follow Hinduism, Christianity or Islam. When someone dies, the family must obtain a death certificate from the government district office after submitting a doctor's medical report. The funeral is arranged by the immediate family of the deceased with the help of the relatives and is usually held at a church or a mortuary. Then the body is buried in the cemetery after the funeral. If the deceased is a Hindu, the body is cremated in an outdoor crematorium; Christians or Muslims are buried in the ground.

In the rural areas, there are various kinds of festivals and ceremonies. For example, in the northeastern part of Mauritius, one can see the ceremony of *Akubashana* or fire walking.

MOROCCO

The Kingdom of Morocco is in western Africa and faces Spain to the north. Most of the land consists of plateaus and plains. The climate is mild, so the raising of stock and agriculture are both prosperous endeavors. The Berbers make up the majority of the people, but there are also Arabs and blacks. Arabic is the official language, but about 40 percent of the population also speak Berber. Many people follow Sunni Islam. In 1956, Morocco became independent from France, but because it was a French colony, it shares many customs with its neighbors, Tunisia and Algeria. The three countries, called the Maghreb, have each developed in their own way. As a result, various customs are practiced.

When someone dies, the body is placed in a boat-shaped coffin, and the funeral is held at the bereaved family's home or at a mosque. After the funeral, the body is buried free of charge in the community graveyard. Flowers are not offered at the burial. The mourning clothes can be of any style, just as long as they are clean. The widow wears a *kaftan* (white dress) and mourns for 40 days.

Because the soul of the deceased is considered to be called away from earth by Allah, the people show no attachment to the body. Except on Holy Friday, the family does not visit the grave very often. Cemeteries are classified by religion. Islamic cemeteries do not allow the burial of people other than Muslims.

Most graves in Morocco are very simple piles of stone and mortar, but the mosques of the *Sidi* (Saints) are notably large, grand structures. The mosque of Mohammed the Fifth, one of the sultans who was said to be related by blood to Ali, the husband of the daughter of the founder of Islam, is especially magnificent. Muslim leaders recite the Qur'an beside the mosque 24 hours a day.

The funeral procedures of the Berbers are similar to other Muslims. The body is placed in the grave with its face turned toward Mecca while the leader (*faqih*) intones an appropriate chapter from the Qur'an. Only men attend funerals, and the kinsmen of the deceased give a feast seven days after the death for the mourners. In the Rif, a widow gives a feast 40 days after her husband's death, which theoretically marks the end of the mourning period.

MOZAMBIQUE

The Republic of Mozambique is located on the eastern coast of Africa. The island of Madagascar lies off its coast in the Indian Ocean. It was a colony of Portugal for many years, but in 1975 it became independent. The name of the country was taken from one of its harbor towns. The capital is Maputo. The population consists mainly of the Bantu Makua, and the official language is Portuguese. The majority of the people follow the native religion, but in the urban areas there are Catholics and Muslims as well. Because missionary work was connected with the colonization by the Europeans, Christian missionaries were deported. Mozambique adopted a socialist system, but it has very strong economic ties with its neighbor, South Africa.

When someone dies, the whole tribe joins the funeral. Because Mozambique is in the tropical zone, the body must be buried in the ground as quickly as possible. In general, the people are afraid of the spirit of death, so prayers of purification by a sorcerer are very common. There are also many taboos. The people hate to touch anything that is taboo or to be photographed. There is no crematorium or custom of cremation, nor is there a custom of offering flowers for the deceased.

NAMIBIA

Namibia is a newly formed country in the southwestern part of Africa. Most of the land consists of the Namib and Kalahari deserts. The population includes the native Name and the San, who are regarded as primitive people, and the

Ouhimba and the Khoi. There are some descendants of German immigrants as well, who live in the cities like Windhoek and Swakopmund. In Namibia there are funeral directors who handle all kinds of funeral services.

The Nama (formerly, the Hottentot) believe that death is the deed of an evil spirit. If the proper ceremony to remove the spirit is not performed, the bad soul will attack. Among the San (formerly, the Bushman), death is the passing into a spiritual realm that is distinct from the material realm. Relatives who have recently died are considered dangerous because their spirits yearn for their kin and may attempt to bring about their early death in order to be reunited; this danger recedes as the memory of the deceased dims with time.

Among the Ouhimba, a branch tribe of the Herero, the people surround the deathbed and cry for the deceased. The body is then carried out of the back door of the house, and it is buried at a gravesite that is designated by the chief. Stones are piled up around the grave, so that wild animals are not able to eat the body. Sometimes they place earthenware in the center of the mound or pile up cattle horns around the grave.

The people believe that the soul of the dead stays in the graveyard, so they choose a remote location for it. It is said that if one points to the ground on his way home, the curse of death will capture him. On the day following the burial, the family moves from the home of the deceased and leaves the deceased's belongings behind. At the funeral, sheep are killed as sacrificial offerings and are served to the mourners. The stomach of a sheep is hung around the neck of the successor of a deceased male. The stomach is entwined with fragrant leaves and then kept around the successor's neck until it rots.

Among the Khoi, the death is reported to the relatives and neighbors in person, and the deceased is buried as soon as possible in the nearby bush. For them, death under exceptional circumstances is often attributed to evil beings or ghosts.

NIGER

The Republic of Niger is a new country that became independent from France in 1960. Its landscape is mostly savanna or desert. Funerals are held according to the tribal traditions.

The Hausa, who make up the majority of Niger's population, follow Islam. They believe that photographs steal away one's soul, so they dislike being photographed. Among the Songhay tribe, funerals are conducted according to Islamic tradition. However, they also observe spirit possession ceremonies, which in some towns occur at least once a week.

The Tuareg, who live in northern Niger, are nomadic people who are said to rob travelers. Though they do not rob anymore, when they dash by on horseback wearing blue robes and veils over their faces, they look quite fierce.

NIGERIA

The Federal Republic of Nigeria is on the coast of the Guef of Guinea. It is hot and humid in general, but to the north of the Jos plateau, in the middle of the country, is a savanna. Slavery was once widespread in Nigeria, but since it was a British colony, it became a country of commerce. Nigeria is a multi-ethnic country with 248 different tribes. In the northern part of the country, Islam is the religion of choice; in the south, it is mainly Christianity, but there are local religions as well.

In the urban areas, a death is reported to the government district office with a doctor's medical report. The funeral is arranged by a relative or a private mortuary. In the case of a Muslim, the body is transported to the mosque, and after the funeral it is buried in the graveyard.

In the case of tribes in remote areas, depending on the place and the tribe, matters concerning the funeral such as the date of the funeral are decided by the chief, who has absolute authority in such decisions, and everyone follows his commands. For instance, when there is a death in the Yoruba tribe, the family and close relatives wash the body and paint it with red dye called *kam*, then they wrap it in a shroud. The body is placed in the house for three days. The family goes to ask the *papalao*, the minister of the *Egungun* (next world), for his instructions, and the body is buried, according to his decision, either under the deceased's bedroom or in a *piaza* (grave). The deceased's clothes and food are buried with the body, to prevent any trouble in the next life. It is believed that the deceased has not died, but has been reborn as a ghost. A couple of months after the burial, a memorial service must be held. If the service is not properly done, there will be a curse on the family. The female family members put white powder and ashes on their faces and arms.

There is no crematorium or custom of cremation in Nigeria. When the deceased is a foreigner, a special permit from the regional office must be obtained, then a mortuary is requested to cremate the body. The mortuary cremates the body in the bush with twigs and branches which they collect there. Within the capital city, Lagos, there are church or private cemeteries. If a foreigner can purchase a grave, especially a private one, then he or she can be buried in the ground. There are many cemeteries for Europeans, where many gorgeous tombstones can be seen.

Among the Igbo, in the south, funerals are rather simple. Only the bodies of the elderly are buried; the others are simply left in the bush. The body of the elderly deceased is buried as soon as possible, and the funerals are elaborate, for old people are believed to have lived well and to have died in a socially acceptable manner.

For the Yoko tribe, the proper funeral ensures a swift journey to paradise; otherwise the transition is delayed. The body is buried outside the village.

Among the Annang tribe, the head of the hierarchical order to which the dead person belongs assumes control of the funeral matters. The body is shaved, washed, and given a change of clothing. Then the body is removed from the house and arranged in a sitting position on a log bench placed between living trees that were specially planted in honor of the dead of the village. While the body is in this position, several cattle are slaughtered before it to honor the dead and to bid his or her spirit to begin its journey to the land of ghosts. Following this rite, strong men carry it off to the nearby graveyard. Not long after the burial, the bereaved family treat the guest mourners with food and refreshments.

PEOPLE'S CONGO

The People's Republic of Congo is located in the central area of the African continent on the equator. One of the largest rivers, the Congo River, flows through the country and creates a basin, which is surrounded by savanna country. Most of the people are of the native Bantu tribe, but there are also Pygmies in the northeastern part of the country. The official language is French, but most of the people speak their own tribal language.

After a long turmoil, the Mobutu Seko rule finally came to end in May 1997, and the country, formerly known as Zaire, was taken over by the rebel leader, Laurent Kabila, and thereafter, changed its name to the People's Republic of Congo.

The native religions in Congo are based on ancestor worship. There are also those who follow the Simon Kimbangu Prophet, which is a locally adapted form of Catholicism, Protestantism and Islam.

The urban areas such as the capital, Kinshasa, are to some extent modernized. Therefore, if someone dies in the hospital, the death is reported to the family, and a professional mortician arranges the funeral and related matters for the family at their request. However, the morticians are rather inefficient, and some even demand a *matabisi*, a tip, prior to the funeral.

There is no custom of cremation, so there are no crematoriums. Funerals for everyone, except for the Christians, are held at the family home or at the cemetery. White flowers are sometimes offered. In the rural areas, relatives and friends get together and hold the funeral according to tribal customs in the community square, and the body is buried in the ground at a designated spot.

Most people believe in the existence of the soul of the dead and are afraid of its curse. Therefore, a magician is often asked to perform an exorcism. The casket that is used by the northern tribes, such as the Bamangala, is made of wood in the shape of the human body.

In general, there is no elaborate ceremony for death, which may be attributed to either natural or supernatural causes. However, the corpse is seen as harmful, and a cleansing ritual is performed to remove the aura of death from the village, as the corpse is buried in the cemetery shared by village clusters.

RWANDA

The Republic of Rwanda is a young inland country that became independent in 1962 from Belgium. The population includes the Tutsi, Hutu and other tribes. The official languages are French and Kinyarwanda. Most of the land is mountainous, and because Rwanda is close to the equator, it is very hot, but the area close to Lake Kivu has lower humidity. Rwanda is said to be the most comfortable and pleasant place to live in Africa.

Because of the European colonization policy, there are many Catholics in the area close to Kigali, the capital of Rwanda. In the rural areas, the people still believe in the native religion.

Funerals are community affairs, and everyone joins in. The people, however, are afraid of the spirit of death (*barimu*), so sorcerers are often called to purify the body, which is usually buried in a nearby graveyard with other remains. The shape of the tombstone differs depending upon the place. At the time of the funeral, the people dress in formal attire and dance in a circle. The Tutsi especially are known to be excellent dancers.

Rwanda does not have a professional mortuary, but there are church graveyards and publicly owned cemeteries in the urban areas. Some of the Christians offer flowers at the funeral, but that is all.

SAO TOME AND PRINCIPE

The Republic of Sao Tome and Principe is composed of the main islands of Sao Tome and Principe and the surrounding islets that are situated off the western coast of Africa. The population is entirely descended from immigrants, as the islands were uninhabited when the Portuguese arrived in 1470. The majority of the people are black Africans, who are Roman Catholic. The traditional religions once practiced by the inhabitants, paricularly by the Bantu, have almost completely disappeared as a result of Catholic evangelical activity.

SENEGAL

The Republic of Senegal is located on the Atlantic coast of West Africa. The country became independent in 1960. Probably because Senegal was a French colony, the political, economic and cultural influence of the French is evident throughout the country. The capital, Dakar, is called "Le Petit Paris D'Afrique."

The population is multi-ethnic and includes the Walof, the Serer and the Peul. The majority of the people in Senegal are Muslim, but there are also Catholics in the cities and French customs are common. The religion of Senegal is called "the black people's Islam," which is a mixture of Islam and the native belief in spirits.

The Islamic leader, called the *malabu*, practices a kind of shamanism and can cure sickness. The religious regulations are not very strict, but as a rule the people of Senegal do not drink alcoholic beverages and do not eat pork. During the Festival of Sacrifice, which is held on the seventieth day after Ramadan, even low-income families kill a sheep to offer to Allah.

When someone dies, the relatives and neighbors are informed in person, and the funeral service is conducted by the *imam*, or priests, at the bereaved family's home. The body is buried in a nearby cemetery immediately afterward, and on the seventh day the relatives and friends visit the graveyard. In Dakar, the capital, there are two major cemeteries, one for Muslims on the coastal Route de la Corniche-ouest, and the other for Catholics in Bel Air. There is no custom of cremation, so there are no crematoriums.

SEYCHELLES

The Republic of Seychelles consists of 92 islands in the Indian Ocean to the north of Madagascar. The islands are surrounded by a white barrier reef, and the aquamarine sea is clear and very beautiful. The Seychelles became independent from England in 1976 as one of the commonwealth countries.

The population consists mainly of Africans and people who are a mixture of African and French. The official languages are French and English, and the majority of the people are Catholic. On the island of Mahe, where the capital, Victoria, is located, there is an international airport, so tourists have begun to visit the island. The other islands are hardly populated, so the natural beauty of the islands remains intact. Almost 90 percent of the population live on Mahe, where there are Catholic parishes with resident priests at Mahe, Praslin and La Digue.

Funerals on the islands are usually held in a church, and the body is buried in a nearby cemetery. Hindu corpses are cremated at an outdoor crematorium, and the ashes are scattered over the ocean.

SIERRA LEONE

The Republic of Sierra Leone is located in the southwestern part of Africa. It became independent of Great Britain in April 1961. The capital is Freetown, and the population includes such tribes as the Sudan-Mende and the Temne, who follow either Sunni Islam or the native religion.

When someone dies, the death is reported to the relatives and neighbors. The divination of the cause of death was usually done in the past, but this custom is now rapidly disappearing. The deceased is washed, oiled and dressed in white cloth, and the funeral takes place immediately after death. The burial usually occurs in or near the family home. The mourning period and the number and form of sacrifices vary depending on the status of the deceased.

Among the Mende, death is a social construct and occurs, as a social condition, at least twice in a person's life. The first time is as an initiate into the primary male and female secret association, the Poro and Sande, respectively, the second, when one experiences biological death.

SOMALIA

The Somalian Democratic Republic extends from the Gulf of Aden to the Indian Ocean at the mouth of the Red Sea. Most of the land is mountainous or desert. In 1960, the British Somaliland and the Italian Trust Territory of Somalia became independent and merged into a single country, which is now ruled by the Somali Revolutionary Socialist Party. The majority of the people are Somalis, who are for the most part nomadic stock farmers. The government recognizes the freedom of religion, though most of the people are Sunni Muslims. However, since the country suffers from poverty and famine, some are too poor to follow the Islamic funeral customs and cannot afford to wash the dead with water and perfume and wrap it in cloth.

When someone dies an accidental or abnormal death, the body must be inspected by a medical examiner and reexamined at a nearby hospital. When there is a death in a hospital, the family must obtain the doctor's medical report, inform the government of the death, and obtain a death certificate, which states the time and date of death as well as the place of burial. In the capital, Mogadishu, there are private mortuaries that assist with funereal matters, but in the rural areas the relatives help prepare for the funeral.

As in other Islamic countries, the deceased usually is washed and wrapped in white cloth, and the funeral, officiated at by the *imam*, is held either at the mosque or at the deceased's home. Then the body is carried in a procession to the graveyard for burial. Men and women are buried separately. When the body is buried, the head must be placed facing Mecca, and stones are placed over the grave with a pointed stone placed at the head. At this time, the mourners repeatedly say "*Allah Akhbar*" (Allah is supreme).

The funeral expenses are usually paid by the family, but sometimes the expenses are paid by the relatives. Also, in the case of a low-income family, sometimes the government pays. After the burial, the relatives and friends gather at the deceased's home for a meal. Memorial services are held every year.

There is a European-style Italian cemetery on the outskirts of Mogadishu. Also, there are a few Indians living in Mogadishu, Brava and Kismayu who work as merchants or technicians. When someone dies among them, the corpse is cremated in the outdoor crematorium.

SOUTH AFRICA

The Republic of South Africa, which is located at the southern tip of the continent of Africa, is called the land of the sun. Most of the country is 900 meters or more above sea level. Since the days are long throughout the year, the air is dry. Colorful flowers bloom all year round. The majority of the people are Bantus. However, Afrikaners, descendants of the Dutch settlers who immigrated there 300 years ago, and others took over the nation and instituted the policy of apartheid, which discriminated against the black population. Recently, however, this policy has been abolished, though its influence has not completely disappeared. The official language of the country is Afrikaans, a development of Dutch, English and several indigenous languages. Most of the people belong to the Church of England, the Catholic Church or the Church of the Reformation of Holland.

Each death must be reported to the district court with a death certificate from a doctor. The native Africans, Chinese and Indians have funerals according to their own cultural traditions. Except for the conservative Jewish population and the fervently devout Christians, funerals mostly take place in private mortuaries. Such mortuaries take care of details such as the coffin, reporting the death, making arrangements for the wake, the funeral site, the request for a priest, and the graveyard. Non-whites may use a mortuary operated by whites, but it seems that they usually request their own community's mortuary for the funeral service.

Most cemeteries in South Africa are publicly operated. Many married couples prefer joint grave plots. In the past, the graves of those who committed suicide used to be separated from the others, where they were buried with the head toward the west.

The fervently devout wish to have the funeral in their own churches, even though it would be more convenient to use a mortuary. The chapel where the funeral is held is filled with hundreds of flower wreaths and bouquets.

South Africa has the highest cremation rate in Africa. Even the rich prefer cremation. Most of the public cemeteries offer such facilities as crematory chambers and chapels. For example, in Johannesburg there is a crematory chamber on Schmidt Street. The funeral is usually two or three days after death. Because it is expensive, people obtain funeral insurance ahead of time, or arrange to pay for the funeral in installments.

Afrikaners are said to be "very naive, kind and religious." Perhaps because of their kind nature, they are known to invite many friends and relatives to very large funerals. The body of the deceased is usually wrapped in white cloth and packed with incense. Then it is buried. Both Caucasians and native Africans go back to the family's home after the funeral, where coffee or tea is offered with light snacks to the mourners.

In Zululand, religion is primarily ancestor worship. Divination is the means of discovering the wishes of the ancestors, and a sacrifice of cattle, the means of propitiation. Sorcery and witchcraft are quite common. In the Zulu tradition, only married women can handle and prepare the corpse, delivering it to the men of the homestead through the doorway of the hut, like the delivery of a child from the womb. A married woman, observing strict restrictions, serves as the principal mourner in the funeral service. Ritual reversals of ordinary conduct also mark the dangerous position of the recently deceased to the ancestral world.

The Xhosa in Transkei and Ciskei are second only to the Zulu in number. They consist of several subtribes such as the Pondo, the Bomvana, the Thembu, the Pomdomiese and others, and include the actual Xhosa tribe itself. When someone dies in the tribe, the funeral service is associated with a set of complex beliefs and rituals, and the contamination has to be removed. If the deceased was the family head, cattle are offered and strict procedures are followed. His spirit is believed to join the previous heads in caring for the well being of the family on earth. Only in certain circumstances are the spirits of women regarded to be of special importance. The funeral procession to the cemetery is always led by the men of the clan, while the women follow behind.

SUDAN

Sudan means "the land of the black people." The Republic of Sudan is located in the northeastern part of Africa. It is now independent from the governments of Great Britain and Egypt, though Arabic is the official language. The majority of the people are a mixture of black and Arab, who believe in Sunni Islam or Coptic Christianity. The customs are very different, depending on the location. Except for the capital, Khartoum, and other urban areas, the people still live in a primitive manner according to the customs of each tribe.

When someone dies in the urban areas, the family must obtain a permit to dispose of the corpse from the registration office of the Ministry of Health.

Among the Sudanese, the main funeral customs of the Berta who live in the western part of Sudan are as follows: when someone is dying, they repose his or her body facing south. When death arrives, the family informs the neighbors, who, being told of the death, join a ceremony of sacrifice, which is held that day or within three days of the death. Usually, the body is buried in a graveyard near the deceased's home on the day of the death, and the funeral is held in the evening. In the case of a person who dies at night, the funeral is held the following morning. If it is a man who dies, the *faqih* (the leader) bathes the deceased. If it is a woman, an elderly woman washes the body. The body is perfumed, and cotton balls are placed in the body's orifices. Then the body is wrapped in a white kaftan.

Young men dig the ground from north to south when making the grave. The body is carried by six men to the grave and buried. The people believe that doing this brings good luck, so many men offer to take turns carrying the deceased. At this time, the head must point south at all times, and the face must be turned toward Mecca. After a simple prayer by the village elder, the mourners join in covering the grave with earth. After the grave is filled, graveposts are placed at the head and foot of the grave. Branches with thorns are placed around the grave to prevent wild animals from eating the corpse.

The mourners are treated to a meal of roasted mutton or goat prepared by the women of the family, and for three days after the burial, everyone joins the family in their mourning. Those who could not join the ceremony of sacrifice attend the seventh or fortieth day memorial service. At these services, the attendees give cash gifts to the family. They also may offer them some food. The animals for the sacrifice are killed by the male members of the family or by the relatives and then cooked. The women of the family prepare the other parts of the meal. The mourners recite the Qur'an in chorus, led by the village elder. In the case that it is a funeral for a rich man, ten to twenty of the *fugara*, specialists in the Qur'an, are invited to the ceremony. The mourners join the *fugara* in reciting the Qur'an. One of the family's cows is also killed and eaten.

The illiterate mourners repeat the name of the god Du'a using the Islamic rosaries, and when they have gone through each of the beads, they say, "As-Salaam." This is repeated 7,000 times in a ceremony called *Jaria*, which is believed to wash away the sins of the deceased. At the same time, the people who are doing the reciting are blessed. The *Jaria* is repeated seven times. Also, on the seventh day, fortieth day and one year after the death, a simple festival of sacrifice is held. This is done for the peace and happiness of the deceased. The *metan*, the mourning period for the family and the relatives, continues for six or seven months. They are to avoid celebrations and are forbidden to wear their best clothes. A widow confines herself to the house for four months and ten days. The people of the village also mourn for two months.

The Fali share with other Muslims reliance on traditional Islamic religious practices. After death, the corpse is washed and sometimes smeared with ocher, and it is placed in a sitting position with the arms extended forward. It is then enveloped in strips of cotton and ox-skin thongs. The hands and feet remain uncovered. The funeral usually takes a day or two, and then the body is buried at a nearby cemetery.

SWAZILAND

The physical environment and being surrounded by South Africa and Mozambique provide major economic and political problems for the Kingdom of Swaziland, which gained independence from Britain in 1968. One major problem is the disparity in the occupational structure between black and white Swazis.

Most of the people are Protestant. When someone dies, the relatives and neighbors are informed in person. Funerals are usually elaborate and expensive, especially when the status of the deceased was high, reflecting his importance in communal life. Swazi funeral services also vary depending on one's relationship to different categories of mourners. A headman is usually buried at the entrance of the cattle enclosure, whereas others are buried in the compound of their home.

Each tribe holds funeral services according to its own traditions, and sometimes buries the dead near their village. In Mbabane, the capital, there is a mortuary that handles funerals for foreigners.

The monarchial rulers of Swaziland, the Mswati family, whose position is challenged by demands for a modern democratic system, visit their ancestral graves on Mount Umjinba in full attire once a year.

TANZANIA

The United Republic of Tanzania is famous for Mount Kilimanjaro, the highest mountain in Africa, which sits at 5,895 meters above sea level. The official languages are Swahili and English. The majority of the people belong to the Bantus, but there are other ethnic groups as well. The people are followers of Islam, Christianity or their native religion. Freedom of religion is assured in Tanzania.

In the case of an unnatural death or accident, inspection by a medical examiner is required, but usually a report to the office is enough. The funeral is held at the home, a church, or a mosque. The native people bury the body in the ground, but cremation is also available for Europeans and Asians. There are several crematoriums in the capital of Tanzania, Dar es Salaam, on the coast of the Indian Ocean. Urns may also be obtained through special order. The graveyard is either privately owned or owned by the church. In the remote areas, the body is buried at a site assigned by the tribe.

Recently, the offering of flowers at funerals has become a custom. In the cities, this custom is widespread. It has especially taken root in the Christian community.

In Nyamwezi, people believe that death is inevitable and everyone knows it swallows every living being like lions do, despite prayer, libation and sacrifice.

Among the Maasai, death is reported to the relatives and neighbors in person. There are no elaborate funerary practices or a belief in the afterlife. Moreover, the corpse is seen as harmful and must be disposed of immediately after death.

TOGO

The Togolese Republic is a long and narrow country on the coast of the Gulf of Guinea. The capital is Lome. Togo became independent in August 1960. Agriculture is the main industry. The population consists mainly of the Sudan-Ewe. Most people there follow Roman Catholicism or the native religion.

When someone dies, the relatives and neighbors are informed in person. Funerals are elaborate and expensive and are important events among other celebrations and feasts. Particularly for the funeral of a high-ranking person or village chief, groups of drummers are hired, and the mourners dance throughout the night for several days in succession.

TUNISIA

The Republic of Tunisia in North Africa looks onto the Mediterranean Sea.

During the time of the Roman Empire, Tunisia was called "the granary of Rome" because the land is very fertile. Houses with white walls and blue window frames are strikingly beautiful under the bright sun. The population is made up of Arabs and Berbers. The majority are Muslims, but there are also Jewish and Greek Orthodox followers. Tunisia has a close relationship with Europe, and as a result the customs and manners of the people are quite Westernized. Among the younger generations, the influence of Islam has gradually weakened.

When someone dies, the family must report the death to the government district office with a doctor's medical certificate. In the urban areas, the people usually ask the mortuary for assistance in preparing for the burial. At the home of the deceased, the body is washed and wrapped in white cloth. The funeral is usually held at one's home or at a mosque, and the body is buried in the cemetery only by men. There is no custom of offering flowers or visiting the grave. The tombstone is for the most part a pile of rectangular shaped limestones, which bear no epitaphs.

In the capital, Tunis, one finds the Kairouan Mosque, the first mosque in Africa, which has become a tourist attraction, along with the Grand Temple in the *souk* (market). Also, in the Central Cemetery of Tunis, there are lines of tombstones, and the bodies of those who died in the General Hospital across the street are carried through an underground pathway to the cemetery. In Ramarusa, there is also a military cemetery for Allied soldiers who died in World War II. In Monastir, a city on the Mediterranean coast, one finds the golden dome mosque of former President Habib Burqiba, which was built before he died.

UGANDA

Lake Victoria occupies one-seventh of the total land area of the Republic of Uganda. Thanks to the lake, although Uganda is on the equator and is located inland, the climate is relatively mild and comfortable. The majority of the people are the Bagandas, who are mostly Christian. There are also Muslims as well as those who follow the native religions. Because Uganda was once a British colony, many British customs and ways of thinking still remain a part of the life style of the people in cities such as Kampala, the capital of Uganda. The official language is English, but the tribal language Swahili is also used outside the urban areas.

When someone dies, the death must be reported to the police, and the body must be inspected by a medical examiner. When the inspection is finished, the body is washed by the family and relatives and wrapped in white cloth. Because the people of Uganda believe that death is caused by the deceased being captured by the spirit of death, a magician is called. He purifies the body by praying that the spirit of death will move to another person. Then a tribal elder instructs the family as to how to arrange the funeral. The body is usually buried within 24 hours, and the grave is often made beside a banana grove. All of the mourners join in the burial ceremony by placing soil on the body.

In the days when the Indians held economic power, cremation was possible just for the Indians. However, since 1972, when they were chased out of the country, cremation became taboo, because in Uganda, the people believe that the soul is destroyed by the fire if the body is cremated.

Among the Iteso, the funerals are simple and the graves tend to be either unmarked or undifferentiated. At death, the spirit of the deceased, called *eparait*, is believed to separate from the body and go on to live in the bush. Moreover, these spirits are believed to be greedy, so they require offerings of food and drink as well as rituals to pacify them. After several years, the bones are exhumed so that rituals can be performed to "cool" them and make them more kindly disposed to the living.

Among the Beganda tribe, the dead body is immediately washed, shaved and wrapped in a cloth made of tree bark, with only the face showing. Friends come later, bringing more of this bark cloth and sometimes muslin to wrap the body. The number of wrappings indicates how important and respectable a dead person was.

The burial usually takes place in the morning and is attended by the chief and senior members of the clan. The body is lowered by means of bark strips into a grave about six feet deep, dug in a nearby banana grove. Dirt is thrown into the grave and piled above it by hand, and then tramped upon or pounded down with poles. If the deceased is a Christian, prayers may be given at the grave after the burial.

ZAMBIA

The Republic of Zambia is in the highlands and is more than 1,000 meters above sea level except for the basins of the country's rivers, which include the Zambezi and the Luapula. The climate is relatively mild and comfortable.

The population consists of various tribes such as the Tonga, the Nyanja, the Mambwe and the Lunda. Each tribe has its own native religion. However, in the urban areas, such as in the capital, Lukasa, there are many Christians, Muslims and Hindus.

The majority of the people bury their dead in the ground, but for the Hindus from India, cremation is also an option. Christians sometimes offer flowers at their funerals.

Zambia was once a British colony, and English continues to be the official language. In the cities, European customs can also be seen. In the rural areas, traditional and local customs are quite strong. For example, the extended family system still exists, so ceremonies such as weddings, funerals or the worshiping of ancestors are held in a grand manner. Moveover, the sense of national and tribal unity is strong, so some outsiders may be given the impression that Zambians are exclusive.

Among the Lozi, the eyes and mouth are kept open until a person is about to die. When the death occurs, the body is bent so that the knees touch the chin, then it is removed from the hut through a special opening on the side of the dwelling cut out for this purpose. As the deceased is taken to the cemetery for burial, spells are scattered on the road to prevent the return of the ghost to haunt the village. Men are buried facing east; women face west. The personal belongings of the deceased are placed around the body and the grave is filled. Then the hut of the deceased is pulled down.

ZIMBABWE

The Republic of Zimbabwe used to be called South Rhodesia. Most of the land rests on plateaus 1,000 meters above sea level, and the climate is mild.

Although the population comprises mainly Bantu Africans, because Zimbabwe was a British colony until 1980 the minority whites still have actual control over the economy and the legal system.

The majority of whites belong to the Anglican Church. Others are either Roman Catholic or Protestant. The majority of blacks believe in the native religion and worship the god Muwali.

When someone dies, the death must be reported to the medical examiner. In Harare (Salisbury), privately run funeral homes, such as Doves or Mashfords, provide all kinds of funeral services. The funeral, though, is often held at the family home or at a church. The body is usually buried in the ground, but there are crematoriums in the capital. Graves must be purchased. In general the mourners wear black clothes to the funeral.

When a foreigner dies in Zimbabwe, it is possible to bury the body in a local graveyard. If the body is properly treated, it is possible to send it back to the home country. If requested, the body can be cremated.

Most graves in the rural areas are insignificant looking, except for those of the rich. In the urban areas, a number of cemeteries are open to all races and faiths. In Bulawayo, Crocker Brothers has a cremation facility. In the rural areas, whole villages participate in the funeral service. When the wife dies, her assets are sometimes returned to her parents.

CHAPTER 4

Middle East

AFGHANISTAN

The Republic of Afghanistan is bordered by four countries: the former Soviet Union to the north, Pakistan to the east, Iran to the west, and China to the northeast. Most of the inland area of the country is either mountainous or desert. The climate is continental, so it is very dry. Generally, it is hot in the summer and cold in the winter. The Pathans (Afghans) are the majority, and they follow Sunni Islam. Languages such as Pushtu and Dari (Afghan-Persian) are used.

The ardent Muslims pray five times a day, facing Mecca. Usually, though, the people pray at least twice a day, at sunrise and again at sunset. They are not to be spoken to while they are praying. They do not eat pork, raw fish, shellfish, crab or shrimp. Only a few people drink alcohol. Women wear a piece of cloth called a *chadal*, which is like a veil, over their faces. The women do not directly speak to men, except for the male members of their family and relatives.

The Afghans consider death as the mercy of the Almighty God, Allah, so death is readily accepted. The body (*Jinaza*) is washed with soap and water, according to the *sunna* of Mohammed, then wrapped in white cloth. In the case of the middle class or higher, the funeral is held at a mosque on the way to the graveyard.

When a foreigner dies, the body is inspected by a medical examiner on the spot, and later an autopsy is performed at a hospital. After the doctors find the cause of death, a medical report is issued, and then they dispose of the body. If cremation is desired for a foreigner, someone from the diplomatic mission in Afghanistan must sign the crematorium register, at which time a medical report must also be submitted.

The Muslims are all buried in the ground. In the capital, Kabul, there is Karacha Crematorium for Hindus. The body is cremated outdoors on a pile of wood, and the coffin is bought at a bazaar. Urns are not available, but it is possible to obtain a jar with a lid that can serve as a substitute.

BAHRAIN

The State of Bahrain is located on the coast of the Persian Gulf. It consists of 33 islands. Bahrain became independent from Great Britain in 1971. The majority of the people are Arabs, and the official language is Arabic. The people of Bahrain are followers of Sunni and Shiite Islam.

As the country has developed its oil fields, it has rapidly modernized. Many immigrant laborers from India and Pakistan live in Bahrain.

The funeral customs in Bahrain are similar to those in other Islamic countries. Funeral occur immediately after death. The corpse is washed by a member of the same sex, wrapped in white cotton, and covered with a prayer rug. It is carried to the nearby mosque, where a blessing is given, according to the Islamic tradition. It is then buried, facing Mecca, stones marking the head and feet. Following a death, friends and relatives visit the family of the deceased to pay their respects.

As an oil-rich country, social welfare work is prominent, and there is free use of cemeteries for the residents near the city of Manama. There are about 85,000 burial mounds in Bahrain that are, literally, all over the island, though many are concentrated in about a half dozen major mound fields believed to date to 2,000 B.C.

CYPRUS

The Republic of Cyprus is a small but strategically situated Mediterranean island off the Syrian coast. Turks settled there in the north of the island during the Ottoman rule from 1571 to 1878, when Cyprus came under British rule. In the 1950s the Greek Cypriots, led by Archbishop Makarios (later president), campaigned for union with Greece, while the Turks favored partition. Most Greek Cypriots follow Greek Orthodox Church, and Turks follow Islam.

For the Greek Cypriots, when someone dies the body is placed on the table at the bereaved family's house, washed, and clothed in a white cloth called *savanon*. At the wake service, the mourners sing ritual laments called *Trisagion*. The corpse is interred within 24 hours of death, with ceremonies at both the family home and the local church led by the priests. The bereaved family usually erects the white marble tombstone in a cemetery.

For the Muslim Turks, the body is likewise buried within 24 hours of death, with ceremonies at both the family home and the local mosque. After several years, the bones are usually exhumed from the ground and placed in a community ossuary.

IRAN

Iran exiled King Pahlevi and established a revolutionary government in 1978, the Islamic Republic of Iran. Since the end of the war between Iran and Iraq, the political situation and the nation's safety have been extremely unstable. The majority of the people follow the national religion, the Shiite sect of Islam, but there are also Christians, Bahais and Zoroastrians.

The funeral customs differ by religion and place, but in the case of the Shiite Muslims, when an ill person's condition becomes critical, the family invites the *muatsura* (leader) who recites the Qur'an. When someone dies, the family, relatives and friends scratch and pull their hair, and go out into the street and wail loudly with intense sorrow. They even tear their clothes. If the person dies on Friday, which is a holy day, the sorrow is even greater. The body is bathed three times by the family and friends with lotus water, camphor water and rose water brought from holy places such as Kalpala and Mecca. The body is then wrapped in white cloth that has been purified by a leader. There is also the custom of placing a red stone inscribed with the names of the twelve Shiite saints in the mouth of the deceased. In urban areas, the bathing of the deceased may be done by undertakers if the family requests it. After the bath, the body is carried to the mosque or cemetery in a specially made hearse.

The body is occasionally carried to the graveyard in a wooden coffin, but since timber is rather scarce and valuable, it is reused. The body is placed directly in the ground or kept in a cave and covered with soil. There are various types of graves. Some graves are simply mounds with bricks or rocks placed on the head or foot of the mound. More elaborate ones are built as well — graves in the form of a miniature mosque with an iron fence, and graves with a picture of the deceased on the tombstone. There is a great variety of tombstones.

In Iran, there is the expression, "Pedar sukhte," meaning "your father was cremated," which is considered the worst insult. This reveals the extent to which most Iranians detest the idea of cremation. For the Muslims, cremation is Allah's punishment for those who have fallen into Hell. In fact, only criminals are cremated.

After the funeral ends, the body is lifted up and down four times and then buried. At this time, everyone recites verses from the Qur'an. The mourners step back seven steps and then go home. Because the graveyard is considered to be impure, the funeral is never held at the grave. The day after the funeral, the relatives gather at the family's home and hold a *hatoum* (memorial service) and recite the Qur'an. When performing the *hatoum*, the men and women must be in separate rooms. On the day of the *hatoum* some people order all 30 volumes of the Qur'an, which they donate to the mosque. Four days after the burial, all of the people who used to associate with or are related to the deceased visit the grave with flowers. The memorial service is held one week, forty days or one year later. For a week after the funeral, a lamp is lit at the family home, and food is offered at the grave. Specially made food is also offered to the mourners. The traditional food is deep-fried kneaded flour dough with butter, honey and spices.

Most of the followers of Islam who are spread throughout the world are authentic Sunni Muslims, and only in Iran are there Shiite Muslims, a group that separated from the Sunnis. Beside the practice of Ramadan (the month of fasting, ninth month of the lunar calendar), there is *Muharram*, a ceremony honoring the martyrdom of Ali's son, Hussein. The *Muharram* is a festival that commemorates the fact that Hussein suffered at Kalbara, a part of present-day Iraq, on the tenth of *Muharran* (tenth month in the lunar calendar) in 680 A.D. Every year around May, men in black robes march, striking themselves on the chest with both hands and on the back with chains. The people stand in the streets and cry when they see these men, for they are reminded of the martyrdom and mourn for the martyrs.

In Iran, there are also about 20,000 Zoroastrians (Parsee), the majority of whom live in the city of Yazd. When they die, the corpses used to be taken to the *Dakhma* (The Tower of Silence) and left on the platform for vultures to eat. Recently, however, the custom was banned for reasons of sanitation. As a result, the body is now buried in the ground.

The most famous grave in Iran is the mosque of Omar Khayyam (d. 1123), a poet and astrologist. His collection of lyrical poems called *Rubaiyat* is famous throughout the world. His mosque is located at Nishapur near Meshed in the northeast of Iran. Also at Tus near Nishapur there is the very large and beautiful mosque for Ferdousi, who was the greatest ethnic poet and pride of Iran.

Sixteen kilometers southwest of Teheran, the capital of Iran, there is a public cemetery called the Beheshte Zahala, which stands beside the highway leading to the holy city of Kom. In the cemetery, flat concrete plates marking graves are neatly lined across the bare ground. There is also a *chelhela chulage* (an altar), which stands on four legs. Flags of red and yellow and other colors or a picture of the deceased are signs that the person was killed in the revolution. The women who come to visit the cemetery wearing black contrast sharply with the colors of the flags.

IRAQ

The Tigris and Euphrates Rivers flow through the heart of the Republic of Iraq, which lies on the Persian Gulf. Because Iraq is bordered by many different countries, it has encountered an endless number of problems and disputes. Islam is the national religion. The number of Sunnis and Shiites are about the same. There are a number of Christians as well.

Early civilization flourished in the land now occupied by Iraq, so there are

many historical sites and ruins. Near the bodies of Neanderthals that were
excavated from the Shanidhal ruins, the pollen of as many as eight different
flowers was found. It is surmised from this discovery that the Neanderthals
were the first humans who offered flowers to the dead.

When someone dies, the body is rubbed with fragrant oil, then wrapped in
white cloth. The family invites a *muller*, who reads the Qur'an and the blessing.
In the Islamic tradition, at the funeral, they do not pray and kneel as they would
when they worship Allah with their heads to the ground. The final bow is made
only to the right. Islam places value on cleanliness, so when they worship, they
always purify their hands, mouth, nose, face, elbows and head in the washroom
of the cemetery or mosque. This ritual is called *wudu*. The funeral is held in a
mosque.

The body is always interred. The most desirable place for an Iraqi Muslim to
be buried is the Hussein Mosque (the child of the founder of Shiite Islam who
killed himself at the death of Ali) in Karbala on the western side of the
Euphrates River or the mosque of Ali (the son-in-law of the founder
Mohammed and the founder of Shiite Islam) in Najaf or the holy places of
Samarra or Kadhimain in the outskirts of Baghdad, the capital of Iraq.
However, because of the recent Gulf War, the country has undergone much
turmoil. Also, because of economic hardship, one cannot freely visit the graves
of such mosques.

Among the Kurds, the funeral takes place immediately after death. The
corpse is washed, wrapped in white cloth, covered with a prayer rug, and
carried to a nearby mosque, where a blessing is given by the shaif (leader). The
body is then buried in the village cemetery. Only men attend the funerals and
the burials. The grave is made up of a simple mound of soil with dead branches
or stones on it, marking the head and feet.

ISRAEL

The State of Israel is surrounded by four Arab countries. Israel, the only
Jewish nation in the world, is a new country, established after World War II by
the Jewish people who gathered from various places around the globe. The
majority of the people are Jewish, but there are also Muslim Palestinians. Israel
won the Middle East War in 1967 and occupied the Golan Heights, the land
west of the Jordan River, and the Gaza Strip on the coast of the Mediterranean.

When a Jewish person dies, the people tear their clothes and drain the water
from all nearby containers. When the body is washed, it is usually rubbed with
fragrant oil, but the Ashkenazic Hebrews rub a mixture of wine and raw egg on
the head of the deceased. After this, the body is dressed in a shroud of cotton
and a shawl, a white cap and white socks. Finally, candle stands are placed by
the head and the feet.

In Denteronomy Chapters 21 and 23 of the Pentateuch, it is clearly stated that the dead should be buried within a day, and conservative Jews strictly abide by this rule. The body is carried out of the house or hospital on a coffin stand and taken to the cemetery. When there is a synagogue along the way, the mourners stop to pray, according to Jewish doctrine.

The rabbi joins in the burial, and the mourners participate in placing soil over the grave. When they leave the graveyard, they pick grass that they toss over their shoulders as they recite, "Ashes we are, and to ashes we shall return." The deceased are all buried in the ground. There is no custom of offering flowers, because flowers are a token of pleasure and happiness. Members of the *Chevrah Kaddisha* (the Holy Fellowship Society) observe a fast on the seventh of Adar, the anniversary of the death of Moses, to atone for any disrespect they may have shown to the dead. Mourning rituals are suspended on the sabbath and holidays. During the initial seven day mourning period, called *shiva* the mourners wear torn clothing. It is taboo to use water in washing anything except one's face, feet, and wear leather shoes. Meals, except for meat and wine, are delivered by someone outside the family. Also, twice a day, in the morning and the evening, the prayer of *Kaddish* (praise for God in Aramaic) is recited. For 20 days after the funeral, they are expected not to shave their beard or cut their hair. For 11 months after that, they must recite the prayer of *Kaddish* daily. On the first year memorial, all of the family members must fast and go to the synagogue to pray.

Jewish communities usually have their own *Chevra Kaddisha*, which are formed for mutual aid in taking care of all funereal matters. They also handle the construction of the tombstone, which can be costly or inexpensive. The Star of David, the symbol of the Jewish people, is carved into the tombstone, and no statues are built. When the tombstone is being made, the members of the group all fast. After all of the members who will join the construction pass around the graveyard seven times, the construction ceremony commences.

Jewish people do not like to be seen during such private events by foreigners, so tourists should be careful. The Muslims hold their funerals according to Islamic customs, and there are graveyards that are used exclusively by the Palestinians. In Saudi Arabia, the worshiping of icons is prohibited, but the Muslims in Israel place icons at the head of their tombstones.

Among the Palestinians, funerals are observed by the family and the entire community. Immediately after death, the corpse is washed, wrapped in white cloth, and carried to a nearby mosque, where a blessing is given. It is then taken to a public cemetery. The Palestinians strongly believe that Jerusalem will be the site of the Day of Judgment, and they consider burial there to be greatly desirable.

At the side of the road below the Hadassah Hospital on Mount Scopus in the northeast part of Jerusalem is the British War Cemetery where soldiers of the Allied Forces who fell in Palestine during World War I are buried. On both sides of the entrance are the emblems of the units whose soldiers are buried here. At the far left are the graves of the soldiers of 16 Germans and 3 Turks.

JORDAN

The Hashemite Kingdom of Jordan was once a territory of the Ottoman Empire, but after World War I it became a trust of Great Britain. In 1946, it became independent, although it was not named Jordan until 1949. The constitution, issued in 1952, established Islam as the national religion. Islam is also taught in the public schools.

The population is mainly composed of Arabs who are followers of Sunni Islam. There are also as many as 700,000 Palestinian refugees, making the return of Palestine an international issue. Arabic is the official language, but English is also used in cities such as Amman. There are Christians in the urban areas, many of whom are government officials, who sometimes mediate in disputes between different Islamic groups.

The funeral customs are very similar to those observed in Syria. The funeral is usually held at the mosque and the body is buried in the cemetery. Also, holy verses from the Qur'an, *Alfata*, are recited in unison. On the fortieth day after a death, a memorial service is held either at the home of the deceased or at a restaurant with relatives and friends. The Christians belong to either the Catholic Church or the Greek Orthodox Church and hold their funerals according to their respective customs.

In Amman, there are the Mosdhal, Shahid and Sahab Public Cemeteries for Muslims, and also the Wahidad Cemetery for Christians. In most cases, married couples are not buried in the same grave. The Muslim people do not have a custom of offering flowers. The elderly are often seen standing by the graveposts and quietly thinking about the deceased. Compared to the graves of the Muslims, the Christian graves are colorful and have a greater variety of styles. There are even tombstones that bear the picture of the deceased. Flowers are also offered at the grave.

The Muslims of Jordan differ from those of Saudi Arabia in that they visit the grave every Thursday as well as the first-year memorial, and sometimes women even spray perfume on the tombstones. Saudi Arabians seldom take care of their graves.

Among the Circassians, who migrated from the northwest of Caucasas, beliefs about death and the afterlife are congruent with the Islamic faith and rite. However, through their ancestral myths of the Narts and of Susoruga (who brought fire to humankind), traces of their distinctive belief in immortality can be seen.

Petra is situated between Amman and Aqaba where the remains of Palaeolithic and Neolithic Period (10,000-6,000 B.C.) were discovered. In Hellenistic and Roman times, Petra was the capital of the Nabataean Kingdom (4th century B.C. -106 A.D.) and became a major caravan center.

KUWAIT

The State of Kuwait is located at the innermost part of the Persian Gulf. The country modernized in a very short period of time. Among the oil-producing countries in the Gulf, Kuwait depends on the production of oil as the mainstay of the economy. The majority of the people are Sunni Muslims, who rigidly adhere to the commandments of their religion.

Serious Muslims never neglect their prayers, which are said five times a day. One can see them praying in the direction of Mecca at dawn, at noon, in the afternoon, in the early evening and at eight o'clock at night. These prayers are called *fajr, zuhr, asr, maghrih* and *isha*. The prayers should not be disturbed, because if they are disturbed, they must be started again from the beginning. Friday is a holiday, and there is a community meeting in the afternoon.

Although there are many foreigners living in Kuwait, the people there do not eat pork or drink alcohol, and during the month of Ramadan, they fast.

When someone dies, the body is bathed, covered with a white robe, then carried to the mosque, where the funeral is held. Then the body is buried in a community graveyard. In the graveyard outside the city, there are lines of tombstones with mosaic designs, encircled by a fence. Next to the graveyard, one sees abandoned automobiles. This scene really gives the impression that this is a terminal station for human life. During the Gulf War, which started with the Iraqi invasion, many people died. The remains of these people are buried in the Riga Graveyard in the southern suburbs of Kuwait.

When death occurs among the workers who are temporary migrants from India or Pakistan, the body is placed in a coffin or cremated, and the remains are sent back to the home country.

LEBANON

The Lebanese Republic is by the Mediterranean Sea and is a crossroads between the Middle and Near East. Throughout its history, Lebanon has been in constant turmoil. Even today, the opposition between the right wing, whose members are mostly Christians, and the left wing, whose members are Muslims, is becoming ever more intense. Moreover, invasion and pressures from outside have further exacerbated its internal social and political problems.

The population of Lebanon consists of the Maronite Christians and the Sunni and Shiite Muslims, who live in their respective residential districts.

When a Christian dies, the family gives the deceased a bath, dresses the body in black, and lays the body on a bed. The head of the bed is decorated with a cross, candlestands and other items. A funeral home is called for assistance. Death notices with black rims are sent out to relatives and friends, and obituaries are posted in the church and in the street. The body is placed in the casket, and after the mourners have gathered it is carried to the graveyard. The procession is led by the minister with the men and women following in two different lines. At the graveyard, right before the burial, the cover of the casket is removed once more for a last meeting with the deceased.

Compared to Christian funerals, Muslim funerals are very economical and generally simple. When a Muslim dies, the family gives the deceased a bath, wraps the body in a white cloth (called *kafan*), and places it in a pine casket (in some cases, it is carried on a stretcher to the mosque). This must be done at the time of the daily prayer, which occurs five times a day. At the mosque, a funeral ritual called *Salat al jinaaza* is performed. After the ceremony, the body is transported in a procession to the cemetery.

The grave is usually constructed with concrete blocks. After the lid and coffin are in place, a ritual ceremony called Talkin is performed by the leader, who asks the deceased questions through two angels, Munkar and Nakir, who serve as intermediaries. The funeral is never held at the cemetery, because the grave is considered a defiled place.

After the burial, coffee and cakes are offered to the mourners. For three days, the mourners visit the family to offer their condolences. On the following Thursday, the family invites the deceased's relatives and friends to their home. This is called *wanisa*, during which time mutton must be served to the mourners. In the case of the Muslims, the funeral is held as early as possible. Since there is no custom of preserving the corpse with dry ice, the burial is held within a day or two of the death.

In Lebanon, cemeteries are generally divided according to religion. In the outskirts of Beirut, the graves of Christians are located in a grove of pines and cactuses. One grave is for everyone in the family and the stone grave has a cross at its head. The Muslim cemetery is located in an area on Basta Street. It is encircled by high iron lattice-work. In the graveyard for the Jewish people are many stone casket-shaped tombstones.

As in some Asian countries, the Druzes, who live in the mountainous areas of southern Lebanon, practice the custom of hiring "crying women." Among the Druze, the custom of *taqiyah* and accommodation to larger protective cultures have helped keep their traditions intact, but in recent years these practices have somewhat declined.

OMAN

The Sultanate of Oman is located on the eastern end of the Arabian Peninsula, directly opposite to Iran, and the Al Rub Al Khali Desert spreads through the middle of the country. It is hot and humid year-round. The majority of the people are Arabs, but there are also Indians and Iranians. Many are followers of Ibadi Kharijites Islam.

Oman was a colony of Great Britain, but in 1970 it became independent. It continues to preserve the old Islamic culture.

When someone dies, relatives and friends gather at the deceased's home.

First, the body is bathed and wrapped in cloth. Then it is cleaned and wrapped again in cloth. The participants recite the Qur'an in unison. The funeral is held at the deceased's home or in a mosque, and then the body is buried in the cemetery.

On top of the Jabal mountain near Salalah, Oman's second largest city and resort town in the south, stands the Mausoleum of Job the prophet, where an Islamic leader recites passages of the Qur'an 24 hours a day. Also, on the coastal road to Marbat, 64 kilometers from Salalah, the onion-domed Bin Ali's mosque is built over the tomb. Around his tomb is a large cemetery with inscribed headstones.

PAKISTAN

The Islamic Republic of Pakistan borders India to the west and was historically part of India. When it became a new country, it based itself on the principles of Islam. The population consists of the Punjabi (as in northern and central India and in Afghanistan) and the Sindhi, who are Indo-Aryans. The official language is Urdu. Although Islam is the national religion, freedom of religion is recognized in Pakistan, and there are also Hindus, Parsees and Christians.

The Muslims, who believe in the existence of the next world, insist that death is not the terminal point of life in this world but just a temporary separation from loved ones. The dead will come back to life and to their loved ones on the Day of Judgment.

When someone dies, the death is reported to the police office in the district. In the case of an accidental death, the body must be inspected. For example, in Karachi the medical examination is made in the municipal hospital or the Jinna Hospital. Then the medical report is issued by the police station. The death is reported afterward to the municipal committee, though this is seldom done in the rural areas.

The family then ties white cloth around the deceased's thumb and puts a shroud, called *kafan*, over the body with green *chadal* (a veil used to cover the face), decorated with roses, and burns agilawood. From a nearby minaret (a tower of a mosque) the death is announced to the neighbors by loudspeaker, and then the body is transported to the *masjid* (mosque). At the *masjid*, all the mourners join in the *namaz-junaza* prayer. After the prayer, the body is carried on their shoulders to the graveyard. The Muslims are always buried in the ground. A hole, about two meters long, sixty centimeters wide and two meters deep, is dug, and the body is then placed there with the head facing north and the face in the direction of Mecca. Each of the mourners then puts two handfuls of soil over the body. This is done three times. Then they offer flower wreaths and water. Finally, the introductory chapter of the Qur'an, *Fatifa*, is read, concluding the funeral. Three days after the funeral (*soyam*), the relatives gather at the family's home and invite the *molbi* to recite the Qur'an. At the end, they all go to visit the grave. After 10 days, 40 days (*chelehem*), 1 year (*Boulsi*) and every subsequent year, the family visits the grave on the day of death and on *Muharram*.

At the graveyard, the burial ceremony (*Salat al jyana*) is held, but the *rak'ah* (bowing one's head deeply) and *sajida* (prostrating oneself) are not performed at this time. At the end of the service, the greeting to pray for the deceased's safety and well-being is given: "*Assalaam Alaikumu Hamatoullar*" (Let God bless you and forgive you for your sins). The burial follows, at which time the people recite: "All that dwells upon the earth is perishing, yet still abides the face of the Lord, majestic and splendid" (Juran 55, All Merciful 26-27).

The Hindus usually cremate the body, while the Parsees prefer "sky burials." The Christians usually bury their dead in the ground, but some request cremation. In such a case, the Hindu crematorium on Manghopic Street in Karachi is used. There are no ready-made coffins or urns, so the family must put in a special order each time.

The cemetery is divided according to religion. The graves of the Islamic saints and the rich are very large, built in the form of mosques or made with cement. In general, however, a heavy rock is placed on the grave and a stick is stuck into the ground in front of the grave. In the Bomboret District, the body is placed in a coffin and left in the mountains. The Hindus do not make graves. After cremating the body in an outlying field, the ashes are scattered over a river.

When a foreigner dies, the family obtains a medical report from the local hospital and informs the local municipal committee. Then the body can be cremated at a Hindu crematory or shipped to its home country.

At the Chaukundi and Thattas ruins, which are 27 and 100 kilometers east of Karachi, respectively, there are over a million graves, mainly made of sandstone and exquisitely carved with geometric and floral designs. Most of these date back to the Summas, the dynasty that ruled the Sind from the mid-14th to the early 16th centuries. Among the graves there is a magnificent mosque that was initiated by King Jahan in 1674 and completed by his son. This mosque is particularly interesting from an architectural point of view.

In Karachi, there is a secluded area called Dakhma in the Defense District, that is used for the "sky burial" of the Parsees, where the body of the deceased is eaten by vultures. The difference between the sky burial of the Parsees and that of the Tibetans is that in the case of the former, only the human flesh is eaten, while in the case of the latter, the entire body with bones is completely eaten.

QATAR

The State of Qatar occupies the entire Qatar Peninsula. The population is for the most part Arab, and the majority live in the capital, Doha and in its vicinity. Income from oil has increased with the development of the Zukhan oil field, which has led to the modernization of this country. The official language is Arabic. Many people are followers of Sunni Islam, who seem to be struggling with their traditional values and rapid modernization.

The funeral is usually held in a mosque, and the body is buried in a nearby graveyard at the earliest convenience. The tombstone is usually very simple. On occasion, stones are piled into a mound, instead of a tombstone.

Migration from the poorer Arabian and Asian countries to oil-rich states has increased, and many of these people practice different customs. When someone dies among them, the body is either placed in a coffin or cremated and is sent back to the home country.

SAUDI ARABIA

Ninety-five percent of the Kingdom of Saudi Arabia is desert, so the country is hot and dry. Because Mohammed, the founder of Islam, is enshrined in Mecca, located in Saudi Arabia, the majority of the Saudis are Wahhabi Muslims, who are the most serious and devout worshippers of the Qur'an. Their commandments are very strict, and the five acts of Islam —*Shahada* (absolute commitment to God), *Salat* (five prayers a day), *Sawm* (fasting in the month of Ramadan), *Zakat* (charity), and *Hajj* (pilgrimage)— are practiced every day without fail. Pork and alcohol are prohibited, and women must wear a *chadal* when they go out.

For a Muslim, death is a fate which Allah has determined for people, and it is nothing more than a temporary sleep. It also means that one has been summoned by God and returns to His house, so it is not a time of grief but a time to rejoice, though in reality the family is usually overcome with sorrow.

When someone dies, the women especially weep very loudly. The neighbors, hearing their cries, rush over. The family then requests the assistance of an undertaker from the *masjid* (mosque), and a *nasi* (stretcher) is delivered from the nearby mosque. The relatives gather at the deceased's home, where the body is washed. The person who performs this act is called *mugasru* (male) or *mugsra* (female), and he or she must wash the feet and hands of the deceased as many as seven times, while verses of the Qur'an are recited. Then the body is sprayed with a perfume called *kaful*, which is similar to camphor, and is wrapped in a white seamless robe.

The men carry the body to the graveyard, while the women stay at home. The body is removed from the coffin and buried in a grave, about one meter deep. The undertakers, playing the role of angels, ask questions concerning religious faith. Then the body is placed on its right side, facing the direction of Mecca. A mound is built on top of the grave or stones are placed at the head and foot of the grave, but no other grave markers are used. When the former

King Faisal died, a simple grave of this sort was constructed at the cemetery in the capital, Riyadh.

On the night of the burial, the bereaved family keeps candles lit throughout the night and burns incense. There is a three-day mourning period after the burial, called *azza*, during which time the family wears white and burns incense. On the last day, they offer the other mourners a meal.

For 40 days, the mourning continues. The family avoid all celebrations during that time and spend their days quietly. The male mourners say, "*Salamt le hatr*" (May Allah comfort your sorrow), whereas the female mourners say, "*Azzam Allah Azukurum*" (May God give you kind blessing). The female relatives wear white and do not wear dark eye shadow. There is a memorial service on the twentieth and fortieth days after the death, and again on the first-year memorial, in which no particular rites are involved.

SYRIA

The Syrian Arab Republic is surrounded by Turkey to the north, Jordan to the south, Iraq to the east, and the Mediterranean Sea and Lebanon to the west. The country is a very important Near Eastern connection between the East and the West. The majority of the people are Arabs, but there are also many Palestinian immigrants. Freedom of religion is guaranteed by the constitution, and there are many Sunni Muslims as well as Christians. There is also a unique religion that is a mixture of Islam and Christianity called *Arave*, whose followers are especially respectful of the five Islamic saints, the *wari*.

Syria prospered in ancient times, and many historical ruins remain today. Among the ruins, Jami al-Umawii (the Umawii mosque), which holds the grave of St. John, and the stone coffin of Salah-al Din, which dates from the thirteenth century, are well worth seeing.

When someone dies, alcohol-free perfume is sprayed over the body, which is then wrapped in white cloth and carried on a stretcher to the graveyard. A coffin may be used, but only the body is buried.

As a rule, an *imam* (prayer leader) is invited to officiate at an Islamic funeral. When no *imam* is available, a *sheik*, an elder of the local area or the head of the family reads a section of the Qur'an. Sometimes a recorded tape is used in their place. In general, the mourning period lasts for three days. During this period, the relatives and friends come to dine with family, but the expenses are shared by anyone who joins the dinner. The grave is visited at any time, but especially at the time of *id al-fatur* right after Ramadan, or at the *id al-dahiiya*, which is held three months after the funeral. All the family members visit the grave, and the head of the family gives money or gifts to the female members of the family. There are no cremation facilities, and all the dead, including Christians, are buried in the ground. Caskets are not often used.

In Damascus, the capital, the government office in charge of funeral matters helps the family prepare for the funeral.

There is an Islamic cemetery at Bob el Sajir, and a Christian one located near the gate of St. Paul's Church at Al Amin.

TURKEY

The Republic of Turkey occupies the far eastern tip of the Balkan peninsula and the Asia Minor peninsula. The climate of the Mediterranean coast is mild year round, but inland the temperatures in the summer and the winter are quite different. The majority of the people are Turkish, but there are also Kurds, Jews and Greeks. Most of the people are Sunni Muslims, but there are also followers of Christianity and Judaism. Compared with the other Islamic countries, there is not the same religious fervor. For instance, the woman's *chadal* (veil) and polygamy are prohibited. Turkey is very European in many ways.

When someone dies, the family reports it to the government office with a doctor's medical report and obtains a burial permit. A mortician usually helps the family with the arrangements for the casket and the burial of the body, which is done within a few days of death. Before the burial, the body is washed and then wrapped in white cloth. All soap and cloth used should be new. According to the Qur'an, the nose, mouth, face, neck, arms and feet must all be washed three times. After wrapping the body in white cloth, the relatives usually tie it with a string, and rub the body with peppermint and naphthaline, and then spray it with rose perfume. At the wake, everyone recites the Qur'an led by the *hoka* (the officiating Islamic leader). The body is then placed in a casket and carried to the *Jama* (mosque). The casket is covered with a piece of cloth on which a verse of the Qur'an is embroidered. When the deceased is female, the cloth is green.

The funeral is usually held at a time which does not interfere with the *salat*, which is performed five times a day. The body is set on the *musala* (coffin stand) in front of the pulpit, and then the *imam* performs the ceremony. At this time, there is no call from the bell tower for prayer, and the mourners do not purify themselves before entering the mosque.

After the funeral, the procession moves to the graveyard. The graveyard is usually communal and it is located close to residential areas. Most graveposts are made of wood and are placed on both ends of the graveyard. People consider it an honor to carry the coffin at least seven steps and are happy to join the procession. At the time of the burial, the family and relatives cover the corpse with dirt and dig several ditches in which they pour hot water. To prepare for the rebirth of the deceased, no stones or tombstones are placed on the grave. Sometime later, flowers may be planted at the grave, because the people believe that they will receive the blessings of Allah. However, there is no custom of offering flowers to the deceased.

At the home of the deceased, candles are kept lit for 40 days after the death, so that the soul of the deceased will not return. During this period, all celebrations must be avoided. When the mourning period is over, the family holds a memorial service and sings the *mebrut* (the song of the hometown of the Prophet) and presents sweets and rose perfume to the people who joined the service. This kind of ceremony is held every year on the memorial day of the deceased.

In Turkey, as it has traditionally been done in Japan, there are the funerary customs of putting a sip of water in the mouth of someone who is dying and placing a knife on the stomach of the deceased. In the past, women were not allowed to join the funeral procession, but today the choice is left to the individual. Even today the women usually do not sit with the men when a funeral is held in a mosque. Since there is no custom of cremation, there are no cremation facilities.

When a foreigner dies in Turkey, the corpse must be kept frozen in the hospital, in a tightly sealed vault. A permit for transportation overseas is required. It is also possible to bury the body in Turkey, but only Muslims are permitted burial in the Islamic cemeteries.

There is the 50 meter high tumulus containing the grave of King Antiochus Epiphanes I of Commagenes on the summit of mount Nemrut, on a plateau 150 meters wide. The mountain is itself 2,150 meters high. It is believed to be the highest graveyard ever built in the world. On the western side of summit there are also giant sculptures resting on high bases, which bore the attributes of more than one god amalgamated into a single figure such as Appolo, Mithras, Helios and Hermes.

UNITED ARAB EMIRATES

The United Arab Emirates, located on the Persian Gulf, include seven hereditary monarchies, which include Abu Dhabi and Dubai. The country has, in recent years, received world-wide attention as an oil-producing country. The climate is hot, and the majority of the land is desert. In the cities on the coast, modernization has rapidly developed because of sudden economic growth, and the number of immigrant laborers has been increasing.

The official language is Arabic, and many follow Sunni Islam and strictly obey the Islamic commandments and precepts. Most Sunni Muslims subscribe to either the Maliki or Hanbali school of Islamic law. Many of the latter are Wahhabis, though they are not nearly as strict and puritanical as the Saudi Wahhabis. The people pray five times a day, and they do not eat or drink in the daytime during Ramadan (the ninth month on the lunar calendar) nor do they eat pork.

The United Arab Emirates is probably the most liberal country in the Gulf, though it is still a very conservative place by Western standards. Most of the women do not wear tight or revealing clothes, and the men do not walk around bare-chested in public. Also the women are very reluctant to have their pictures taken.

When someone dies, the family reports the death to the police station. The family bathes the deceased, then wraps the body with white cloth and sprays it with perfume before it is placed in the coffin. Because more people today die in hospitals, the hospital staff often bathe the body for the family.

For the funeral procession to the mosque and community graveyard, the mourners used to walk, but today they go by car. Because of the hot climate, it is necessary to bury the body in the ground as soon as possible. As in other Islamic countries, the deceased must face Mecca. There are several public cemeteries around major cities; in Dubai, there are also Christian and Jewish cemeteries.

It is customary for a widow to observe a mourning period of 40 days after her husband's death in order to determine paternity in case of pregnancy, although it is possible to divorce and remarry .

YEMEN

The Republic of Yemen is on the southwestern tip of the Arabian peninsula. The population consists of mainly Arabs, who are followers of Sunni or Shiite Islam. Because of a coup d'etat in 1962, the monarchy fell and North Yemen became a republic. In 1967, South Yemen became independent from Great Britain. Since then, the two countries have been involved in repeated power struggles. In 1990, however, the Yemen Arab Republic (North Yemen) declared unification with South Yemen and as a result a new country was born.

Because Yemen lies in the tropical zone, and also because of Islamic custom, the body must be buried as quickly as possible. In the cities, such as San'a, the family may ask a private mortuary for assistance. After the family bathes the deceased for the last time, they wrap the body in cloth. If the deceased is male, the cloth is white, and if female, green. Then some fragrant oil is sprinkled over the body. After that, the *imam* recites verses from the Qur'an.

The funeral is usually held at a mosque and the body is buried in a community graveyard. Female mourners wear black. Men can wear anything so long as it is clean. There is no custom of offering flowers. A simple gravepost is set in the sand to mark the grave. In the case of a Muslim, the body is buried in a cemetery used exclusively by followers of Islam, so there is no need to purchase a gravesite. Cremation is not a custom, so there are no crematoriums or urns.

Chinese, Somalians and Indians in Yemen hold funerals according to their own religious customs. The nomadic Veddoid who live in the inland areas of Yemen are itinerant, so they have no need for established cemeteries. When a foreigner dies in Yemen, the body may be sent back to the home country if the bereaved family so desires.

CHAPTER 5

Europe

ALBANIA

The Republic of Albania is located on the coast of the Adriatic Sea in the southwestern part of the Balkan peninsula. Seventy percent of the population once followed Islam. After World War II, however, Albania became a socialist country, and antireligious sentiment became stronger than before. At the convention of the Communist Party in 1966, Albania officially stated that it was the world's first country without a god. All the churches were taken over by the government, and all priests were forced to retire from the priesthood. Until recently, Albania kept its borders closed, and almost all foreigners were forbidden entry.

Islamic customs were formerly practiced by the people, but now they eat pork, drink alcoholic beverages, and ignore the ritual of fasting. The people toast with glasses of *raki* wine, and say "*Gzwar*" (to happiness) even in the middle of the day. The Albanians claim that by denying religion it became possible for the first time to forget their feudalistic system and history.

When someone dies in Tirana, the capital, a very simple secular funeral is held at the family home or at a gathering place. A representative from the mourning party gives a speech of condolence, and the body is buried in the graveyard. A memorial service may also be held.

In the rural area, wailing, scratching one's face, cutting or tearing out one's hair, and wearing clothes inside out, are recognized modes of mourning. This ritualistic behavior is exhibited by female dependents and neighbors, rarely by men, and sometimes female mourners are hired. However, these customs are now disappearing.

ANDORRA

The Co-Principality of Andorra is a small country in the Pyrenees between Spain and France. Tourists from all over Europe enjoy the beautiful scenery and the tax-free shopping. The majority of the people are Catalonian Spanish, who are mostly Roman Catholic. Funerals are usually held in a Catholic church and the body is buried in a cemetery. In the capital, there are three public cemeteries. There is no crematorium in the country.

AUSTRIA

Austria lies in the heart of Europe. The majority of the people are German-speaking Austrians, but there are also people originally from Croatia, Hungary, Slovenia and the Czech Republic. The overwhelming majority are Catholic, though there are also many Protestants, Jews and Greek Orthodox Christians.

When someone dies in Austria, the necessary legal procedure is a coroner's inquest (*Totenbeschau*), which has to be carried out in all cases of death. Since this is not a federal but a state matter, the detailed provisions differ in the nine Austrian states. The inquest is usually carried out by a specially authorized medical doctor (*Sprengelarzt*). The purpose of the inquest is mainly to establish the fact that the person in question has actually died, to determine the cause of death, to check for contagious disease, and so forth. An official death certificate is then released by the General Register Office. After the inquest is completed, the dead body is usually taken care of by a mortician. An autopsy, a practice established during the reign (1740-1780) of Empress Maria Theresa, is performed in special cases only.

Three days to a week after death, the body is moved from the morgue to the chapel, and the funeral is held there according to the wishes of the family or the deceased. The funeral costs have to be borne by the person ordering the funeral. In most cases such costs are fully or partially covered by social insurance or by life insurance. Under the Trade Regulation Act, the head of each of the nine states has to fix maximum rates for funerals. The funeral director may apply those maximum rates for his state when he is rendering services accordingly. After the funeral, the coffin is transported to the graveyard and is usually buried. Catholics generally hold a memorial service in the family church a few days later.

Austrians often visit the cemetery. On days such as the birthday of the deceased, Memorial Day, and on Christian holidays, such as Christmas and Easter, the family lights candles at the grave of the deceased. They also offer flowers such as carnations and roses. Some even go to the cemetery as often as three times a month.

As in France and Germany, cremation has been practiced mostly by people of the working class. Recently, however, cremation has become more popular, and many public mortuaries have crematory chambers. After cremation the ashes are kept in the cinerarium for many years and not immediately buried in the ground.

Today in Vienna there are 10 church graveyards and 46 public cemeteries. The largest one is in Wiener Zentralfriedhof (Vienna Central cemetery). It occupies approximately 2,400,000 square meters, and is renowned as one of the locations in the movie *The Third Man*. It is a tourist attraction, also being known as the cemetery in honor of world-famous Austrian musicians. For example, on the left side of the central entrance (Section 32-A), are the tombstones of Beethoven, Schubert, Mozart, Strauss, Brahms, Suppe, Wolff and others. Mozart's grave is merely a cenotaph; the body itself is said to be buried in St. Marx cemetery (Third district). In the case of Beethoven and Schubert, their remains were transported here from the cemetery of Waehring (Eighteenth district) in 1888.

In the catacombs under the Capuchin's church, the monks still preserve the funeral sites of a large number of members of the Imperial Habsburg family. Most caskets are beautifully modeled from pure zinc. The funeral for Zita, the wife of Karl the last Emperor of the Habsburgs, who had for many years ruled over much of Austria, was held in this church in a grand style on the first of April, 1989.

On Goldeggasse Avenue in Vienna, there is a Funeral Museum, which is a must for people who want to learn about the history of funeral customs in Austria. On Graben Street is a monument built by Leopold I in 1683 to commemorate the end of the Black Plague in 1679. Thousands of victims of the plague were buried here. The graves of many plague victims in the city of Salzburg can be found bordering the cemetery in the back of St. Peter's Church.

BELGIUM

The Kingdom of Belgium, situated in the west of Europe and facing the North Sea, consists of plains and gentle slopes. It is populated mostly by the Flemish, the Walloon French and the Dutch. Most of its people are Catholic.

When a death occurs, a report, together with a medical certificate, is filed at the nearest Census Registration office to obtain a death certificate, stating that a period of 24 hours has lapsed since death. There are large and small private mortuaries. The body is generally not embalmed. It is clothed in ordinary clothing (sometimes in white) and then put in a coffin and decorated with flowers and a cross. It is then placed in the family home or in a mortuary until the funeral, which normally takes place in the family church two or three days after the death.

Unless it is the expressed wish of the deceased, in most cases a burial is conducted at a cemetery. Crematory facilities are available in the capital city of Brussels, but for the devout Catholic adherent, burial is preferable unless the death had been caused by a contagious disease. In cases when cremation is desired, the body is occasionally transported to neighboring Germany or France. Cemeteries play an important role in community life and are visited around November 1 on All Saints' Day, each year. Evergreen wreaths symbolizing resurrection to eternal life are placed on the grave by the bereaved family members or relatives.

BOSNIA AND HERZEGOVINA

The Republic of Bosnia and Herzegovina used to be a member of the Socialist Republics of Yugoslavia. It consists of northern Bosnia and southern Herzegovina. The capital is Sarajevo. In March 1992, the country declared its independence, but three elements in the population—the Muslims, the Serbians and the Croatians—have been hostile to one another, and the disputes between them have developed into an ethnic war. The United Nations is now working as a mediator, but this dangerous situation still continues.

The funerary practices of Bosnian Muslims are similar to those of Turkish Muslims. They have independent community cemeteries that are separate from those of Serbian Orthodox or Croatian Catholic members.

BULGARIA

The Republic of Bulgaria lies on the Balkan peninsula in the southeast end of Eastern Europe. A mountain range divides the country into northern and southern Bulgaria. The southern area has a Mediterranean climate and is very mild, whereas the northern area has an inland climate that brings severe winter temperatures.

The majority of the people are Bulgarians, but there are Turkish people and gypsies as well. Most follow Bulgarian Orthodox Church or Islam. The traditional Pomak religions retain Christian and pre-Christian elements and are grounded in the agricultural cycle. The Gypsies do not tend to be devout followers of any one institutional religion but rather practice an eclectic folk religion that combines Muslim, Christian and pre-Christian customs. Since 1946 when Bulgaria became a communist country, the people have become less and less religious. Funerals are most often held in a non-religious manner. In 1989 there were pro-democracy demonstrations, and as a result the Zhivkov regime, which had been in power for 35 years, came to an end. The new government is now trying to make the country democratic.

At present, a funeral is held in a public cemetery or in the chapel of the funeral home (*Progrebalno Bureau*). It is a simple affair, and the body is buried in the cemetery. If the family requests it, the funeral may be held at a church and the body buried with the priest in attendance. In the rural areas, religious funeral services still occur. After the funeral, the family may serve light snacks to the mourners. If the deceased was well known, a memorial service is held on the day of the death.

Such services are held by national groups. In graveyards that antedate the revolution, there are traditional tombstones, representing both religions. More recent graves are rather standardized. For instance, the graves of communists are very simple: red, triangle-shaped tombstones with the mark of a star. However, the grave of a person of distinguished service is an exception. The body of the first Prime Minister of Bulgaria, Georgi Dimitrov, for example, is in a mausoleum covered with yellow bricks in front of the September 9th Square.

CROATIA

The Republic of Croatia is a new industrial country that became independent of Yugoslavia in June 1991. The capital is Zagreb. Croatia has often fought with its neighboring Serbia. The majority of the people are Catholic Croatians, but there are Serbians as well. The Croatians and the Serbians are hostile toward each other, and although the United Nations have tried to mediate, they have had no success. Tourist attractions like Dubrovnik, on the Adriatic coast, have been partly devastated by the war. In Dubrovnik, there is a public cemetery (Novo Groblye) with different religious sections.

CZECH REPUBLIC

The Czech Republic is located in the heart of western Europe. It is a multiethnic country, including the Czechs and the Slovakians and many other groups. Originally Catholicism had a strong influence in the country, but after 1946 when the communist regime was established, the government banned those religious activities, which were in conflict with national policy. Accordingly, many of the churches, theological schools and convents were used for other purposes.

In 1989, a large scale pro-democracy demonstration erupted. As a result, the Jakes government, which was the successor of the Husak government, collapsed. At that time, the present coalition government, which includes a citizens' forum, was established, and the anti-establishment writer Vaclav Havel was elected as the Czech president.

When someone dies, the family reports the death to the government district office in order to obtain a death certificate. In the urban areas, the family holds a wake, and then holds the funeral at the mortuary of a public cemetery. The remains are buried in the cemetery or the ashes are preserved in a niche. Outside the cities, a priest may be invited by the family to hold a religious ceremony.

The practice of traditional funeral customs has been waning. In the large cities, about 25 percent wish to be cremated, but in the rural areas interment is much more common. A gravesite can be rented for five years at a low cost, and this contract period can be extended. The graves of unknown people or those without families are buried together in a mass grave.

Religiously and historically significant buildings and cemeteries are preserved at the government's expense. The Jewish cemetery and the Vyshehrad Cemetery, where Dvorak and Smetana are buried, are well cared for and are even tourist attractions. The Olshanske Cemetery has a crematorium (*Vinohrd-sky Hrbitovy*).

The cemetery's mortuary has the responsibility of placing the death notice on the town bulletin board. The note contains the deceased's birthday, the names of the family members, their relationship to the deceased and the deceased's religion. Also, there is a monument to honor the people who died in World War II protecting the city against German troops. Flowers are offered at the monument almost every day, which is a very impressive sight.

In the community graveyard in Praha, there are some unique tombstones. For example, there are tombstones with a stone dove, symbolizing peace or tombstones with a broken propeller, marking the grave of a pilot who died in battle.

When spring comes, many beautiful flowers such as tulips, pansies and hyacinths bloom in profusion in the graveyards in the Czech Republic. Around the time of the festival of Easter, the cemeteries and graveyards bustle with people visiting graves. Also, the first of November is a memorial day called Doshichiki. It is said that the soul of the deceased returns from the other world on this day.

DENMARK

Situated at the entrance to the Baltic Sea, the Kingdom of Denmark is separated by a small strait from Sweden. Although a small country, it has a very dense population. Lutheran Gospel Church is the national religion of Denmark.

When a death occurs, it is reported to the government office and a health certificate from the doctor is submitted. Then a certificate of death is issued. This practice is similar to other Western countries; however, the arrangements for the funeral are placed completely in the hands of the mortuary.

The deceased, if male, is clothed in a suit; if a female, most often the body is wrapped in her wedding dress. A minister is invited to direct the encoffining ceremony in the presence of close relatives. After the body is placed in the coffin, it is transported to the affiliated church or to the crematorium, which is situated within the cemetery. Funeral services are held on the next day. If the deceased was a labor union official, or if there are many funeral attendees, the funeral services may be held in the Labor Union Hall or in the City Hall.

Several years ago, there were 24 crematoriums established within Denmark; but presently, it seems, this number has increased. The cremation rate in the capital Copenhagen has risen to 76 percent (as of 1995), but even today, there are places outside of the cities where burials still take place. Increasingly, the cremated ashes are buried in common graves, and it is said that in Copenhagen the number has climbed to 60 percent.

The royal family and the nobility are customarily buried in the mausoleum at Roskild Cathedral, but such mausoleum-type burial is uncommon for the general population. Outside of the cities, many burials are performed in church-affiliated cemeteries.

After the burial and before the attendees leave, a snack is served either at the home of the bereaved family, a restaurant, or other gathering place. For the family, there is no strictly set mourning period. The expenses, including the cremation fees, are about 3,000 kroner (as of 1995), which covers the honorarium for the priest. In the case of a Lutheran Gospel church member, the conducting minister's honorarium is paid by the government.

Ashisutan Cemetery, within Copenhagen, is thickly covered by trees that shadow the grounds. Entering its front gate, one can see the graves of Hans Christian Anderson (1805-1875) and Danish philosopher and theologian Soren Aabye Kierkegaard (1813-1855).

The Faroe Islands, a self-governing region of Denmark since 1948, is situated in the North Atlantic between Iceland and the Shetland Islands. The majority of the people follow the Evangelical Lutheran tradition, and observe their funerals accordingly. Also, in Greenland, another autonomous region of Denmark, a death is reported to the community office (*communi arafia*) and the funeral rite is observed at the church, followed by burial at the cemetery nearby.

ESTONIA

The Republic of Estonia is bordered by Latvia and the Russian Federation. Its terrain is flat, boggy and partly wooded, and includes more than 1,500 islands in the Baltic Sea. In March 1990, Estonia became independent from the former Soviet Union and joined the United Nations in September of the same year. The capital of Estonia is Tallin. In association with the Balto-Finnish Estonians, the country was given the name Estonia, which means "est" or "east" in Old Filisia. The Estonians are ethnically close to the Finns, and, culturally, they feel strongly that they are part of Northern Europe. As in Finland, many belong to the Lutheran Church.

Since its independence, the country has become liberated very quickly. The majority of the people are Finns, and the language is also similar to Finnish. During the time when Estonia was under Soviet rule, there was no religious freedom, so many people became non-religious. Recently, however, religion, beginning with Lutheran Christianity, seems to have made a comeback. Since 1988 the activities of various Christian groups have become more prominent. However, funerals are still mostly held in a non-religious manner.

In Talinn, there are four public cemeteries—Metsa, Siselinna, Rahumae and Liiva Kalamistu—on the outskirts of the city. The graves are lined up in rows.

FINLAND

Situated in the northern extremity of Europe, 70 percent of the Republic of Finland is a forest zone; scattered within it are lakes and marshes. The population, beginning with the great majority Finns, includes Swedes and Lapps. Finland is a progressive nation with an advanced social welfare system. Most of its population are members of the Protestant faith and belong to the Lutheran churches. Situated on a hill in the heart of its capital, Helsinki, and towering into the sky is the Great Cathedral of Saint Nicholas, which is the headquarters of the Lutheran Church.

When a death occurs, a death certificate is obtained by presenting the doctor's examination certificate at the government office. The funeral arrangements can be made by a nearby mortuary. The wake is carried out at the family's home, but the funeral service is conducted the next morning at the family's church, attended by surviving family members and other mourners wearing black mourning clothes. After the funeral service, the body is usually buried in the church cemetery, although the number of cremations has increased. If the body is cremated, it is done at a public crematorium, and the remains are buried in the cemetery. Lilies ordered from the florist are most common as floral offerings. Memorial feasts are held six weeks and one year after death.

Within the city of Helsinki there is a public cemetery near the western seacoast where the grave sites are sectioned according to the family's religion. Here you can find the grave of Baron Carl Gustav Emil von Mannerheim who is beloved as the founding father of Finland. On Christmas Eve, candles are lit before the grave and reflect on the surrounding snow, creating a majestic atmosphere.

Many of the Lapps who live in the Arctic Circle belong to the Russian Orthodox Eastern Church or the Lutheran Church. In the past, when a death occurred, the deceased's possessions were packed into a bag and buried with the body. The body was either buried in a grave or placed in a roofshaped wooden coffin and left on the ground with a wooden cross standing at its head.

FRANCE

France is a land of gently rolling hills in western Europe, bordered on the south by the Mediterranean Sea and on the north by the English Channel. Although the majority of the people speak French, in Brittany some speak the Breton language. Most present-day French are of Celtic and Latin descent. The Catholic religion is overwhelmingly predominant, but with increasing secularization. Especially within the working class in the cites, religion seems to have become a mere formality. However, among the older generation, there are still reverent believers, and there still remains the custom of conducting grand and solemn funerals. The funeral is the last ceremony they must attend.

When someone dies, a death certificate is obtained from the local medical doctor and submitted to the Bureau de l'etat Civil. One can obtain a certificate of permission for burial, but there is a rule that forbids burial within 24 hours after death. The mortuaries are privately owned and operated. Usually after the wake at the family home a funeral is performed at the church or at the cemetery morgue.

In the era when Napoleon ruled the country, funerals were performed exclusively by the church, but in 1904, this right was transferred from the church to a self-governing local body which, today, has taken control of the business of funerals outside the church.

The largest mortuary in the world, the Pompes Funebres Generales SA, has obtained exclusive rights to the French funeral business. The company has 5,500 employees, and it is said that the company brings in a yearly sum that exceeds two billion francs (based on figures from 1989). Recently, two British companies, Hodgson Holdings and Kenyon Securities, have also merged with this company.

The techniques successfully used to restore the appearance of the corpse in America are seldom used in France, except for renowned people, and the formalities are complex. If an American dies in France, the restorative process is performed on the corpse before it is transported back to the United States.

The French coffin is boat-shaped, and although a variety of wood may be used, the ordinary model is pine, whereas high-priced coffins are made of mahogany or ebony. The coffin is placed along with candles in the mortuary or in the room of the family home where the wake is held. This area is enclosed in black curtains. If the deceased is an adult, a black cloth covering is draped over the coffin; for a child, white is used. An ornament bearing the deceased's initials is placed on the coffin of an adult.

As a general rule, one must be buried in a public cemetery within 24 hours of death. If the place of burial is further than 125 miles from the place of death or if more than 24 hours from death passes, the inside of the coffin is fitted with a metallic shield to better preserve the body. Customarily, it is the duty of the police to seal the coffin.

Formerly, when the funeral procession assembled on the day of the funeral, bearers slowly carried the coffin in a carriage from the home of the deceased to the funeral hall; but this is now a thing of the past. Today efficiency is the rule, and hearses are almost always used. The cemeteries are publicly managed and one customarily obtains a five-year lease for the gravesite. The contract expires after 35 years at the longest, but it is possible to renew it. The percentage of deserted graves, which have not been renewed even though five years have passed since the burial, has risen to about 65 percent. The remains of the deceased are removed from there and are buried together elsewhere.

In Paris, up until the time of the French Revolution, there was an area called the Innocent Cemetery adjoining the central marketplace, where the city's commoners were simply buried in the earth in the same way as domestic animals. However, after a fixed time had elapsed the remains were unearthed and the bones were placed in the loft of the outer wall of the cemetery.

The cemetery for the pre-Revolution monarchs was in Saint Denis Abbey on the outskirts of Paris. The top of the stone coffin was carved with a life-size image of the deceased lying down, but this practice, called *gisant*, gradually disappeared. Before long it became the fashion among the rich to make life-size standing images called *transi*. After the Revolution, they began moving the images or statues of the deceased and the coffins that had been installed in the abbey to the outside.

Today it is still customary to be buried, although cremation is also an option. For example, in the Pere Laches Cemetery in Paris's Twentieth Ward there is a crematorium attached to the large cemetery. The philosopher Jean-Paul Sartre and the actor Jean Gabin were cremated here. It is believed among the Christian denominations that had Jesus Christ been cremated rather than buried after his crucifixion the miracle of his resurrection could not have taken place, and therefore burial is preferable to cremation. The Catholic Church in particular strictly observes this tradition, and when one reads statements such as *if the will asks for cremation, you should not conduct the cremation and if the will asks for cremation, do not go against that wish, but the church will not perform the ceremony*, one understands that the Catholic Church regards cremation as a serious breach of faith. However, since the 19th century, members of the intelligentsia, who denied the resurrection of Christ, requested to be cremated. For those who were trying to undermine traditional Christian practices, cremation may have been the final act of defiance.

In the same Pere Laches Cemetery there are many graves of renowned people. Among men of letters, here rest Moliere, La Fontaine and Balzac, and among composers, Rossini, Chopin and Georges Bizet. In the cemetery that lies west of the hill of Montmartre are the graves of Berlioz and Offenbach. When All Saints' Day arrives on November 1 and All Souls' Day on the following day, crowds of visitors pay their respects by laying flowers at these graves.

On the street corners of Paris one can spot monuments and plaques celebrating the memory of those who sacrificed their lives in the French resistance during World War II. In the center of the basement of this dome-shaped church for veterans lies the stone coffin that held the body of Napoleon Bonaparte, on an altar of green granite. The stone was a gift of the Russian Tsar Nicholas I, and the coffin was made from a 3.98x1.82x1.27 meter slab of red stone mica. Surrounding his coffin rest eight other coffins, two of which belong to his elder brother, the Spanish King Joseph, and the famous World War I General Bertrand Durse. During the summer, Paris' famous outdoor laser show, "*Son Lumiere*" takes place along with the performances of Beethoven's symphony "Eroica" on the front lawn of this memorial.

The war dead are also remembered in Verdun, about 180 kilometers east of

Paris. The 18-month battle between the French and the Germans during World War I left more than 700,000 dead and nine villages wiped off the map. At Douaumont, 10 kilometers to the north, an unusual memorial tower rears up over an endless sea of graves.

The Bretons, who live in the westernmost region of France, tend to prepare for death, ensuring well in advance that their cemetery plot or place in the family vault is secure. Cremation is rare. Many superstitions are practiced when a close relative passes away. For example, the doors and windows are left open to permit the soul to easily leave.

Among the Gypsies, it is taboo to call the deceased's name once he or she dies. The mourners take part in the wake for three days and nights; during those days, the men do not shave and the women do not cook. Before the burial, all the belongings must be burned and no trace of the deceased should be left in this world. When visiting the grave, the mourners play a dirge on the violin and openly shed their tears. Afterward, they remain in mourning for a year, during which time they refrain from listening to music or to the radio and from watching television.

GERMANY

In Germany, which is situated in the central part of Europe, there are gently sloping plains, except for along its southern border. Germany was reunified in 1990 after years of division between East and West following the defeat of the Nazi regime in 1945. The majority of the people are Christian. Those in the north are for the most part Protestants, and many in the south are Catholics. The preface of the Organic Law, which was promulgated in 1949 and revised in 1966, advocates freedom of religion. The National Treasury gives support to the Lutheran Church and the Catholic Church. However, there has been a decrease in the rate of Sunday church attendance among the young and, in general, interest in religion has been decreasing.

When death occurs, as in other developed countries, a death certificate from the attending doctor must be obtained and submitted to the General Registry office. The death is reported to close relatives and friends by telephone, and for the general public an obituary is generally placed in the local newspaper.

There are both public and private mortuaries in the districts from which the family of the deceased can choose. After the enactment of the Free Trade Law in 1860, independent mortuaries began operating their own establishments. In 1928, it is said that there were 80 public cemeteries, 3 crematoriums and 3 public mortuaries in Berlin, which managed 60 percent of all funerals in the city. After World War II, private industry was encouraged, and the mortuary business began to flourish. Private mortuaries spread all over the country, and the German Mortuary Business Association was organized. Some of the private mortuary companies serve as funeral insurance agents that provide low-premium coverage of funeral expenses. In the city of Munich, most of the cemeteries have changed to public management.

The coffins are generally made of pine or teak. The eight-sided, boat-shaped coffins are painted either black or brown, and the inside edges are covered with either paper or silk. A mattress and pillow filled with wood shavings are placed in the coffin under the body, which is sometimes embalmed before being placed in the casket so it can lie in the family home for several days. However, in most cases, the body is immediately transported by hearse to a morgue within the cemetery and is placed in a room equipped with refrigeration facilities. Mourners may view the body through a glass partition. In a corner of the district church-affiliated cemetery, there is a small cottage called the "House of the Dead," where the deceased is kept until the funeral or burial.

Funeral processions are scarcely seen in the cities, but in the rural areas one can see funeral processions from the house of the bereaved family or from the church, heading toward the burial ground. The members of the family and the mourners in the procession wear black funeral robes. The sight of six bearers slowly transporting the casket, while the church bell tolls, is solemn and impressive. The funeral is held in the funeral hall within the cemetery grounds or in the family church, and a minister of their religion is invited to conduct the funeral service. In recent times, many funeral services in the city are held in the cemetery. If it is desired by the bereaved family, the church or the mortuary may arrange for musicians and singers to provide the funeral music.

The cemeteries are either public or church-operated. They are systematically sectioned with white birch or evergreen trees, so they give the impression of a park. Also the burial grounds are leased according to size: a 25 year contract for single graves; a 30-60 year contract for family graves; and a 60 year contract for solid, impregnable graves. The lease contract is renewable. On renewal, the rent is reduced by half, and payments can be made in installments. Remains in a grave with an expired lease and without surviving families are reburied and the headstone is removed. It is customary that after a certain period of time human remains at negected graves be transferred to a mausoleum called *knochenhaus,* in the cemetery. People love to plant flowers at the grave, and often visit there to reflect upon the deceased. Each town has private mortuaries, called *bestattungshaus* or *bestattungsinstitute,* which handle all kinds of funeral procedures. There is a Federal Association of German Undertakers, called Bundesverband Bestattungsgewerbes e. V. in Dusseldorf.

Generally, funeral services are held after the grave diggers have finished their work. At the end of the service, the officiating minister sprinkles some soil on the casket, and then the family members and mourners follow his lead. When the coffin is buried, soil is heaped up to form a mound. Some ivy and flowers are planted on it or around it. As for tombstones, crosses as well as many other different shapes and sizes of stones can be ordered from the stone merchants. From the distant past, gravesites have been separated along denominational lines — Catholic, Protestant and Jewish religions.

Eastern Germany had traditionally been a stronghold of Lutheran Gospel churches, but after it became a socialist country, the separation of church and state was promoted. Article 39 of the recently abolished East German Constitution, which was promulgated in 1968, recognized freedom of religion. In 1990, the Berlin Wall was destroyed, and since East and West Germany have been joined, the one-time socialist structure is being dismantled.

When death occurs in eastern Germany, a medical certificate must be obtained and filed with the government office in order to obtain a death certificate with which the government mortuary may be requested to undertake funeral preparations. Many bereaved families request a non-religious type of funeral service to be carried out at the funeral hall within the public cemetery. However, when the family belongs to a specific religious sect, they may request a minister from this sect to conduct the funeral service.

After cremation, the remains are buried in the grave. The graves are under a leasing system and contracts are renewable every 12 years. Compared to western Germany, the expenses for funeral services and burials are lower, and many of the tombstones are simple. However, exceptions are made in the case of those who had made noble contributions to the country, science or the arts. For instance, for many years, the great musician Johann Sebastian Bach, who died on July 28, 1750, at the age of 65, was buried in Leipzig's Saint John Cathedral, but because the cathedral was destroyed in the air raid of 1943, his remains were transferred to Saint Thomas Cathedral in commemoration of his 264th birthday in 1949. Since then he has been magnificently enshrined in the sanctuary altar, which has been open to public viewing since 1964.

In the past, when someone died, the hands of the clocks were stopped and mirrors and windows were covered, but today these practices have become obsolete.

The Bavarians bounded to the northwest by the state of Hessen, are generally pragmatic about death. They observe funeral services normally found in the Roman Catholic or Protestant liturgy. Also, the deceased is remembered on November 1, All Saints' Day, when the family members gather in the cemetery to clean and decorate the graves and to participate in a religious service.

GREAT BRITAIN

The United Kingdom occupies the major portion of the British Isles, including the nations of England, Scotland, and Wales, and of northern Ireland and several outlying islands. The United Kingdom is separated from the Northwestern part of Europe by the English Channel and the North Sea. The majority of the people are English, followed by the Scottish; Britain's ethnic minorities account for less than 5 percent of the total population.

When death occurs, based on the "Birth and Death Registration Act" enacted in 1853, a death report together with a doctor's certificate of death must be submitted within five days after death (eight days in Scotland) to the census registration office, but a period of fourteen days is allowed for full registration to take place. In the case of an accidental death, an autopsy must be conducted in the coroner's office of the respective district seat. The body is laid out in the mortuary of the hospital where the death occurred or in the morgue of the coroner's office. The deceased's body may be removed with a Certificate of Death. Whether burial or cremation is chosen, or in the case of foreigners, whether the body will be sent to the home country, is decided according to the wishes of the bereaved family.

Death and funeral notices are made by telephone to close relatives, but one usually places a notice in a local newspaper when wider-scale circulation is required. If a private funeral is desired, the obituary omits the date, time and place, reporting only when the death occurred. When relatives and close acquaintances are numerous, another date may be chosen to conduct a form of memorial service after the private funeral is observed.

Ordinarily, the site of the funeral is at the cemetery or in the chapel of the crematorium, but the living room of the deceased's home is occasionally used. Other than for cases of funerals for ministers or persons of prominence, city or urban churches are hardly ever used.

Flower wreaths are displayed around the coffin, and the general practice is for relatives and friends to send flowers through a florist or the mortuary, and those flowers are later taken to the grave or are donated to places like hospitals. If one does not want flowers, it must be clearly stated in the funeral notice. If contributions to charities are desired in place of obituary gifts, the name of the organization and its address should be clearly stated (there is not necessarily a practice of those attending the funeral service to make obituary gifts of money to the bereaved family nor is there a return token of acknowledgement). On occasion, snacks are served to the guests.

The mortuary is in charge of all the arrangements relating to the funeral from the moment of death to the burial, as well as all business matters for the bereaved family. Aside from the Jewish People's Mutual Aid Association for Funerals and Celebrations, most bereaved families turn to a nearby mortuary. Presently, about 2,500 large and small mortuaries are affiliated with the Mortuary Service Association of Great Britain. Also, the members of the National Association of Funeral Directors of Great Britain provide an extensive list of services to their clients; they make arrangements for the cremation or burial, the priest, the hearse, the cemetery, food and drinks, the collection of life insurance and so forth.

The mortuary staff, after receiving just a phone call, will come to the family home and keep the body until the funeral services and the burial or cremation are completed. This service generally includes bathing the corpse and changing it into clothes for burial, but rarely do they apply make-up to the face of the corpse as they do in America. In England, improving the appearance of the corpse would serve no purpose, because the English dislike having a last viewing at the funeral service. Consequently, orthopedic preservation is not performed in England, unless it is necessary to transport the body to a distant land or the bereaved family specifically requests it. Caskets made of inexpensive synthetic materials to expensive oak are available at the various mortuaries and can be selected from a catalog to meet one's budget and choice. There has been less demand recently for the traditional boat-shaped casket and the general preference is the rectangular-shaped one.

The greater portion of the funeral expenses are borne by the family, but the mortuary must act under the compulsory directions of the Fair Trade Commission of Great Britain. The mortuary must show in written form an itemized account of funeral expenses and obtain the family's written agreement.

Among the intelligentsia, there were people who, for economic reasons, advocated doing away with funerals. According to these people, funeral services were a meaningless anachronism and an empty shell of a ceremony. They insisted that the real value of the funeral had been lost, and it helped only those who want to gain commercial profit from it. The argument that funerals were useless not only gave an impetus to the simplification of funeral services, but also inevitably brought a change to the laws concerning what was done with the cremated body, as the practice of cremation was rapidly spreading.

In England, the corpse is completely burned to ashes. The bones lose their original form and the remains cannot be placed in a mortuary urn and buried in a grave nor, except in a few cases, can the remains be placed in the columbarium. After cremation, 65 percent of the ashes are scattered on the ground. One section of the crematorium grounds is set aside for a memorial cemetery park where ashes are scattered. Here, the remaining ashes are scattered over the earth. Occasionally, roses or other flowers are planted and a small monument is erected, and the name of the deceased is recorded in the mortuary register. Often the ashes are scattered over the ocean or on a site that was memorable to the deceased. Currently, most cemeteries provide regulations that set the size, form and the content of inscriptions of the tombstones, and prohibit people from encircling the grave with a fence, as well as burying the body within church property.

Nowadays it is unusual for more than 20 people to attend a funeral service; it is becoming brief and informal, with attendees going directly to the grave or the crematorium. There is an increase in the memorial service type of funeral, and this tendency is striking among the intelligentsia and the middle class. The attendees, except for close relatives, do not wear mourning clothes; many appear dressed in everyday clothing. The mourning period for close relatives has been shortened, and even during this period few restrain themselves from attending social events. Some remarry immediately after a spouse's death. Except for the Irish, a wake is generally not held.

Early in this century, the Swiss psychologist Jung declared that in a highly civilized society, customs relating to the dead will be simplified. It is not an exaggeration to say that in England what Jung predicted has come true.

In the past, death was ever-present for the British. They constantly faced the reality of death and were amazed by it. Many entrusted their hopes to a life after death, but now such a view of life and death seems to have faded. The very moment of meeting death is, indeed, the time to close the record of one's life. In that moment, one is assailed with various temptations that must be overcome. At the moment of death, it is important that one achieve a calm mind. It seems that this kind of individualizing and internalizing of death has caused the traditional customs surrounding the occurrence of death and burial customs to have been simplified and made meaningless.

In English society today, there has been a gradual change that may affect these views of life and death. This is due to the fact that most of the British no longer die at home, watched over by their nearest and dearest relatives and friends, but in the hospital. In other words, the initiative of saving life or terminating it is now in the hands of the doctors and hospitals. Originally, death was expected to be dramatic, but now it is handled in an isolated sickroom. Because no one can take our place in death, we must willingly accept the loneliness of death and endure it with strength. Even when facing the death of a beloved friend, the British believe that the anguish and sorrow of parting are something that they must bear and deal with by themselves, and not be assuaged, comforted or deadened by societal customs or burial practices. Therefore, weeping in public or expressing the sorrow of parting is thought to be a shameful exhibition.

Concerning this same matter, A.C.A. Hall, who is in the mortuary business in England, made the following observations:

On the occasion of a funeral, it is hard for an English family to understand the concerned who rush to them offering condolences, I, too, belonging to this typical group, find it intolerable to do so, and in a personal way, am an unpopular mediator of life.

Toru Kuroiwa, a Japanese jounalist, gave a similar account:

I felt alienated by the way the English dealt with death. So I related my feelings to a Spanish friend. Immediately he replied: 'The English are a very strange group of people. When my English friend suddenly died of a heart attack, I went to his house to console his wife and found only a Jewish friend there. None of his English friends had come. . . In Spain, it's different, you know. Even in Israel, I understand, it is not like that. Everybody joins together to mourn the dead. That way, wouldn't the bereaved family members be consoled? To shed tears when sad, to laugh when happy, and let everyone see it, isn't this what human society is all about?" (Quoted from *Yutakana Igirisujin* (Affluent British) Tokyo: Chuo Koronsha, 1984, pp.151-152.)

It appears from the standpoint of the British that those who have subdued emotions are stronger as human beings. However, such an individualistic attitude sometimes tends to be considered cold in the eyes of foreigners. The attitude that the British recently showed toward the death of former Princess Diana was an exception.

The view of life and death by the British may create strong people who will not be defeated by the misery of death and will respect the independence and dignity of each person. At the same time, however, there is also the possibility of creating a people who cannot bear such misery in death. For the former, even though one does not leave behind any form of oneself in this world, through the simple fact that that person is doing his or her best during one's lifetime, that person would be able to close his or her life in peace and contentment. However, in the case of the latter, who is discouraged by death without being able to receive any sympathy or words of encouragement, he or she would have to endure the grief of life and death alone.

The custom of grieving for the dead has become simplified, as though the process were carried out on a conveyer belt: the body is first cremated, then the ashes are scattered. Perhaps it is not a coincidence that debates relating to death then began. These debates have triggered similar debates over euthanasia, the sanctity of death and the hospice movement.

The American religionist Thomas Lukemann, seeing the phenomenon of secularization in modern society, and the religion of former times moving toward secularization, observed, "The new social form of religion supports the dehumanization of the social mechanism, but at the same time it sanctifies the liberation of human consciousness that is not restricted by social structures." If this theory is applied to England's present state of affairs in funeral attendance, it can be said that a death that can be seen is in the process of moving toward a death that cannot be seen. This would expand the autonomy of individual existence; at the same time it would cause an extreme polarity that would break the bonds of social life. It will be interesting to see how the British will balance and preserve the rivalry and harmony between the individual and society at large and how they will deal with the present trend of alienation.

Funerals and burials in the districts of Scotland are similar to those in England and Wales, but here the cemetery is under the supervision of local self-government and there are no facilities for worship. In the event of a burial, it was the custom from the old days that the mourners would tie a silk cord around the coffin and lower it into the ground. A mattress was placed on the coffin so that you could not hear the sound of soil dropping on the coffin. This practice comes from the old custom of placing grass on the coffin.

Since 1965, regulations relating to cremation have been standardized throughout the nation. However, it is said that until the last century, when there was a death in English homes, employees of the mortuary were hired to guard the body and the front entrance of the home until the coffin had left the residence. For the purpose of exorcism, a dish filled with salt was placed on the stomach of the deceased and candles were placed beside the dish. The candles were kept lit for the duration of the ceremony. The funeral rites were conducted at midnight.

The Enactment of 1678 set the regulations that decreed that burial clothes should be of woolen cloth. Linen and silk were forbidden. The covering of the coffins of children and the unmarried was to be white, whereas the covering for adults was black. Six pall bearers would shoulder the casket and proceed to the cemetery. On the way, the procession stopped often and all the mourners in unison raised their voices, saying, "Lord, have mercy! Christ, have mercy!"

Offering flowers at funerals and burials was also an old custom. Downy myrtle, ivy, roses and primroses were the flowers of choice. To protect the grave from rain, wind and wild animals, evergreens such as yew and cypress were planted. There was a time when the rich hired a professional poet to recite the praises of the deceased at the funeral, but now this is the job of mourners.

The British, who are strongly individualistic, dislike causing trouble to others and generally, unlike the Americans, do not invite a large number of people to their funerals. They prefer to have the funeral attended by members of the family.

As for graves as well, although there is King Edward's ornately decorated casket, for the general public, simple ones are most common. Perhaps because marble is an expensive, imported item, many tombstones are made from more common stone with brass plates inserted on them. Nevertheless, inscriptions on the tombstones are interesting, because they reflect the national character of the British, who love humor. For instance, at the Hereford Cemetery, there are the tombstones of a husband and wife. The wife, who had died first, had the following inscribed on her tombstone: "Dear husband, please do not grieve. I have not died, but I am sleeping here. Wait patiently and prepare for death. Soon you will be coming to join me." In return the husband inscribed his reply to her message: "My dearest wife, I am not grieving. I have taken a second wife, therefore, I cannot go to your side. I am going to hers."

There are even enthusiastic collectors who take detailed rubbings of such inscriptions. These are called brass rubbings and are produced by taping flock paper over the surface of the stone, then rubbing the surface with paraffin wax, making a copy of the convex part of the inscriptions. In the basement of St. James Cathedral, on Piccadilly Street, in London, there is a rubbings folio center where this process is taught.

In the case of burials as well, at the newly established government cemetery, the form and scale of tombstones are standardized and those imaginative, individualistic types of the past can no longer be seen. The humorous tombstone epitaphs have completely disappeared.

Cremation had been legalized before the war, but in 1940 the cremation rate was still at 3.9 percent of total deaths. In 1950, it surged to 15.6 percent; in 1960 to 34.7 percent; and in 1980 to 64.48 percent. The magnitude of the increase in rate was considerable indeed. In fact, for the realistic English citizen who values the traditional religious belief that a corpse is simply a body without a soul and who wants to protect the environment and secure an adequate amount of living space, it is natural to choose cremation.

Nevertheless, it is also true that there are even now religious orders and believers who remain unchanged in their religious beliefs and are fervently against cremation. Some of the reasons given for their objections are that the decomposition of the body is in best accord with the laws of nature and that cremation would impede the resurrection of the body at the second coming of the Lord. Also they could not bear the instantaneous destruction of the body.

There is great disparity in the degree and extent of permission or approval by religious organizations relating to the practice of funerals, as well as cremation. A general outline follows. (Quoted from C. J. Polson and T. K. Marshall *The Disposal of the Dead*, London: The English Universities Press, 1975, pp. 264-285.)

Armenian Orthodox Church

The church does not forbid or encourage cremation. After death, the body is wrapped in a shroud (black for males and white for females), and a prayer book is placed on the encoffined body. A priest is summoned immediately after death, and the remains are removed to the church as soon as possible. If an Armenian Orthodox church or priest is not available nearby, a priest from a Greek Orthodox church or an Anglican church may be permitted to officiate at the funeral rites.

The priest blesses the grave site and the graveyard before the committal rites and throws earth on the coffin and prays, "Stay as you are until the second coming of the Lord." Before dispersing, those attending the funeral service kiss the cross held in the priest's hand and receive his benediction. After the burial, the grave is visited on August 14, on the anniversary of the burial, and on the day immediately after the church's great festivals.

The Baptist Church

Formerly against cremation, the Baptist Church tacitly approves of it today. The Baptists follow the same rituals as the other Protestant churches, except for the English Anglican Church. The funeral services are held at the house of the deceased or in the church that the family belongs to, but a priest from another Christian church may be requested to conduct the services.

The Baptist Society (The Strict and Particular Baptist Society)

Burial rites are given to the dead. When a priest from their church is not available, a fellow church member or a minister of an Evangelical Protestant denomination may be asked to officiate. A Catholic father is never asked to officiate at the funeral in place of a Protestant minister.

Christian Science

Interment is legally performed, conforming to the wishes of the family and respecting general practices. Interment is never done at the church, and the memorial services are left to the discretion of persons concerned.

Christian Spiritualists

Burial is in accordance with general practices; however, in the case of cremation, it is deemed desirable that it be performed at least three to five days after death. Burial rites, performed mainly to provide comfort to the bereaved family, are accepted and under any Christian ritual. The Spiritualists see the human body as the vessel of the spirit, and they show little concern for the body that no longer houses the spirit.

Church of England (The Established Church)

Both cremation and burial rites are sanctioned. The funeral is conducted by the Anglican priest or by the minister of a church that is similar in doctrine. Those attending the services take part in the ceremony and sing hymns, recite passages from the Scriptures (Book of John: 11, 25, and 26; Book of Job: 19, 25-27; Paul's First Letter to Timothy: 6, 7; Song of Solomon: 90, 39, 130; Acts of the Apostles; (1 Corinthians: 15, 20-58; 2 Corinthians: 4, 16 to 5, 10)), read the Lord's Prayer, and receive Holy Communion. They also listen to the sermon of the officiating minister who eulogizes the earthly virtues of the departed, and gives a short period of silent prayer. The service closes with a parting hymn, which is sung by the entire congregation.

Churches of Christ

Burial is the common practice, but legal cremation is allowed. Funeral services may be conducted under the rules of any Christian church but an Anglican or a Free Church minister is preferred. The Churches of Christ have a cemetery for church members in Chetter and Soghall.

Congregational Church

The way the body is handled is left to the discretion of the bereaved family. When a Congregational church minister is not available to conduct the funeral, a minister from another Free church may fill in.

Eastern Orthodox Church

There are divisions such as the Greek, Polish and Serbian branches, but there is no great difference in funeral customs. The Greek branch members have exclusive use of a cemetery in London, whereas the members of the Serbian branch use a private cemetery at Cardiff.

Elim Church

The process of disposing of the dead is left to the discretion of the minister, but the selection of the grave is made by the bereaved family. Funeral services under other Christian churches are also allowed.

Free Church of England (Reformed Episcopal Church)

Burial is left to the discretion of the bereaved family, and the funeral service may be held under any Christian church ritual.

Free Presbyterian Church of Scotland

Cremation is prohibited, being deemed the custom of non-Christians. Funeral services need not be held, as long as Christian practice is adhered to when the body is buried. Importance is attached to the deceased's life-long relationships with the people around him or her.

French Protestant Huguenot Church

The church does not impose any special prohibitions regarding the manner of the disposition of the dead and conforms to general practices of other Free churches. Funeral rites are left to the discretion of the bereaved family. When a priest from their church is not available, the service may be conducted according to the practices of other Protestant Free churches.

Jehovah's Witnesses

This sect is also known under the names of International Bible Student's Association, Watch Tower Bible and Tract Society. Disposal of the body is left to the discretion of the members, who may seek funeral rites conducted by ministers of other Christian churches.

Lutheran Church

There is no particular opposition to cremation. There are cemeteries in Cardiff and in London for Norwegian members, but burial may be in any cemetery, and funeral rites may be conducted under Christian practices of other churches.

Methodist Church

There are no specific requirements for the disposition of the body. Burial, cremation or burial at sea may be chosen. When a pastor from the church is not available, any Protestant minister may be called to officiate at the funeral rites.

Moravian Church

Traditionally, disposal is by burial; however, the church is not opposed to cremation or burial at sea. This sect maintains private burial grounds, which are divided sectionally for males and females. Only one body is buried in each individual plot. Standardized tombstones, 18 inches by 24 inches, are uniformly inscribed with the name, age and the date of death. An Anglican or Free church minister may be asked to officiate at the funeral rites when a pastor of the Moravian Church is not available.

Evangelical Christian Churches

A burial service is observed with the usual customs. Prayers for the deceased are not said. A minister from another Protestant church may be asked to conduct the services when the minister of their church is not available.

Plymouth Brethren

This sect does not favor cremation.

Presbyterian Church in Ireland

A short service is held at the deceased's home before the funeral service at church. After the funeral rites are performed, an interment service is held at the burial ground. If their own pastor is not available, a Protestant minister may be asked to conduct funeral rites.

Presbyterian Church of Wales

Funeral rites are generally held both at the house of the deceased and at the grave. In the case that the deceased is a minister or a person of consequence, funeral services are held at the church using the Book of Common Prayer, which was prepared in conjunction with the Presbyterian Church of England. If a minister from their church is unavailable, one from another Christian church may be requested.

Roman Catholic Church

The church formerly opposed cremation. However, since 1963, when Pope Paul VI gave his official approval, cremation has been allowed, so long as it is not done deliberately to deny the teachings of the Catholic Church. After 1966, the restrictions against priests conducting services at the actual cremation have been eased.

As a general rule, funerals are held in the parish cemetery. When death occurs elsewhere, the services are held in the nearest Catholic church. Customarily, bodies of priests and nuns are buried in their parish church or burial in the church grounds of the town where they were born. Burial for the general church member takes place in the reserved burial grounds set aside for them by their church, or even in burial grounds elsewhere. Great importance is placed by Catholics on the sacrament for the dying. Only an ordained Catholic priest can perform the last rites for the dying. This denomination often refuses to perform funeral and burial rites for apostates, heretics, atheists, and criminals. These people are buried in unconsecrated ground.

On the occasion of the funeral services, the body is placed before the altar with the feet toward the sanctuary. In the case that it is a pastor, the legs face the transept. The priest attends and officiates at the burial rites.

Russian Orthodox Church

Burial is the general rule. Cremation is allowed, but the church does not approve of it. If still conscious, the dying must confess his or her sins in order to receive the last rites. After the body is washed, the priest makes the sign of the cross on the forehead, chest, hands and ankles. The body is clothed in a shroud, and icons are placed in the hands. Hymns are sung at the burial, and memorial services are held twice daily. Greek and Romanian churches permit their members to receive the last rites from Anglican priests, but are opposed to Free church ministers.

Serbian Orthodox Church

Except for death at sea, burial is obligatory. The body is usually buried 48 hours after death. Following the general practice of the Eastern Orthodox Church, the dying member confesses his or her sins and receives absolution. The body is washed, shrouded, and an icon is placed in the hands. Although Anglican funeral rites are accepted, the ritual of the Roman Catholic Church is not sanctioned. Also, the church will not conduct funeral rites for murderers and excommunicates.

Seventh-Day Adventists

There are no special regulations for the disposal of the dead. If a minister from the sect is not available, any minister from a Protestant church may be asked to officiate at the funeral.

Society of Friends

The Friends stress simplicity in the funeral rites. Thus, there are no flowers offered. The funeral is in the form of a memorial meeting, which is held by the bereaved family either at the grave or at the meeting house. Ever since churches of different sects denied the burial of members of the Friends church in their graveyards, the Friends have had their own private cemetery, but burials in public graveyards have become more common. The inscriptions carved on the tombstone are standardized with a name, age and the date of death.

Swedenborgian Church (The New Church)

There is little concern regarding the method of disposal for the body after the spirit has left it. Mourners read the Bible and pray either at the home of the bereaved family or at church that the soul of the deceased will ascend into heaven. The funeral is conducted with respect and simplicity.

Swiss Protestant Church

The funeral is conducted simply, avoiding ostentation. It follows the established regulations of the Christian church and holds a strong belief in the resurrection of the soul. The doctrine of this sect is most similar to that of the Presbyterian Church.

Unitarian and Free Christian Churches

The church is not opposed to cremation. It does not question whether one is baptized or whether one is a confirmed Christian. It does not accept the belief in the resurrection of the soul. When funeral services are conducted by officiants from other churches, the Unitarian and Free Churches are preferred.

United Free Church of Scotland

The church's funeral rites are based on the ceremony of the Anglican Church. However, the rites of any other Christian church are accepted if an Anglican minister cannot perform the funeral service.

Buddhism

The form of Buddhism that is followed for the funeral depends on the area in which one lives. Most Buddhists choose to be cremated, conforming with the ancient lore that the Buddha, after entering Nirvana, was cremated. Buddhists in the West do not particularly oppose cremation. Generally, monks and priests are asked to conduct services at funerals, and after the burial, the Buddhist Wheel of Law is carved on the tombstone. When Buddhist rites are not observed, a burial service is held, which excludes Christian-type elements or prayers, and those attending join together in reading from Buddhist Scriptures.

Hinduism

Cremation is the orthodox Hindu method of disposing of the dead. By following this method, it is believed that the spirit is released to ascend to the celestial sphere. When a Hindu living in England dies, after cremation, his ashes are sent to his family in India. At a later date, the ashes are cast into the Ganges River. In general, a Hindu priest is asked to officiate at the funeral, but if the family does not call a priest, it conducts its own memorial service.

Judaism

Funerals and burials are performed based on detailed regulations and are normally managed by the Jewish burial societies. The deceased is washed and wrapped in white cotton shrouds. If the deceased is male, a cap is placed on the head before the body is placed in the coffin.

Cremation is opposed, based on the Old Testament (Deuteronomy 11:23), and the burial must be conducted as quickly as possible. However, on the Jewish sabbath and holidays, (Saturdays) funerals are not held. There is no difference in the funeral rites held for the rich or the poor and, simplicity being the rule, there is no practice of offering flowers.

During the period between death and the completion of the burial, the deceased's family members must abstain from eating meat and drinking wine. They must wear mourning dress for one month. If the deceased is one's parent, the mourning period must be continued for a year.

Islam

Muslims believe that, after death, the spirit remains in the body for about three to forty days. Cremation, which is considered to be unclean, is not practiced. Soon after death, the preparations for burial begin. The face is turned toward the holy land of Mecca. An officiating leader is summoned to conduct a ceremony praising their god, Allah, and His Prophet, Mohammed. The funeral is held at the mosque or at the gravesite. There is a cemetery at Brookswood exclusively for Islamic followers.

Zoroastrianism (Parsees)

The body of the deceased is washed and clad in clean white garments, which include the sacred shirt. The materials must be inexpensive and no distinction is made between rich and poor, for in death all are equal. The whole of the body except the face must be covered, When it has been prepared for disposal the body should be touched only by professional bearers.

As stated, numerous religious organizations carry on these activities within England. Each organization recommends that the congregation that belongs to the churches in their jurisdiction conform to the funeral rites and practices based on their own doctrines. Nevertheless, since World War II, it is said that the number of people who have left the church is phenomenal.

It is said that, according to the Religious Public Opinion of the 1980's, England's total population of about 58,000,000 can be divided in the following manner:

Christians

Church of England	32,000,000	Protestants	8,600,000
Catholic	7,500,000	Other Christians	1,000,000

Non-Christians

Jews	460,000	Muslims	860,000
Hindu	380,000	Sikh	210,000
Buddhists	200,000		

However, these figures do not necessarily represent the number of faithful believers. For instance, only 15% (1985 Survey) of the adult members of the Church of England regularly attend services. Moreover, during the ten years after 1977, it is reported that about 500 churches attached to the Church of England fell into financial difficulties and 200 were eliminated, while 150 received financial aid from the church maintenance fund.

The Church of England is not the only church facing this type of rapid estrangement. It is probably a world-wide trend. In particular, the Church of England considered funeral practices a worldly matter and did not aggressively participate in them. Consequently, the local self-governing body and private mortuaries have taken over the major duties connected with funeral services. Churches and ministers were able to perform only supplemental roles, and in turn, this became one of the causes of the weakening of the economic base of the Church of England.

Increasingly, more people have left the church or have become non-religious, but when confronted by deaths in their families, they sometimes face the necessity of having a minister officiate at a funeral service of some kind. On such occasions, if they put in a request to the Humanists' Society of England, the Rationalists' Society of England or the Society of Non-Religionists, for a fee, a minister suitable to their needs is dispatched. However, a funeral service is not conducted, but often shortly after the burial or cremation, friends and relatives get together for a memorial service.

On the outskirts of Oxford, there is a military cemetery with the graves of German soldiers who died in World War II along with the graves of British soldiers.

GREECE

The Hellenic Republic of Greece is a country on the southern end of the Balkan peninsula. It includes many islands in the Aegean and Ionian Seas. Over 98 percent of the population are Greeks, who follow Greek Orthodoxy, which has penetrated deeply into the daily lives of the people.

When someone dies, the family takes a doctor's medical report to the government office and receives a death certificate. At the same time, the family must get a burial certificate from the police department. Additionally they must arrange with the church for a service and ask the funeral home to make the necessary preparations. The body is bathed and wrapped in a white cloth, called *savanon*, before it is placed in the casket, which is kept at the family home for

24 hours. Decorative flowers surround the body, and the forehead is wrapped with a band, called a small crown, bearing the images of Jesus Christ, the Virgin Mary and Saint John. Also an icon of Jesus Christ is placed on the chest. At the wake, people who were intimates of the deceased gather and recite a prayer, called *Trisagion*, for the deceased's eternal rest. Then the people read a part of the Psalms of David from the Old Testament. The Greek Orthodox funeral is elaborate.

The priest, dressed in the proper vestments, stands before the casket after it has been placed in the church. Then he praises the Lord and sings *Alleluia* in a mournful key. Then the assistant priest continues the prayers, and another hymn is sung in a minor key. The Gospel of John and congratulatory words are read. The priest places a tablet inscribed with these words into the hands of the deceased. This is said to be proof that the person's sins were forgiven when the deceased was judged by God. Following this, the choir sings the parting hymn, *Stihira*, and the priest reads the purgatorial prayer. Next, the priest says the last prayers and recites a poem that pleads for the deceased's eternal rest. Parting with the doleful melody *Eternal Memory*, the casket is taken out of the church. At the burial, mourners light candles and pray around the casket, which signifies that the deceased should seek the eternal light of heaven. After the burial ceremony performed by the priest, holy water is sprinkled over the body, which is then buried. Cremation is not customary in Greece. Three years after the burial the remains may be taken out of the grave and reburied.

The tombstones are varied in shape. There are many magnificent ones. In the First Cemetery near the Acropolis in Athens, the white marble tombstones are well worth viewing.

The religiously devout Greeks have a custom of eating a piece of bread and drinking wine as a token of forgiveness from Jesus when they leave a church or cemetery. The home of the bereaved family has a black flag placed outside to indicate that there has been a death in the family. In general, the mourning period is long for close relatives of the deceased. In the case of parents or siblings, the period is three years. In the case of distant relatives, the period is 40 days. Men wear black armbands and women wear black dresses and veils. Once in a while, a widow who has lost her beloved husband will wear black clothes for the rest of her life. In the case of a man who has lost a wife, the mourning period is only 40 days.

Among the Cyclades, death continues to be commemorated with a long mourning period (usually for three years) marked by periodic services (mnimosyna). At the end of this period, it is the custom on at least some of the islands to disinter the bones and place them in an ossuary, at which time the formal mourning period ends.

HUNGARY

The Republic of Hungary is in the central part of Europe and is bordered by five Eastern European countries. It was a partner country of the Austro-Hungarian Empire from 1699 to 1918, when Austro-Hungary was defeated in World War I and the monarchy collapsed. The history of Hungary's independent statehood in the 20th century from 1918 to the present day was interrupted by the German conquest during the World War II, then to some extent in 1949 when Hungary became a Soviet people's republic. In 1956 the only anti-communist revolution in history was carried out by the Hungarians and was defeated by Soviet troops. In 1989 liberalization and democratization developed, and Hungary started to adopt a Western European-style democracy At that time, its present name "the Republic of Hungary" was established.

The majority of the people are Magyars of Asian origin, who used to belong to the Catholic Church, but today the younger generation is not very religious. King Istvan I, the founder of the state, took up Christianity and was canonized by the Roman Catholic Church. He was crowned the king of the Christian Kingdom of Hungarians, which survived for a century until 1918. St. Istvan Church, erected in his memory in the heart of the Pest District of Budapest, was completed in 1905, and its impressive spire is a full 96 meters tall. At the front of this church hall is a statue of St. Istvan, the object of respect and prayer.

When someone dies, the family submits a report of the death with the doctor's death certificate. In the cities, a publicly operated funeral home prepares for the funeral. In the rural areas, old customs are still preserved. When someone dies in the village, the church bell is rung. If the deceased is Catholic, the family invites their priest to rub holy oil over the deceased. The feet of the deceased must be turned toward the doorway. Also, all of the windows are opened, while the doors of the cabinets and appliances must be kept shut. This symbolizes forcing the soul out of the house and along on its journey after death.

When the body is placed in the casket, some belongings are also placed in it. In the case of an unmarried woman, the deceased wears a wedding dress. Perhaps because the Magyars love bright colors, the casket is usually blue, green, red or white. Only the caskets for old people are black.

At the wake, drink is offered to the mourners. There was a time when a woman was hired to wail. The next morning, when the casket is carried out of the house, it goes head first; then the door to the house is opened and shut three times. Men with white and black spears lead the procession. The immediate family and relatives bury the body in the graveyard. After the burial, all the mourners must return home by roads other than those on which they came. At the family home, the mourners are treated to food and wine, and they talk about the deceased. However these customs are unfortunately being forgotten.

The tombstones that used to be built behind the graves were various shapes and colors. Today, there are only small standardized tombstones. Many people cremate the body and put the ashes in niche-type graves. In Budapest, there are several community cemeteries, and even in small villages there are usually several graveyards according to the religious composition of the population: Catholic, Protestant and Jewish. Many people visit these cemeteries throughout the day.

ICELAND

Iceland, which lies in the North Atlantic Ocean, is the world's northernmost island country and is famous for its glaciers and volcano. It is also one of the countries with the greatest life expectancy. Despite its latitude, the climate is temperate and its average atmospheric temperature is one degree centigrade because of the influence of the Gulf Stream. Immigrants from places like Norway and Denmark live in Iceland. The official language is Icelandic, and the national religion is Lutheran Church, which is followed by most of the inhabitants. The minister's honorarium and the greater half of the church maintenance are borne by the National Treasury. Since even the church-built schools receive assistance from the National Treasury, a church tax is levied upon its residents. Freedom of religion has, of course, been recognized, and a small number of the people belong to the Catholic Church, the Lutheran Free Church, the Pentecostal Movement and the Watch Tower. There are three public cemeteries in Reykjavik, the capital. A cemetery is called *Kircher Gardor*, meaning "church garden." In former times the corpse was buried, but now cremation has become more common.

When death occurs, a doctor's certificate is obtained and filed with the government office. In Reykjavik, the mortuary is kept busy conducting funerals at the church. The deceased is either buried in a cemetery or cremated and buried. Because Iceland is a cold land, many graves are simple cairns built with a cross.

Most modern Icelanders are confirmed in the Icelandic State Church, a major rite of passage. The clergy have social as well as religious roles. The church is tax-supported, but individuals who do not want to support the church may so indicate on their tax returns and their taxes are used for other purposes, such as the operational funds of the Icelandic University.

IRELAND

This Republic occupies the major portion of the island of Ireland. The majority of its people are Irish, and Catholicism is the dominant religion.

Dying Catholics receive extreme unction, one of seven sacraments a priest performs at the time of death. When someone dies, it is the custom for the family to place a white card with a black frame at the entrance to the home. This card is kept there until the funeral ends. The coffins are made of such woods as chestnut, elm and oak. Coffins made of metal are not commonly used, except when the body is being transported long distances.

It is a matter of course to report the death to the municipal office with a death certificate from a doctor. At the wake, the mourners usually visit the bereaved family's house and stay awake for a couple of days eating and drinking. This custom has been continued even today in the countryside, showing the people's intimacy when they most need to express their togetherness. The body is placed in a coffin and carried to the family church, and then it is buried after the funeral. Automobiles are used as transport to the cemetery for the mourners, who proceed in the following order: the family, the hearse, and then the other mourners. The priest recites the memorial address in both Gaelic and Latin, and the people pray with rosaries. The regulations concerning burial are almost the same as those in other European nations or the United States. For example, there are public cemeteries in the city of Dublin and its outskirts, a member of the Office of Health attends the funeral, and the coffin must be buried at least three-feet deep in the ground.

About 10 days after the burial, the head of the family usually puts a thank-you note in the local newspaper addressed to the mourners. The mourning period is about six months, during which time the members of the bereaved family must wear mourning clothes, black ties or other garments that signify that they are in mourning. They must also avoid attending social gatherings. The mortuary takes care of reporting the death to the municipal office, arranging things needed for the funeral, the hearse, the obituary and the burial. As for requesting the church and a priest, the family must do it directly. It is not customary to cremate the body, but if one insists on doing so, the body must be transported by boat to a crematorium in England, such as the one in Liverpool.

If the corpse must be preserved for three or four days, or be transported to a country overseas, it is necessary to embalm it and then to get a certificate from the medical examiner stating that the body is free of any contagious disease, as well as written permission to transport it.

The funeral is usually held at the home of the bereaved family, but occasionally it is held at church. In either case, the body is buried after the funeral. Recently, more people in Ireland have requested cremation, which may be due to British influence.

ITALY

Italy is shaped like a boot and extends out into the Mediterranean Sea. The majority of the people in Italy are Catholic, but with varying degrees of devotion to the faith. The young, especially, are rather non-religious.

In Italy, about 56,000 people (as of 1995) die each year. Catholics are expected to receive the extreme unction from a priest at the time of death. This practice is, however, gradually becoming a mere formality. In the case of death in a hospital, the body is taken back to the family and bathed. Afterward, the family puts a cloth over the body, which is then placed in the casket for the wake. During the wake, all the mourners say prayers with rosaries. The next morning, the family transports the body to the church. After the funeral mass, the priest leads the procession to the cemetery. The car is decorated with flowers, and the hearse and close relatives follow the family and priest by car.

The coffins are mostly made of oak, pine or mahogany. For burial in nearby cities, a coffin with boards thicker than 2.5 centimeters must be used, and the nails must be hammered in 20 centimeters apart. When a body is buried in a remote area, it is transported by car. In the 1920s in Milan, a black and white hearse transported the bodies. In Venice, the city of canals, even today a gondola or motorboat is used in place of a hearse.

Today in Italy there are about 4,000 privately operated mortuaries registered in the Italian Mortuary Union (in Verona), which was established in 1965. These mortuaries are small because most of the hearses and graveyards are public, and funerals are often held at a church or hospital. There are, however, public mortuaries as well.

Compared to the northern part, which is an industrial region, the people in the southern part of Italy, an agricultural region, are serious Christians and preserve their traditional customs. The older generations are especially devout. However, in spite of the fact that Italy is a country in which Catholics are most dominant, not many people attend church, even on Sundays. In the urban areas, the number of families asking the mortuary, the *Pompe Funebri*, for cremation has been increasing. In the rural areas, however, the funeral is held at a church, and the body is buried directly in the ground.

In Sicily, parents go back to their hometowns in order to visit the family graveyard. The cemeteries, *cimitero*, are usually on the outskirts of town, where cypress trees are planted. In the past, there were many family-unit mausoleums, but things have gradually been simplified, and as a result, there are more flat tombstones and niches.

In the rural areas cemeteries are operated by the church, whereas there are public cemeteries in the urban areas. The memorial cemetery near Porta Garibaldi Station in Milan is very beautiful and contains gorgeous white mausoleums and carvings neatly arranged in rows. The body of the deceased is usually buried in the ground, so although there are crematory chambers in the big public mortuaries in the urban areas, less than 1 percent of funerals involve cremation. The majority of the gravesites in the cemeteries are rented. Usually the lease is for 10 to 30 years. After 30 years the remains are removed and kept in the cinerarium.

People prefer to bring white chrysanthemums when they visit a cemetery. On November 1, All Saints' Day, cemeteries are thronged with visitors.

There are many historical funerary ruins in Rome, one of which is the catacombs under the Santa Maria Church on the street of Beneto in Rome, where the remains of about 4,000 Capuchin monks are held. These catacombs were built at the time of the Roman Empire when Christians were persecuted. Even around Rome the catacombs extend out over 100 kilometers. The catacombs were not only burial sites, but also underground holy places where Christians reinforced their beliefs. When Christianity was officially recognized in 313 A.D., churches and cathedrals were hurriedly built. The common people as well competed to be buried in such churches, but due to a shortage of space, only the wealthy or people with religious authority were allowed to be buried there. Underneath the Catholic churches built during medieval times, burial places for such people with epitaphs carved on the floor can be found. Visitors often nonchalantly walk over these floors. Santa Angelo Castle, which sits at the entrance to the Vatican by the Tiber River, was built in 139 A.D. and is where Roman emperors such as Hadrian are buried.

At Monte Casino, between Rome and Naples, there is a military cemetery for American, German and other soldiers who died in World War II.

Among the Sicilians, death notices are often released in the local press. They also observe the funeral services of the Roman Catholic liturgy. After the service, the deceased is placed on a bed of rose petals in the casket and is carried through town to the cemetery. The mourning period varies depending on the relation to the deceased. Traditionally, when a husband died, the widow wore black mourning clothes for the rest of her life.

LATVIA

The Republic of Latvia is named after its people, the Latvians. It is said that "Latvia" is from the word "*lav*" meaning "the land of the law." In August 1991 Latvia became completely independent of the former Soviet Union. In September of the same year, Latvia joined the United Nations. Among the three Baltic countries, Latvia is the most successful industrial country.

Predating World War II, there were influences from countries like Germany and Poland, and people mainly belonged to the Catholic or Lutheran churches. When Latvia was under Soviet rule, the authorities looked upon religion as an anti-communist force and tried to discourage it through the educational system and propaganda. Many churches were closed and worship activities were severely limited. However, in the 1980s many restrictions were dropped, and after years of decline, church attendance increased markedly. In 1994, there were 291 Lutheran churches, 192 Roman Catholic churches and 100 Russian Orthodox churches registered in Latvia.

Funerals are usually held in a cemetery. In Riga, the capital, there are several public cemeteries, the most famous ones being Raina and Mezza Kapi. The funeral services are taken care of by the private funeral directors called *Apbedisanas Birojs*.

LIECHTENSTEIN

The Principality of Liechtenstein is a small country surrounded by Switzerland and Austria. In 1867 it declared its permanent neutrality. The majority of its people are of Germanic descent, but there are also Italians and Spaniards. As Catholics are overwhelming in number, funerals are usually held in a Catholic church, and then the body is buried in a nearby cemetery.

When someone dies, the death certificate is issued by the attending medical doctor and the burial permit is issued by the Town House, *Rathaus*. Since there is one small public hospital, the country has concluded agreements with its neighboring Swiss and Austrian regions that ensure the availability of beds in hospitals there. There is only one private mortuary in Vaduz, called *Kintra Bestattungsinstitute*, which handles all kinds of funeral procedures. There is no crematorium in this country. If the bereaved family so wishes, the body is taken to a crematorium in Switzerland.

Traditionally, when a villager died, all work in the community was prohibited, and periods of wearing black in mourning were prescribed by degree of relation to the deceased. Now, the mourners, except for the bereaved immediate family members and relatives, attend funeral services at the church in ordinary clothes.

LITHUANIA

The Republic of Lithuania lies at the southern end of the three Baltic countries. In September 1991 it became independent. Many people follow Catholicism or Russian Orthodoxy.

When someone dies, the bereaved family must report to the Bureau of Civil Registration (*Civilires Metrikaajos Biurus*) with the death certificate issued by an authorized medical doctor.

The Lithuanian State Jewish Museum on Pamenkalnio Street in Vilnius, the capital, houses an exhibition that is a homage to the victims of the Holocaust. In the early 20th century, 40 to 50 percent of Vilnius's population was Jewish. However, during World War II, 94 percent of Lithania's Jews were exterminated by the Nazis.

In the suburbs of Siauliai, 140 kilometers north of Kaunas, there is an unusual Hill of Crosses, where for many years thousands of crosses have been planted by the Lithuanians as a memorial for the people deported to Siberia. In the Soviet era, the crosses were repeatedly bulldozed, but they were always replaced by the new ones.

LUXEMBOURG

The Grand Duchy of Luxembourg is a small country surrounded by France, Germany and Belgium. The official languages are Luxembourgish, German and French. Recently, there has been a resurgence of interest in learning and speaking Luxenburgesh, a local dialect of German with roots in the Moselle Frankish language once spoken in western Germany. Luxembourg is a constitutional monarchy governed by the Grand Duke or Duchess, a prime minister and a chamber of deputies. The majority of the people are Catholic.

Funerals are usually held in the church, and the body is buried in a nearby cemetery. If a private mortuary is used, it will take care of all the arrangements for the funeral and burial. There is only one crematorium in Luxembourg, which has been operated since 1995 by the Pompes Funerabres Erasmy at Hamm. Public cemeteries are usually located next to churches in all localities.

On the outskirts of Luxembourg, there is the American Military Cemetery where the remains of U.S. soldiers who died during World War II are buried. Set into the granite paving at the center of the memorial terrace in bronze letters is the following inscription from General Eisenhower's dedication of the roll of honor in St. Paul's Cathedral in London:

> All who shall hereafter live in freedom will be here reminded that to these
> men and their comrades we owe a debt to be paid with grateful remembrance
> of their sacrifice and with the high resolve that the cause for which they died
> shall live eternally.

In Clervau, 100 kilometers north of Luxembourg City, stands a monument in memory of the American soldiers who were killed or wounded in the Battle of Ardennes, one of the most hard-fought battles between the Allied Powers and the Nazis during World War II in Europe.

MACEDONIA

The Republic of Macedonia was one of the members of the Socialist Republics of Yugoslavia. Macedonia means "the plateau people" in ancient Greek. In September 1991, it declared its independence, but because Greece strongly opposed the use of the name "Macedonia" which comes from the Greek, Macedonia's entry into the United Nations was delayed. The country therefore tentatively named itself the Former Yugoslavia Macedonia Republic. The majority of the people are Macedonian Orthodox Christians.

The sister republic of Yugoslavia once accounted for 70 percent of Macedonian trade, and Serbia is still one of its strongest allies. Macedonians fought alongside the Serbs as partisans in the anti-Fascist forces in World War II, and Tito encouraged the development of the Macedonian language and culture.

Among the Slav Macedonians, the 12 days from Christmas to Epiphany are dedicated to the reverence of the dead, but there are also a substantial number of Slavic Muslims who fallow Islamic tradition.

MALTA

The Republic of Malta is a rocky island that lies in the center of the Mediterranean Sea. Since 1964 Malta has been an independent country. The majority of the islanders are Italian and Catholic. There are as many as 365 Catholic churches for a population of about 350,000. Generally the people speak Italian, but the official languages are English and Maltese.

Although Malta is a small nation, its location is geographically and militarily important. It became a trading post and functioned as the site of negotiations and meetings during World War II.

Because Malta is close to Italy, North Africa and the Middle East, it has been influenced by various cultures, and because of its historical background, the funeral customs of Malta also show various influences from Europe and Arab countries. When someone dies, the family and close relatives stay inside the house without using fire for cooking, light or heat for three days. During that time people from outside the home deliver food and drinks to the house. They also have the custom of hiring "crying women."

Until recently, the Maltese used to close the deceased's eyes and place a dish of salt on the stomach of the corpse. Women in the family would mourn for 40 days, and the men for 7 days. During the mourning period, they avoided going out of the house and combing their hair, and the bedroom lights were kept on at all times. These rules, however, have been simplified.

When someone dies, the family reports the death to the medical doctor and the police. They also place the notice of death at the corners of streets in town and announce it in the newspaper. Such business is taken care of by the mortuary, called *lehina*, and the funeral is held in a church. The public cemeteries are located on the outskirts of town. There are Roman Catholic, Protestant and Islamic cemeteries.

MONACO

The Principality of Monaco is located in the southeast of France near the Italian border. It is a resort country on the Mediterranean Sea. Monaco became a principality under the protection of France in 1861. The national religion is Roman Catholicism. Since the climate is mild all year around, and its citizens are exempt from taxes, rich people gather here from all over the world.

When one dies in Monaco, the preparations or arrangements for the funeral are taken care of by a private mortuary, and the funeral is held in a church. When the Princess of Monaco, the former actress Grace Kelly, died in 1982, the funeral was held in Monaco Cathedral, where the Prince and Princess had married. Her body was buried in the Royal Cemetery in Monaco.

NETHERLANDS

The Netherlands is situated in northwestern Europe and is known as the "land of dairy farming." As the meaning of its name, "the country underneath," suggests, one-fourth of its land is below sea level. There are vast agricultural lands, but the population density is high. The Dutch language, which resembles German, is the official language, but the languages of neighboring countries are also used. Although there are non-religionists, the majority of the inhabitants are Catholics or Protestants.

When death occurs, a doctor's examination certificate is filed with the government office, and a death certificate is received through the mortuary. The processing and filing of the obituary notice in the newspaper, the notification of the people concerned, the transferring of the body to the morgue, and other such duties are taken care of by the mortuaries of the family's religious sect or by their neighbors. The funeral is conducted at the church, the mortuary or at the grave site.

When the funeral is held at the church, the casket is placed near the altar, and the deceased's family members and closest relatives sit in the front row. On both sides of the aisle, gifts of flowers or wreaths, sent by various groups and old friends, are displayed. After the minister's prayers and sermon, the attendants from the mortuary, dressed in black top hats, black suits and wearing black gloves, silently remove the casket from the church and transfer it to the hearse and head toward either the cemetery or the crematorium as instructed by the will of the deceased or as desired by the family.

The hearse and following cars in the funeral procession, uninterrupted by traffic lights, move slowly through town. At the cemetery, often the minister reads from the *Book of Common Prayer*, but in the case of a non-religious ceremony, someone from among the mourners will greet the group and make a memorial address, followed by a representative of the family, who will express the family's gratitude. Before departing, the attendees never fail to shake hands with the family members saying, "*Ik Condoleer U*" (Please accept my sincere condolences).

After the burial, it is the practice to offer a light meal—usually only pieces of buttered bread with a slice of cheese between them and coffee. Processed meat is never served.

Today Holland has seven crematoriums. The cremated ash remains are placed in an urn, which is then placed in a grave or ossuary, but some are scattered on the gravesites of those without surviving relatives. Today, people do not wear black mourning clothes when attending funerals as they did in the past. Also there has been an increase in families declining floral offerings for the funeral. In such cases, the family clarifies this beforehand in the obituary notice.

In the 20th century, traditional or institutionalized mourning has lost much of its force, while the personal side of mourning has been accentuated and privatized. Whatever the belief of the individual he or she now dies or grieves in settings that are secularized and in process of being humanized.

NORWAY

The Kingdom of Norway, bordering on the Atlantic and Arctic Oceans, is known for its fjords, the narrow inlets of sea between cliffs and steep slopes. The Arctic Circle crosses the country, and most of northern Norway is located above it. Its climate is comparatively moderate, influenced by the warm currents of the Gulf Stream. The Norwegians are very practical and hardy people.

When there is a death, it must be confirmed by a doctor or by the hospital; the police and the church must be notified, then the mortuary is contacted. Mortuaries are privately operated, and, if requested, they will take the necessary steps to expedite the funeral. Burial or cremation must take place within eight days. It is not common to hold a wake at the family's house. After the death, the undertaker takes custody of the body until the funeral takes place. Funerals, therefore, will usually be held within eight days regardless of the time of year. Although mourners wear black mourning clothes when they attend the funeral, it is the custom to purchase colorful wreaths and floral sprays to be delivered by the florist to the church.

During the winter, an electric thawing machine is used to dig the grave. Though in recent times, the number of cremations has exceeded the number of burials. The cemetery is on a rental agreement plan, but if a set period has passed without a renewal of the plan, the remains are removed to be buried with other bones. The tombstone is also removed.

POLAND

The Republic of Poland is on the Baltic coast of Europe. Most of the flat land area is at an elevation of less than 300 meters. The climate is very unstable, because the continental climate meets there with the oceanic climate. Poland has had a bitter and miserable history due to its location. The majority are Polish and the national language is Polish. It is a very monolithic country and even today 90 percent of the population are Catholic.

The country has always been embroiled in the power struggles of the countries that border her to the east and west. In the 1989 election, the first liberal election in Eastern Europe, the first government led by a non-communist power was established and Poland became one of the most liberated countries in Eastern Europe.

When someone dies, the death is reported to the government district office with a doctor's medical certificate, and a public mortuary takes care of the funeral as well as other related matters such as obtaining permission for burial and transporting the body. A flower wreath is placed at the entrance of the bereaved family home to indicate there has been a death in the family, then a minister is called to give extreme unction. Also, it is customary to place money and gifts in the casket because many believe that the soul of the deceased has need for such things in the afterlife.

Normally, three days after the death, the casket is moved from the house to the cemetery in a funeral procession. Many people die in hospital, nowadays, so their bodies are carried directly by a hearse from the hospital to the cemetery. The funeral is held in the chapel of the cemetery and then the body is buried.

The body is usually buried in the ground, but there are also some local places where the body is cremated if the deceased or the family requests it. In the cemetery, there are niche-type graves in the ground and also underground graves over which stand unique personalized tombstones.

The people of Poland never forget about war victims. In Saski Park in front of Victory Square is the Tomb of the Unknown Soldier. One always finds flowers there. Especially on August 1, which is the anniversary of the Liberation, memorial services are held at various places around the country.

Representative cemeteries include Povonski Cemetery, the Jewish cemetery next to the Povonski, and a large cemetery for unknown soldiers near Parmili Village in Campinos. On All Saints' Day on November 1, graveyards are covered with snow and a bright sea of candle light.

Approximately 60 kilometers southwest of Krakow are the ruined concentration camps of Birkenau, Trelinka and Auschwitz. During World War II, thousands of Jews, resistance fighters, and prisoners of war died there. The systematic mass murder that took place claimed victims from all over Europe. On the sites of the concentration camps there are photo displays and film material from the camp archives. The camp of Birkenau has been left as it was. The Treblinka memorial in honor of the 800,00 victims of Fascism was erected by the architect Adam Haupt and the sculptor Franciszek Duszenko in 1964.

The traditional Pomak religion retains Christian and pre-Christian elements, and is grounded in the agricultural cycle. Therefore, rituals such as weddings and funerals combine elements of both Christian and pre-Chrisitan practice.

PORTUGAL

Portugal is a country in southern Europe. On one side is Spain and on the other side a mountainous shoreline. The climate is mild and warm. The majority of the people are Portuguese, a mixture of various races such as the Iberian and the Celtic. The national language is Portuguese, and the majority of the people are Catholic.

When someone dies in Portugal, the death is reported to the Registro de Obito with a doctor's medical report. The wake takes place at the family home, and then the funeral takes place at the church. The body is usually buried in the ground, but there is also a crematorium in Lisbon.

The Portuguese funeral customs are similar to those in Spain. However, whereas the body must be buried within 48 hours in Spain, in Portugal the burial usually takes place after more than 48 hours. Except for the case of celebrities or bodies that have to be transported to distant places, it is rare that the body undergoes any preservative treatment.

Coffins are made at a factory that is run exclusively by the mortuaries. The materials used for the coffin are usually mahogany, oak or pine. Some coffins are very beautiful and elaborately engraved. In some cases, the cross, the candle stands, the coffin with its attachments and the altar are all made of metal, and are rented out for the wake. The cloth cover for the casket is black or purple velvet. An unusual thing is that at the wake, everything hanging in the room is hung upside-down or placed inside-out.

The hearse used to be pulled by eight horses, which looked very elegant. Today, however, automobiles are used. The first car is for the minister in charge of the funeral. Then the hearse and the cars with the mourners, wearing black, follow. At the funeral or burial, chrysanthemums and wreaths are offered in memory of the deceased.

Seven cemeteries are operated by the city of Lisbon. The cemeteries, however, have become too crowded, so remains that have been buried for five years are exhumed and placed in niches or underground graves with the remains of others. Many of the graves of rich people are constructed in a mausoleum style. All Saints' Day is an occasion for special reverence to departed loved ones, and the cemeteries bustle with people bearing flowers.

In the villages, the tolling of church bells inform villagers that a neighbor (*vizinho*) has died. In some areas, the gates and doors of the deceased's home are opened inviting neighbors to offer their condolences. Relatives also gather there to wail. There are also several burial societies (*confrarias*) to help defray the costs of the funeral and commemorative masses that continue for several years after death.

On the island of Madeira, which is situated off the western coast of Africa, there is no crematorium. Those who wish to be cremated must be shipped to Lisbon. In Funchal city, Funerarias Madrilenas will handle such services.

ROMANIA

Romania is located in the northeastern part of the Balkan peninsula. The topography of the land is quite varied. The majority of the people are Latin Romanians, but there are also Magyars and Germans.

In the past, many followed Romanian Orthodox Church, one of the branches of Greek Orthodox Church, and the country's traditions and customs were well preserved. After Romania became a socialist country, such customs began to be forgotten. In 1989, there were anti-government demonstrations in the central part of eastern Europe. The crisis spread all over Romania, and the Ceausescu government collapsed, leaving the real power in the hands of the National Salvation Front.

When someone dies in the capital, Bucharest, a public funeral home and the relatives take care of the funeral and prepare for a service in the cemetery (*Cimitirul Bellu*) for the immediate family. In the rural areas, neighbors assist the family. After giving the body its last bath, they dress it in its best clothes and put candles and an icon of Jesus Christ in the deceased's hands. Then the body is positioned for the wake with its feet toward the doorway.

Most of the priests and a cantor from the church join the funeral when it is held in the middle of the family's yard. After the funeral, the mourners, dressed in colorful ethnic attire, march to the graveyard. The procession is led by a flag at half mast and flower wreaths, as the mourners carry candle stands and the casket. A band may play mourning hymns along the way. Upon the grave, they place a wooden cross. After the funeral, the family treats the mourners to ring shaped bread at their home. When someone dies in a remote place, the grave may be located in the deceased's hometown. When death was due to a traffic accident, a cross used to be erected at the site, but that custom is not very common now.

In the village of Sapuntza in the Malamresh District, a man called Stan Batrash makes unique tombstones. His products are very colorful and indicate the deceased's occupation. Batrash has been working on tombstones on his own since 1935.

SAN MARINO

The Republic of San Marino is a small country in the Chita Mountains on the Italian peninsula. It is protected by and dependent on Italy. The population is approximately 20,000, and the majority are Catholics. Generally funerals are held at a Catholic church in the city of San Marino, the capital.

SLOVAK REPUBLIC

In 1918, the country was founded as Socialist Czechoslovakia, but in 1989 the Communist Party, which ruled the country, collapsed. As a result, the Slovak Republic, which lies close to Hungary, became independent from the Czech Republic in January 1993.

Many Slovakians are Catholic and believe in an afterlife. Burials are primarily inhumations in conventional cemeteries. Pre-Christian Slovaks cremated the dead and placed the ashes in ceramic urns, which were interred with grave goods of various types, and then covered with clay and stone mounds. In the recent past, the deceased was washed and prepared for burial at home. A wooden coffin was made as soon as possible and brought to the house. The family then kept vigil with the corpse through the night. Visitors came to pay their last respects the next day, at which time religious services would be held in the church and then the coffin would be carried off for burial. Normally, a funeral procession would form and walk through the village, accompanied by the village band.

SLOVENIA

The Republic of Slovenia, which lies near Austria and Italy, was a part of the

Socialist Republics of Yugoslavia, but in August 1992 it became independent. Slovenia is an industrial country, and among the former Socialist Republics of Yugoslavia, it has the highest standard of living and is relatively stable and peaceful.

Since Slovenia has traditionally identified with the alpine countries such as Austria and Italy to the west than its Balkan neighbors, there are many Catholics. Funerals follow traditional Catholic customs. The body is placed in an open coffin in the house for 48 hours while friends and relatives pay a visit and sprinkle holy water or salt on the deceased. This is followed by the funeral mass at the church, a graveside benediction by the priest, the burial, and then the funeral feast. For eight days thereafter friends visit the family of the deceased and pray, eat, and drink together. Finally, there are additional requiem masses 13 and 18 days later.

SPAIN

The Kingdom of Spain is located in the southwestern corner of Europe and occupies most of the Iberian peninsula, the Balearic Isles in the Mediterranean and the Canary Island chains. Although most of the people are Catholic, the influence of the Catholic Church on personal behavior has declined.

When someone dies in Spain, the death must be reported to the Registro Civil with a doctor's medical certificate. After the legal proceedings are completed, the funeral is arranged. The deceased's body must be buried within 24 to 48 hours. If the burial is delayed, the body is required to be frozen and preserved.

Although many in the urban areas are not very religious, they are customarily Catholic and call a Catholic priest in order to receive extreme unction. The preparations for the funeral are made by the mortuary. At the wake, candles are lit around the casket, and flowers are offered. Mourners say words of sympathy and condolence to the family, and then bid farewell to the deceased through a small window in the casket. In the past, the wake was held at the family home, and the funeral mass was held the following day in the church. After the mass, the people would proceed to the cemetery.

Nowadays, however, in the big cities both the funeral and mass are often held in the mortuary. In order to meet this demand, Madrid has built a public funeral assembly hall in Sui de Caravanchel Cemetery. About 10 percent of those brought to this assembly hall now use its crematorium (another is in Barcelona), and the number is increasing despite the Catholic tradition. The mortuaries are either privately or semi-publicly operated, and they take care of the necessary business related to the funeral for the family. There are two kinds of interment: one is the burial of the body directly in the ground after the wake and the funeral, and the other is the burial of the body in the cemetery ground after the funeral held in the church. In either case, it is expected that the casket will be carried into the cemetery by hearse, followed by relatives and friends. It is necessary for the minister and members of the mortuary to attend the funeral.

Most of the cemeteries in the cities are public, and there are two kinds of graves: niches, which are above the ground, and those underground. In either case, people have a choice of purchase or rental, and there are a variety of styles of tombstones. Rich people usually have ornate tombstones, but compared with the tombstones of the Italians, who have shared the same Latin culture, the tombstones in Spain are rather simple.

Exhumation is not allowed for two years in the case of a natural death, and for six years in the case of death from an epidemic disease. Funeral masses are usually held on the third day, the seventh day and one year after the burial. It is common for the people to visit the cemetery with flowers on November 1, All Saints' Day and on November 2, All Souls' Day.

In the Canary Island chain, which is situated off the western coast of Africa, there are quite a number of Hindu immigrants from India who wish their bodies to be cremated at the time of the funeral. There are crematoriums at Las Palmas on Grand Canary Island and Santa Cruz City on Tenerief Island. Each city has Pompas Funebres that handles all kinds of funeral services.

SWEDEN

The Kingdom of Sweden is located in the eastern half of the northern European Scandinavian peninsula. More than half of its land, which extends from north to south, is a forest zone. In winter the nights are long, and in the summer the nights, called "nights of the midnight sun," are short. Public welfare is scrupulously practiced. Most accept Swedish as the official language; a small portion of the people speak French or Lappish. The Lutheran Gospel Church is the national religion, and the inhabitants pay church taxes to the government, which pays the salaries of the clergy.

When there is a death, the doctor's medical certificate must be filed with the census registration office or the nearest police department. A burial permit is then issued and either a private or a semi-public mortuary is solicited to undertake the funeral arrangements. A coffin that meets one's specifications and budget can be selected from the mortuary catalog, which carries a variety of caskets from cheap pine to expensive beechwood coffins.

When cremation is desired, the cremation certificate, attested to by the doctor, must be obtained from the Police Department. When burial is desired in other than a public cemetery, a burial permit must be secured from the Real Property Division of the regional office. If a church member buries the body in the family church cemetery, there are no costs; generally, however, the gravesite must be bought or leased in a publicly operated cemetery.

The notice of death may be sent to the local newspaper or may be sent out individually. This may be taken care of for the family by the mortuary.

Male mourning clothes include a black dress suit and white tie, and a black mourning band is worn around the left arm. Females wear a black gown and a black veil. It is the custom to send, direct from the florist to the funeral site, a flower wreath with a short note of sympathy, with a pennant in the colors of the Swedish flag of blue and yellow attached.

In the church, the family members sit on the right side, while the other mourners sit on the left side. The minister's readings include, from the Old Testament, Psalms 103, Psalms 130:1-6, Psalms 139: 23, 24, and from the New Testament, John 11: 25, 26; 1 Corinthians 15: 20-58. The music most often used is Handel's Funeral March.

After the funeral services, the attendees move from the church to the cemetery for the burial. The procession moves in the following order: the hearse, the car with the flower wreaths, the cars carrying the immediate family members, close relatives and other mourners. During the burial, after the minister offers prayers, he shovels three spades of soil on the coffin, and the assembled mourners then offer flowers. In the case of cremation, prayers are offered by the coffin; then the coffin is slowly lowered to the strains of a funeral march to the basement cremation furnace. A light meal is served at the family home after the service, sometimes even supper is offered.

At present in the urban areas as well as in the remote areas, cremations are more common, and burials are more common in the rural areas. In Lapland, the ground is frozen for half the year, so burials are practically impossible. Those who desire burial preserve the body by freezing it. Within the country, there are crematoriums in some 20 or more places which are run by the Church of Sweden. In the capital city of Stockholm, there is a crematorium in the Subranka Public Cemetery and also one in the modern Ensukado Public Cemetery, which was recently built in the suburbs and was designed by Gunal Aspurando.

There is a plot on a hill at the Ensukado Cemetery where, in keeping with the expressed wish of the deceased and the family, the ashes can be scattered. However, not a single grave marker can be found there, showing the Swedes' practical side. To avoid the sinking of the ground caused by the foundations of the gravestones, the law provides that headstones in public cemeteries may not be set up until six months after the burial. A 25-year lease agreement is available and can be renewed. Recently, many people tend toward the choice of a family grave that can contain two to four bodies instead of a single grave.

In Sweden, the bereaved family makes contributions to the Elderly Welfare Fund, which includes money from funerals and from the inheritance from the deceased. This fund was established in May 1921 and, since then, many homes (apartments) for the elderly have been built on Stockholm city lands.

The Saamis and the Tornedalians in the north still practice a traditional funeral service. Immediately after a death, the family, neighbors and close friends gather around the deceased, in his or her home. Afterwards the formal funeral takes place in the church.

SWITZERLAND

The Swiss Federation is located in the foothills of the Alps, the "roof" of Europe. Switzerland is a tourist resort known for its scenic beauty, and its terrain is spotted with lakes and marshes. It has the reputation throughout the world for being the cleanest country and for its management of its public facilities. The majority of the people are of German origin. Some are of French, Italian and late Romansh origin as well. German, French, Italian and Romansh are spoken. In Switzerland, a country of religious freedom, it is hard to generalize, but the Germans are usually Protestants and many of the French, Italians and Romansh are Catholics.

When there is a death, a doctor's death certificate is obtained, then the mortuary makes all the legal arrangements for the family and organizes the details of the funeral rite and burial. Normally, people view the deceased in the hospital mortuary, and before cremation or burial, a funeral service takes place at the deceased's church. The law states that 48 hours must pass after death before cremation or burial can take place. The proportion of those who choose cremation to those who choose burial is nearly even, and there is a crematorium in most cities.

The mortuary service fee is more than 2,000 francs (as of 1995) and includes the transportation of the body, the preparation and filing of documents, the cremation and the urn, among other things, but this does not include the cost of the casket and the honorarium for the celebrant. Unless specifically requested by the family, the body is encoffined without taking any measures for the cosmetic preservation of the body. Generally, the body is clothed in a white-laced shirt and a specially made pillow is placed beneath the head. On occasion, in certain places, a local self-governing group will prepare the coffin without charge. Because cremation is so widespread within the German-speaking area, a simple coffin lined with cotton is used. However, a deluxe casket lined with silk or velvet may also be purchased.

When the bereaved family does not desire to purchase a grave, there are also cemeteries without a burial fee. Generally after a period of 20 years the remains are transferred to an unclaimed grave section. The family grave is leased for 50 years, after which time renewal is possible.

Among the Swiss Italians and the Swiss Romansch, the funeral rites are shaped by the Cathoric tradition. In villages today the deceased is no longer kept at home until the funeral, and wakes are less common. A community home is now used for this purpose. The bodies are interred at public cemeteries.

VATICAN

The Vatican City State is located in Rome. Although the Vatican seems far from our image of a "nation," it is a miniature-size country with a population of fewer than 1,000 people and the pope as the nation's sovereign. It became independent from Italy after the signing of the Lateran Treaty in 1929, and at present the Vatican has diplomatic relations with over a hundred countries. The center of the nation is St. Peter's Basilica, the headquarters of the Roman Catholic Church. The foundation of the present cathedral was laid in 1606 at the site of the early basilica, which was started in the 4th century by Constantine and completed in 1656. There are graves of former popes, starting with St. Peter, a disciple of Jesus.

The daily life of the people actually depends on the city of Rome. When a priest dies, the funeral is arranged by a mortuary in Rome. There is only one old German graveyard behind the cathedral, where priests other than the popes are buried. There is no other cemetery in Vatican City.

YUGOSLAVIA

Yugoslavia is located in the southeastern part of Europe on the Balkan peninsula facing the Adriatic Sea. A large part of the land mass is mountainous. Plains are found only in the north along the Danube River. Yugoslavia is a socialist country that consists of six republics. The majority of the people are the Serbians and Croatians. There are also Slovenians, Macedonians, Montenegrins and other ethnic groups with different languages.

Since World War II, religious concerns have abated, but in the Serbian and Montenegrin areas people follow Serbian Orthodox Church, which derives from Greek Orthodox Church, whereas in the northern area and the coastal areas of the Adriatic Sea, the people follow Islam. Freedom of religion is recognized as long as it does not conflict with national policy.

When someone dies, the family reports the death to the government district office and receives assistance with the funeral and burial from the funeral officers. The majority of the burials consist of interment, but in the capital of Belgrade about 25 percent choose cremation. There are about 10 graveyards, which are separated according to religion. The notification of death is made possible with a black-framed picture on the community bulletin board. They used to ring the church bell five times, if the deceased was a male, and two times, if female, in order to inform neighbors of the death. At the deceased's house, women weep, and candles are kept lit throughout the night. Then the funeral is held and the body is buried in the family grave. The funerals are usually held the day after death, which continues to serve an important integrative function both in terms of lineage recall and lineage solidarity. Large graveyard feasts are traditionally held one week, 40 days, six months and one year after the death.

The mourning clothes are generally black, but in the Bosnian area women wear white. The mourning period is one year, during which time joyful events must be avoided. Once it was taken as a sign of good behavior to allow one's hair and beard to grow, but the custom is rare now. Among the followers of Serbian Orthodox Church, there is a saint's day called *Sraba* to protect the family. On memorial days, the people make a ring-shaped bread and invite their relatives and friends to their home.

The people also used to believe that if someone suffers when he or she dies, it is because he or she is paying the price for the sins committed during life. Moreover, the people believe that if someone dies with the eyes open, he or she will become a vampire. Also, the place where someone dies is considered to be impure, so the priest must purify it with holy water and incense.

In Belgrade, there is a mausoleum of former president Josip Broz Tito, who founded the country, on a hill in Topchitel Forest Park. Roses are in bloom year-round, and there is an endless stream of visitors to the park.

CHAPTER 6

Commonwealth of Independent States

ARMENIA

After the collapse of the Soviet Union, the Republic of Armenia declared its independence in September 1991. Armenia made Christianity the national religion as early as 301 A.D., but it subsequently came under the rule of the overwhelming forces of the Romans, Persians, Sarasens, Mongols and Turks. After the Russian Revolution, Armenia regained its independence, but it joined the Soviet Union. Since the dissolution of the Soviet Union, the Armenians have been fighting with their neighbors, the Azerbaijanis. The majority of the people follow Armenian Orthodox tradition.

When someone dies, the death is reported to the Civil Registration Office (ZAGS) with a death certificate issued by the attending medical doctor. The funeral (*pokhorony*) then takes place at a nearby graveyard, where the mourners bow deeply three times to show respect for the dead. The men of the bereaved family are prohibited from shaving or cutting their hair until the fortieth day after the death. Food, alcoholic beverages and flowers are common offerings for the dead.

AZERBAIJAN

Situated on the western coast of the Caspian Sea, the Republic of Azerbaijan was the first Soviet Republic to declare independence in 1991. In December 1991, Azerbaijan became self-reliant after the Soviet Union collapsed. Because its neighbor, the Nagorno Karabakh Autonomous Oblast, declared its independence from Azerbaijan, the two have been at war. The majority of the people are Azerbaijanis and followers of Islam.

Today Azerbaijan is more than three-quarters Shiite, less than one-quarter Sunni Islam. Therefore, Islamic ceremonies in mourning and burial appear to be practiced universally. A commemoration is held on the fortieth day after death.

BELARUS

The Republic of Belorussia (Belarus) is a flat country that spreads across the Russian plain. The name originated from the Slavic word "*bela*" meaning "white." At the beginning of 1991, Belarus became independent as the "White Russian Republic," but in September of the same year the name returned to "Belorussia." The majority of the people are Byelorussians, and they follow either Russian Orthodox Christianity or Catholicism.

The traditional funeral rites included many magical elements. The dead person was buried on the third day after death. Salt, a pipe and copper coins were usually put into the coffin. After the funeral and on the sixth, ninth and fortieth days, and half a year after the memorial, ritual dinners (*trapeza*) were held at the bereaved family's home. *Kutsa* (a sweet barley porridge) would always be prepared for these events.

GEORGIA

The Republic of Georgia is a mountainous country on the shore of the Black Sea. After the collapse of the Soviet Union, Georgia declared its independence in April 1991. The majority of the people are Georgians, who follow the Georgian Orthodox Church or Islam. The Georgians are very resentful of the Russians, and there has been continuous rebellion.

The Georgians prefer to die in the company of their families and be buried in their native land. As a person is dying, relatives place a bowl of water beside the bed and open a window so the soul can be clean and fly away.

KAZAKHSTAN

The Republic of Kazakhstan is an inland country in the northern half of Central Asia. After the dissolution of the Soviet Union, Kazakhstan joined the Socialist Soviet Republics in December 1991. The population is made up of mostly Russians and the Kazakhs.

The Kazakhs observe funeral services that are a mixture of Muslim customs with pre-Islamic beliefs. The relatives and neighbors of the deceased take part in the funerary ceremonies by placing the deceased, washed and wrapped in a white shroud, into a separate yurt specially put up for this event and keep constant attendance until the burial. Those who gather for the funeral pray under the guidance of a *mullah*.

The Russians who settled here follow the Russian Orthodox tradition.

KYRGIZTAN

The Republic of Kyrgiztan is a mountainous country in the southern part of Central Asia. After the collapse of the Soviet Union, Kyrgiztan joined the Soviet Socialist Republics. The population is mainly made up of Kirgiztanis and Russians, who follow Sunni Islam or Russian Orthodox tradition.

The Kyrgiztans practice standard Islamic ceremonies and rituals. The Sufi orders have their own *murshids* (leaders), who take care of Islamic ceremonies and rituals. The wealthy and the politically powerful hold large, well attended ceremonies to commemorate the death of a family member.

MOLDOVA

The Republic of Moldova is an inland country surrounded by the Ukraine and Romania. The name of the country is associated with the river Moldova, which flows through the eastern part of Romania. The Moldovans are pro Romania, but are very resentful of the Russians. Moldova became independent in August 1991. The majority of the people are Romanian Moldovans, many of whom follow Russian Orthodox tradition.

When there is a death in Moldova, the dead are dressed in their best clothes. Young unmarried women are buried in a wedding dress. The corpse has to be watched during a three-day-and-three-night vigil. As death is seen as a voyage, a silver coin is often placed on the chest or in the hand of the dead person, to pay the customs for passage into the other world. The body is placed in the grave and the priest pours a bottle of wine over the body in the form of the cross. The traditional food prepared for a funeral is called *coliva*, which is made of cooked wheat, sugar and lemon peel. Nine days, 40 days, and six months after the death, and then once a year, memorial services are held for the dead.

RUSSIA

The Russian Federation occupies half of the Eurasian continent from Europe to Asia. The majority of the people are Russian, and some are of Asian descent.

Before the dissolution of the Soviet Union, because of the anti-religious policy of the communist government, the number of religious believers had become very small. However, so long as believers did not violate national policy, freedom of religion was allowed. Among the older generations, many still follow the Russian Orthodox Church or Islam. Kroedof, chairman of the Council for Religious Affairs, said in *The Literary Newspaper* that 9 to 10 percent of the adult population were active followers, and that half of them were Russian. Since the collapse of the former Soviet Union, Russia has had both social and economic problems. Because of the failure of the Communist Party, which was the hope of the people, many are now in a state of anxiety. As a result, the Russian Orthodox Church, which provides spiritual and moral support, has begun to regain its influence and authority.

When someone dies, the death has to be reported to a nearby government district office, called the *Pokhoron-noe Byuro,* with the death certificate. This office also functions as the national mortuary, which helps the family to prepare for the funeral.

At the time of death, candles are lit and placed around the casket. The family, relatives and friends gather around the casket and kiss the deceased. In general, interment is considered the preferable form of disposal. According to Russian Orthodox custom, the family, relatives and friends get together after seven days, forty days and a year, to hold memorial services. At this time, some vodka is poured into the deceased's glass, and all the participants drink vodka and make toasts. An iron fence is placed around the graveyard to keep out wild dogs. Also, candles are lit when the gravesite is visited. Recently, graves have become less elaborate and locker-style niches are being built in different areas around the country.

Usually, only close relatives and friends join the family at the wake. In cities like Moscow, most funerals are held in a funeral home with a crematory. Such a funeral home also has a publicly operated cemetery. The funeral is generally non-religious and simple. The head of the deceased's union reads messages of condolence and a representative of the family expresses their thanks to the mourners. If the family wishes, they may also invite a band to play music like Grieg's *Peer Gynt* and Chopin's *Funeral March.* The funeral expenses depend upon such things as the material of the casket and the number of musicians.

Currently, systematic funerals are common in Russia. The casket is placed on a table in the middle of a funeral hall, and the mourners line up in the hall. Then the casket is sent down to the basement crematory chamber on an elevator, while funeral music is played by a band. After several hours, an urn containing the ashes is given to the family. After that, the ashes are buried in a cemetery. This type of crematorium is found in such places as the Donskoi or Nikolisko Arhangelskoi Public Cemeteries in Moscow.

In Moscow, finding a site for a graveyard has become difficult, so cremation is popular. Also, because existing cemeteries are full, publicly operated cemeteries have been built in the suburbs, in places such as Habinska, Kalinin, Stalin and Wagankovskoi. In the cemeteries, same-size niches are neatly arranged.

Many buy flowers at the flower shops by the entrance of the cemeteries and visit the graves of famous people. Especially on Easter Sunday in the Russian Orthodox Church, one of the Sundays from April to May, people visit cemeteries with specially baked round bread called *creech,* colored eggs and bouquets of flowers. In Zagorsk, which is about 70 kilometers northeast of Moscow, is the Troitz Sergei Monastery, the headquarters of the Russian Orthodox Church, where the devout followers come during Easter and other religious holidays.

In the case of important people, like the former president of the Soviet

Union, Leonid Brezhnev, a grand funeral is held in Red Square. Then the body is buried in a special cemetery behind Lenin's mausoleum, and a statue of the deceased is placed on the grave. According to the importance of the person's contribution to the country, the body may also be buried in historically important cemeteries like the one belonging to the Nobodevici Monastery. Elaborate tombstones are built for VIPs, but otherwise tombstones are generally simple.

Nikolai Lenin's mausoleum at the Red Square in Moscow is still in good shape, although there are no longer parades of changing guards or long lines of visitors. There is speculation that in the near future his mummified body will be transferred to the Bolkovo Cemetery and buried beside his mother's grave there.

Throughout the country, cemeteries contain graves of unknown soldiers who died during World War II. Most of the graves are obelisk types, and in front of the graves burn eternal flames. Also, colorful flower wreathes lie in offering. It is a custom for couples who have just been married in the government marriage hall to pay a visit to this kind of cemetery. In Moscow, there is a graveyard for unknown soldiers near the walls of the Kremlin. Brides with white veils and flower bouquets and their bridegrooms were often seen by graveyards such as Lenin's mausoleum in Red Square.

In the suburbs of St. Petersburg, which faces the Baltic Sea on the western side of Russia, one finds the vast Piscarior State Cemetery. It was built in honor of the more than 400,000 people who died of starvation in the city during World War II, when the German army surrounded it and cut off the supply lines that brought food in. There are no tombstones or crosses, just concrete plates with the dates of death. Near the center of the cemetery, a tombstone marks the grave of the poet Olga Bergolitz; its epitaph says, "*I will not forget even one person; I will not forget anything.*" There is also a statue of Mother Russia there. At the end of Nevskii Avenue, next to the Alexander Nevskii Monastery, there is a famous cemetery where the remains of Dostoyevski and Tchaikovski are buried.

When a foreigner dies in Russia, a doctor must determine the cause of death. As a rule, the same ambulance that takes the doctor to the dying can take the body to the morgue of an "on duty" hospital, where a pathologist examines the body. Deaths are registered at the Civil Registration Office (ZAGS).

The Outlying Districts of Russia

In Central Asia, there are about fifty million Muslims, and even under national control, they have kept their own beliefs and customs, being separated from other Slavic peoples. When a Muslim dies, the funeral is held in a mosque. Muslims prefer to be buried in a graveyard exclusively used by followers of Islam. Once the government tried to bury some non-Muslim Kazakh soldiers, who died in Afghanistan, in the public cemetery in Almaty, but the people protested violently, and the situation escalated into a near riot.

The Jews and Buddhists there also follow their own customs. Most Jewish people live in the western part of Russia, but there are also some communities for Jewish immigrants from these parts in Central Asia. Buddhists are found in places like the Bryat Self-Governing Territory, centering around Ulan Ude, and they adhere to their own beliefs and customs.

In Siberia, there are many Asian minorities. Their funeral customs are diverse, so it is impossible to give a general account of them. However, it is said that shamanism and animism, which even today reflect on the ways of wisdom, are practiced in this area. For example, when a member of the Nivf tribe, whose home is in the northern part of Sakhalin and Amur River area, dies, the family keeps a fire burning and holds a wake with relatives and friends. Usually, the family stays by the deceased without sleeping. When the deceased is male, they stay up for three days; when a female family member dies, they stay up for four days. After that, the body is carried to an outdoor crematorium. When the body is carried out of the house, the feet must go out first. On the way to the crematorium, the carriers stop three times if the deceased is male, four times if the deceased is female. At the crematorium, the carriers turn around three times from east to west, and then place the body on a funeral pyre. The body is then cremated. A dog is also put into the fire as a sacrifice. The mourners eat the dog meat with gruel. Then the deceased's bones are buried in a cave of the community graveyard with his or her possessions, which are all broken up or crushed before the burial. The people believe that if they do this, the deceased may use them in the next life. Finally, a wooden statue, a symbol of the deceased, is placed upright on the grave.

TAJIKISTAN

The Republic of Tajikistan is a mountainous country. Most of the country's land rests on the Pamir Plateau, which is called the "roof of the world." After the dissolution of the Soviet Union, Tajikistan joined the Soviet Socialist Republics in December 1991. This is the poorest country of all the associated republics. The people are Tadzhiks, but there are also some Uzbeks. Many of the Tadzhiks follow Sunni Islam. It is customary for funeral services to be conducted according to Muslim custom and for burial to take place in a Muslim cemetery.

When someone dies, the relatives and friends are informed in person, and the death is reported to the Civil Registration Office (ZAGS). There are no professional undertakers. The dead body is washed and wrapped in a white shroud by the neighbors and is placed in a separate yurt, which is put up for this purpose. The funeral (*osanoza*) takes place in this yurt on the third day under the guidance of a *mullah*. The body is constantly attended until the burial. After the funeral, the male neighbors carry the body to a nearby graveyard on a special stretcher. The women are not allowed in the graveyard. The first-year memorial is observed solemnly with many people coming together.

TURKMENISTAN

The Republic of Turkmenistan is located in the southwestern part of Central Asia. The western area of Turkmenistan is flat land on the coast of the Caspian Sea. "Turkmenistan" is a compound word that joins *Turkmen* with the Persian word *stan,* meaning country.

In December 1991, after the dissolution of the Soviet Union, Turkmenistan joined the Soviet Socialist Republics. The majority are Turkmen or Russians, who follow Sunni Islam or Russian Orthodox tradition respectively.

When someone dies, the relatives and friends are informed in person, and the death is reported to the Civil Registration Office (ZAGS). The deceased's body is washed and wrapped in a white shroud and is immediately carried to a nearby cemetery for burial. The funeral (*gurgaziyan*) takes place on the third day after the death at a neighbor's house. Funerary feasts in memory of the deceased are held on the third, seventh and fortieth days after the death.

The Russians living in Turkmenistan follow most of the same procedures as the local people. However, the funeral (*pokhorony*) is arranged by a professional undertaker (*mogilshik*), and it takes place at a Russian Orthodox church. The grave usually consists of a stone pillar monument with a picture of the deceased. Funerary feasts are also held on the third, seventh and fortieth days after the death. On these occasions, a glass of vodka and bread is prepared at the dining table for the deceased as well as the participants.

In Ashkhabad, the capital, several memorial statues are erected in memory of the victims of the great earthquake on October 6, 1948. The statue of Lenin is still standing at the Central Park (former Lenin Park). It is the only one of its kind remaining in the former Soviet Union.

UKRAINE

The Republic of Ukraine is bordered by seven states; to the south it lies on the Black Sea and the Sea of Azov. After the Soviet Union collapsed, Ukraine became independent and joined the Soviet Socialist Republics. Most of the people are Ukranians, who follow Ukranian Orthodoxy, but some follow Russian Orthodox tradition.

Death brings about a change in the behavior of people and the use of cultural markers (for example, a white sheet is hung out, young women let their hair down, men do not wear any headgear). Traditionally, an unmarried young woman is buried in a wedding dress.

UZBEKISTAN

After the Soviet Union collapsed, the Republic of Uzbekistan joined the Commonwealth of Independent States. The majority of the people are Uzbeks, who are Muslims. Uzbekistan was prosperous in the past as a trade port on the Silk Road. Many cities, such as Samarkand and Bukhara, preserve the inheritance of Islamic and pre-Islamic culture.

The Uzbeks, even those who do not consider themselves ardent believers, participate in a number of Muslim religious ceremonies. It is customary for funeral services to be conducted according to Muslim tradition. The cult of tombs of holy men (*mazar*) is widespread in Central Asia. After independence, the Uzbeks have continued to follow Islamic customs and rituals.

The ancient custom of mutual help, *khashar*, is the expression of comradeship and mutual aid. A fraternity called *Makhallya* assists with funerals in the neighborhood in town, and in the country it is a *Kishlak*. Although such analogous institutions exist in the other CIS countries, the *Makhallya* and Kishlak in Uzbekistan are the strongest and most organized.

When someone dies, the death is announced in person in the neighborhood and is reported to the Civil Registration Office (ZAGS). The body is wrapped in a seven-meter-long shroud and is taken to a nearby cemetery on a special stretcher by male participants. If the color of the shroud is white, the deceased is an adult; if it is red, the deceased is an infant, so people passing by can tell who died. Then the body is lowered into the grave and buried. Women are not allowed at the cemetery at this time.

The funeral (*ulik*) takes placed at a neighbor's house on the third day after death. Sometimes professional crying women are hired. The mourners are given bread, candies or eggs as a token of appreciation. If a family member passes away, the mourning period for the men in the family is usually three days, and the women are expected to mourn for a year, during which time they wear a blue dress with a white veil.

After the funeral rite, the burial takes place at nearby cemeteries, men carrying the deceased body. Only female next of kin might decide to attend, but are ordered to walk at the back of the procession. The body can be seen lying on the bier in its white wrappings. No coffin is needed or wanted.

The graves are simple mounds of soil with a headstone at the front. In the Urgenchi region, where the soil is contaminated with salt, the body is laid in a concrete Quonset-hut style tomb. A memorial feast is held at the bereaved family's house one year after the death. Thereafter, people rarely visit the grave.

CHAPTER 7

North and Central America

ANTIGUA AND BARBUDA

Antigua and Barbuda lie in the West Indies in the Caribbean Sea. More than half of the 84,000 people are members of the Anglican church. Belief in the magical Rastafarianism, which is a religion among Jamaicans, is popular.

When someone dies, the body is taken care of by the mortuary. When a rich man dies, some families request facial make-up for the deceased. The body is viewed at the wake. After the funeral, the body is buried in the cemetery. At this time, all the mourners sing hymns and offer flowers.

Many people adopt the large family life-style. The relatives and friends are very closely united. Family events such as weddings and funerals are taken care of by the family members. Women who are close relatives of the deceased wail loudly, oblivious to the other mourners. For the Antiguans and Barbudans, weddings and funerals are very important and elaborate events that take place at the church to which they belong.

ARUBA

An island in the Carribean, located in the westernmost of the Lesser Antilles, north of Venezuela, Aruba is an autonomous part of the Netherlands. The people follow Christian, Hindu, Muslim, Chinese and Jewish traditions and conduct funerals accordingly.

BAHAMAS

The Commonwealth of the Bahamas are located in the northern part of the West Indies, close to the Florida peninsula. It includes over 700 islands of all

West Indies, close to the Florida peninsula. It includes over 700 islands of all sizes and many shore reefs. The Bahama islands, because of their mild climate, have become a resort. The majority of the people are black and speak English as the official language. There are many Christians who belong to various churches.

When someone dies, the death is reported to the relatives and neighbors in person or by telephone. Funerals are held at the church to which the bereaved family belongs. Afterward, the mourners form a procession and go to the cemetery, where the body is interred.

The unique custom of *Obeah*, the spirits of the dead, has been practiced in this country to harm rivals, to protect one's property and person, and to raise the spirits of the dead. Nowadays, this practice is rare.

BARBADOS

Situated in the easternmost part of the Caribbean Sea, Barbados became a British colony in 1627. Sugar production, which once used African slave labor, is the major industry.

When someone dies, the death is reported to the relatives and neighbors in person or by telephone. Funerals are usually held at a Christian church to which the bereaved family belongs. More than half the population belongs to the Church of England. Others are Methodist, Roman Catholic or Seventh Day Adventists, and a small number of people with diverse backgrounds practice Islam, Rastafarianism, Hinduism and Judaism.

BELIZE

Formerly British Honduras, Belize was the last Central American country to gain its independence from Britain in 1981. It lies on the eastern shore of the Yucatan peninsula and shares a border with Mexico along the River Hondo.

Almost half of the population can trace their roots back to the Africans brought over in the 17th century. Catholic, Anglican and Methodist are the major religious denominations that prefer burial of the deceased at the time of the funeral. There are also immigrants from India, who practice Hinduism and prefer cremation.

BERMUDA

Bermuda is an archipelago in the West Atlantic, comprising low-lying coral islands and islets. It was colonized by English settlers in 1612 and has had an internal self-government since 1968. Because of the mild weather year-round, it attracts many tourists, and increasingly it has become an international business center. Most of the people follow the Christian tradition.

CANADA

The vast land of Canada stretches from the Pacific Coast to the Atlantic. Its land mass is second only to Russia's. Eighty percent of the population live in the south near the American border. About half of the population is British Canadian, who live in Ontario. The French Canadians are the next largest ethnic group, and for the most part they live in the province of Quebec. Most of the people are either Protestant or Catholic.

When a death occurs in the family, a funeral director is asked to arrange the funeral, dispose of the body, and take care of other pressing matters. With a doctor's death certificate, permission can be obtained from the provincial office to dispose of the body, which is then taken to the mortuary. There the body is properly made-up, and the family and friends gather in the chapel of the mortuary. In the case of an unnatural death, a legal autopsy must be performed by the police. In other cases, the family has a wake or funeral in the mortuary chapel. This has been a common practice in the urban areas of Canada since World War II. In the rural areas, however, sometimes when the wake or funeral is held in a church. The mourners who are Protestant usually attend only a wake, funeral, or burial and prefer to have the funeral at a funeral home. Especially during the cold winter months, since the heating in churches is often not very good and it is expensive, people seem to use mortuaries more often than churches.

In the Vancouver and Toronto areas, there are many Canadians of Japanese and Chinese descent. When the family is Buddhist, usually the last rites are given at the hospital. The wake takes place in the deceased's home with family and friends and ends around ten to eleven o'clock. The funeral customarily takes place two or three days after the death and is usually performed at a Buddhist temple. In the past, the mourners lined up and proceeded to the graveyard after the funeral by carriage or sled. Today, however, if traffic conditions allow it, the family uses a hearse.

Graveyards are usually owned and managed by a church or public organization, but there are also some privately managed mortuaries, which are regulated by law so that they do not run the business only for profit. The private graveyards used to be divided into three sections: Protestant, Catholic and Jewish. In the newly built public cemeteries, however, there is no such division. Most commonly, a family or an individual purchases a section for a grave. In the past, Catholics built either mausoleum-style or niche-style tombstones, and Protestants built standing-style tombstones. Recently, as in memorial parks in America, flat tombstones have became more common. In the areas, where they have snow and the ground is frozen for a substantial amount of time, the corpses are kept in a chamber until spring comes, because it is almost impossible to bury a body in the frozen ground.

In Canada, about 85 percent of the deceased are interred, and the rest are cremated. Among Buddhists, Protestants and those without a religion, cremation is more common. A cemetery near a large city usually has a crematory chamber. The dead in most cases are cremated 48 hours after death.

Since the majority of residents in the east of Quebec are Catholic and cremation is not common in this area, there are only two crematoriums. One is in Montreal, the other in New Brunswick. In Quebec, there are many immigrants, and both French and English are official languages. However, even in the funeral rites, traditional French customs are well preserved. The word "hearse" in English originated from the old French word *herce*, meaning "a frame for holding candles." There was an old Catholic tradition of placing a candle stand on the coffin, and because the stand looked like a rake turned upside down, an actual rake began to be placed on the coffin in its place. In Quebec in some Catholic churches, this custom of placing a rake on the coffin is still practiced. The Catholic church generally holds the funeral in the morning, whereas Protestant funerals are more often held in the evening.

Canada's native population, the Inuit, who live in remote areas in the north, generally believe that when someone dies, the spirit, personality, soul and name are freed from the decaying body, and that they survive until they pass into a new body and follow a new life. Although their funeral practices differ from one area to another, they usually build a cairn over the body, because the frozen tundra is too hard for burial, and then erect a cross on it. There are also places where they build a wooden fence, so that they may protect the body from wild animals.

In the eastern and northernmost areas, the body of someone who dies during the summer is placed directly on the ground right after the funeral. Then stones are piled up on the body to form a mound. During the winter months, the body is just left in the snow. In some areas, the body is placed on a stand with the deceased's personal belongings, and the arms and legs are bent into the fetal position. Even among Christianized people, many believe that the spirit of the deceased will be reborn into the world and not ascend into heaven after being judged by God. They also believe that not only human beings but also animals have spirits. The animals choose to be hunted by people as a favor and allow people to catch them. Therefore, people need to hold feasts and festivals in order to appease the spirits of the animals. They carve wooden statues of human beings and animals, which are placed on graves for this same purpose.

In *The Hare Indians*, Hiroko Hara, an anthropologist, tells us that the goal of the Hare Indian's life is to die with a beautiful face, because they believe that only those who die with a beautiful face can be reborn.

Among the Montagnais-Naskapi, who live in the southern part of Canada, the deceased are wrapped in robes or birchbark and buried along with their personal belongings. In winter, the corpse is placed on a scaffold and buried later. The dead are buried facing west, the direction of the home of the dead in the sky, to which the deceased's soul journeys after death.

COSTA RICA

The Republic of Costa Rica, called the Switzerland of Latin America, has a very mild climate. The majority of the people are Spanish. The official language is Spanish. Although freedom of religion is recognized, the constitution, promulgated in 1949, made Catholicism the national religion. Therefore, all of the national and formal events, such as the inauguration of the president, are held in the Catholic style.

When someone dies, the death is reported to a municipal office. All matters involving the funeral are taken care of by the mortuary at the family's request. The funeral is most often held in a church after the wake. Mourners usually deliver flowers and bouquets, but they do not offer any money. Black is the color of mourning.

Only closely related people join the procession going to the cemetery. There is no custom of cremation, so everyone is buried in the ground, but the bones are sometimes removed and kept apart from the grave in a niche. One week after the death, a memorial mass is held in the church. On All Souls' Day, November 1, everybody goes to the cemetery, where flowers are placed on graves.

In the capital, San Jose, there is a public cemetery near the national gymnasium, and most of the deceased in the city are buried here. Some families make public announcements of memorial masses for a few years. Most people believe the life of the soul is eternal.

CUBA

The Republic of Cuba is the largest among the islands of the West Indies in the Caribbean Sea. In 1898, after a revolution, Cuba became independent from Spain. After the revolution led by Fidel Castro, Cuba in 1959 became the first socialist nation in Latin America. The majority of the people are Spanish Cubans, but there are also black people and those who are a mixture of different ethnic groups. The official language is Spanish. The people of Cuba are very strongly united. The nation had been under Spanish rule in the past, so, as in other Latin American countries, Catholicism is the dominant religion. Because of the strict separation of religion from politics and the government's anti-religious policy, freedom of religious belief was established under the new constitution. However, the younger generation is less interested in religion.

When someone dies, the family obtains a medical report from a doctor and then reports the death to the Registri Civil. The public mortuary takes care of matters surrounding the funeral for the family.

Family and friends of the deceased gather at the funeral, which is held at the mortuary hall or church with the family, relatives and friends, and then the body is buried in a cemetery. In Havana, the capital, there is the vast Christobal Colon Memorial Park Cemetery, built in 1871. It is famous for its architectural,

artistic and historical value. The huge portal in Romanesque style was constructed by the Spanish architect Calixto de Loira, who drew up the first
pantheon of the cemetery where he himself was buried in 1872.

In the Revolution Square stands a huge monument in honor of Jose Marti,
the apostle of Cuba, who died in 1895 during the battle of Dos Rios, the
independence war against the United States. In prewar cemeteries, we can see
elaborate mausoleums, but since World War II, they have just placed tombstones
in equally divided sections. In the Santa Efgenia Memorial Cemetery on the
outskirts of Santiago de Cuba, is the grave of Jose Marti, the founding father of
Cuba.

Afro-Cuban Santeria, a syncretic religion that draws on both the Yoruba and
Catholic cultural heritages, is deeply ingrained in Cuba. Funeral services also
reflect the combined Santeria and Roman Catholic tradition.

DOMINICAN REPUBLIC

The Dominican Republic occupies the eastern two-thirds of the island of
Hispaniola, which is in the middle of the Antilles Islands, between the Atlantic
Ocean and the Caribbean Sea. As the name suggests, the island has traces of
Spanish culture, a result of the discovery of the New World by Columbus in
1492. The population consists mostly of people of mixed descent of Spanish
and Africans. The official language is Spanish, and the majority of the people
are Catholic. However, most people of the younger generation do not attend
church on Sunday, as was common in the past. Freedom of religion is assured,
though Catholicism was given official national support by the constitution
promulgated in 1966. There are also followers of the First Assembly of God and
Seventh Day Adventists.

When someone dies, the family reports it to the Registro Civil and obtains a
death certificate. The wake, funeral, and related matters are handled by the
mortuary. The funeral service is held in a church. Family members wear black.
After the service, a procession heads to either a private or church cemetery,
mass is held, and the body is buried. Tombstones are usually simple wooden
crosses. After the funeral, the family offers the mourners a light meal.

EL SALVADOR

El Salvador on the Pacific coast of Central America is located in the tropics.
The capital city, San Salvador, is 682 meters above sea level. It has low
humidity, although the temperature is high. The country is narrow and national
resources are scarce. El Salvador is also overpopulated, and illegal activities
involving extreme left-wing guerrillas are very common, so there is not much
peace for the people in El Salvador. The population is mainly native Indian and
mestizo. Freedom of religion was recognized by the constitution that was
promulgated in 1962, but the national religion is Catholicism.

When someone dies in El Salvador, the death is reported to the Registro Civil with a doctor's medical report and the death certificate. Usually the mortuary handles the funeral arrangements for the family. The coffins are prepared differently according to the material being used. The cheapest ones are pine and the most expensive ones are usually mahogany. Because the humidity is high in the coastal areas of this country, if the body is not properly preserved within 24 hours of death, the funeral and the wake are not allowed.

A Catholic funeral is usually held in the family church. Also, there is no custom of cremation or facilities for it in El Salvador. In the family home, the body is put in a casket in the living room, and relatives and friends place candles and flowers on top. Then they invite a priest to pray for them. The family repeatedly prays with their rosaries throughout the night. The following morning the casket is moved from the family home to the graveyard. The procession is led by the priest. The casket, decorated with flowers and bouquets, is buried in a hole about six feet deep.

As in other Latin American countries like Mexico and Cuba, people buy a gravesite in the public cemetery or choose a seven-year rental agreement. In the rental system, three bodies are buried in one section, and a tombstone is erected in seven months to one year. Because they create very elaborate tombstones, it is said that most of the funeral expenses go to the tombstone. The family goes to the grave every day for nine days after the death. On All Souls' Day, November 2, people visit the cemeteries with flowers.

GRENADA

A British colony since 1783, Grenada became independent in 1974. The most southerly of the Windward Islands, Grenada also includes the islands of Carriacou and Petite Martinique. It is the world's second largest producer of nutmeg. Since the removal of the Marxists, emphasis has been placed on privatization of wealth and industry, with the aim of attracting foreign investors and increased production for export. About 65 percent of the population are Catholic, and the remaining 35 percent are Anglican, Presbyterian and Methodist.

GUATEMALA

The Republic of Guatemala is a mountainous country located in Central America. Guatemala has many cultural aspects in common with other Latin American countries. Catholicism is the national religion, and there are many Catholic churches in Guatemala. The people also tend to follow the foreign religious beliefs and worship statues of Christ, the Virgin Mary, angels and saints. However, it is unique among Central and South American countries in that the Mayan population have kept their traditional life style and customs, and many follow the native religion in which the spirits and souls of the dead are worshipped.

In the urban areas, a death is reported to the Registro Civil. The funeral is unique and full of ethnic color. According to a report by an American anthropologist Charles Wagley, in the Chimal Tinango village of Santiago the women cling to the deceased's body and cry out so loudly that their voices can be heard throughout the town. The men, however, stay very calm. When a man dies, a bell is rung three times, and when a woman dies, it is rung only once. The body, wrapped in a funeral cloth, is laid on a bench and covered with a blanket. Candles are lit and placed by the head of the body. Flowers and postcards are placed on both sides of the body for decoration. People close to the deceased gather at the wake. Wine made from corn or sugarcane is served to the mourners. The wake is accompanied by dirge music played by a marimba band. Other mourners come to bid farewell to the deceased. Coffee and snacks are served, but the mourners leave soon afterward, because the soul of the dead may attack them if they stay too long.

The next morning, the funeral procession, led by the marimba band, heads to a nearby cemetery. The body is carried on a coffin board, and the procession stops from time to time and the women cling to the body and cry loudly. At the graveyard, songs of mourning are sung in Latin and accompanied by violin and guitar. Wine is served here as well, and the singing voices echo far and wide. On the following day or on the twelfth day after the burial, the same singer is hired to sing at the graveyard. The people say that the soul of the dead is comforted by this, enabling it to escape from its loneliness. For one month after this, the singer may be called to sing every five days. All Souls' Day, November 2, is set aside for the dead. The people decorate the entrance of the family home with marigolds, and they also go to the cemetery with offerings and flowers. At night, a party is held with marimba music.

Among the Chuj, a Mayan tribe living in northwestern Guatemala, death is the transformation to "ancestral spirits." Funeral customs continue to reflect the combined traditional Mayan and Roman Catholic heritage. The spirits maintain an interest in the affairs of their families and can be approached for advice and aid, either at family altars, cave entrances or hilltops.

HAITI

The Republic of Haiti occupies one-third of the island of Hispaniola in the Caribbean Sea and shares the island with the Dominican Republic. The majority of the people are black, but there are also many *mulattos*, who are a mixture of black and French blood. Because of the strong sun, typical of the tropical zone and the tradewinds, the climate is very good and comfortable. Haiti has created some unique social customs that combine the French life style with African traditions. However, Haiti is also the poorest country in North and South America, and its rate of illiteracy is also the highest.

The national religion is Catholicism, and many people are baptized. But many also follow the Voodoo religion, which originated in Africa. Voodoo was founded by Macamdaner, a Muslim who was brought from Africa as a slave, in the 18th century. His goal was to overthrow the autocracy of the white people and to free blacks from slavery. When Macamdaner was arrested and prosecuted in Limbe in Northern Haiti, he began to be respected and was considered a hero. The believers, who seek the salvation of the spiritual God Loa, who was prophesied by Macamdaner, passionately dance and go into a state of possession as a group. When a Voodoo believer dies, the Voodoo priest is invited to perform the secret ceremony of death and rebirth. After the ceremony, the body is buried in a cemetery.

In the urban areas, funeral matters are taken care of by either a public or private mortuary, and the funeral itself is held in the mortuary or a church. It is customary to offer red roses. Most of the cemeteries are public or belong to churches. No cosmetic or preservative treatment is performed. The body is simply buried right after the funeral. There are no facilities for cremation or keeping urns.

When a foreigner dies in Haiti, and the family wishes the body to be sent back to their own country, they must apply for special permission, and the body must be treated in a hospital so that it does not decompose.

HONDURAS

The Republic of Honduras is the most mountainous country in Central America. The majority of the people are *mestizo*—a mixture of Spanish and the Indians who are native to Honduras. The official language is Spanish, and the majority of the people are Catholic.

When someone dies, the family obtains a death certificate from a doctor, and then asks the mortuary to take care of all the necessary business arrangements. The mortuary does not beautify the corpse in any way. The government provides free coffins to low-income families.

The funeral is held in a funeral hall in the mortuary, and then the burial takes place in a cemetery. The mourning clothes are black, though casual wear is becoming more common even at the funeral. There is no custom of cremating the body nor are there the facilities for it. The cemeteries usually belong to the Catholic church, and graves marked with a simple cross are most commonly seen.

The people of Honduras go to the graveyards with flowers on All Saints' Day, All Souls' Day, and other days of observance.

Along the eastern coastal region of Honduras are the Miskitos, who believe that death can be foretold by dreams or omens. It is also thought that the spirits of the deceased continued to live among the living for a while. Elaborate funeral rites were traditionally observed, though today simple Christian rites are more commonly followed.

JAMAICA

Jamaica in the West Indies is known for tourism and sugar cane. It is a land of everlasting summer. It is a newly formed country that became independent as a self-governing commonwealth of Great Britain in 1962. The majority of the people are of African descent. There are also people who are a mixture of African and white, Indians from India, and Chinese.

Most belong to the Anglican, Baptist, Methodist and Catholic churches. Some, however, believe in the native religions such as Bocomania and the Sion Reformist.

Bocomania values reciting the Holy Bible and its interpretation. The Sion Reformist, on the other hand, emphasizes ceremony, magical treatment and group possession. In both cases, the churches try to attract followers by baptizing them. Probably the blacks were cruelly treated and persecuted because of their religion in the old Spanish and English colonial days. Perhaps such an unfortunate experience has impelled them to follow these religions.

The people hold funerals according to their own religious customs. In the urban areas, the mortuary helps the family prepare for the funeral. Recently, funerals in the mortuary hall are very common. After the funeral, the body is buried in the cemetery. After that, most people visit the graveyard every year on All Saints' Day or All Souls' Day.

Among the Jamaicans, ghosts of the deceased are widely feared. Some of the black Jamaicans believe in a good soul that goes to Africa after death and a bad one that lingers as a duppy, particularly around cotton trees. A festive wake is held to pacify the deceased and render the ghost harmless.

MEXICO

Mexico is the largest country in Central America. The population mainly comprises *mestizos*, who are people of Spanish and Indian blood. The official language is Spanish. The people are for the most part Catholic. However, because a policy separating church and state was adopted some time ago, the church does not have much influence over politics, education, labor and social life.

When someone dies in the city, the death is reported to the nearby Registro Civil with a doctor's report. If the bereaved family uses a mortuary, all business matters are taken care of by the mortuary, which seem to be used more often by low-income families. Among private mortuaries in Mexico City, the Gayosso Mortuary does the most business, handling 5,000 to 6,000 funerals each year.

When the mortuary receives a request, the body is immediately transported to the mortuary chapel. After the wake in the chapel, the funeral is held in the hall or in the graveyard of the cemetery with the services of a minister. Bodies are usually buried in the ground, but cremation is also possible, if the family requests it. The body is buried in a public cemetery within 24 hours. The grave is rented for seven years, and if the family does not renew the contract, the grave will be deemed deserted.

Traditional customs are preserved in the rural areas. For example, the Nahuatl tribe of Central Mexico believes that a child's death is the birth of an angel, so death is not considered a sorrowful event. The dead child's body is decorated with flowers and is placed in a casket painted red, white and gold. At the family home happy music is played and sometimes even a party is given. When an adult dies, the casket and the candles are black.

In the Otomic tribe, the funeral is postponed until an animal passes in front of the house. This is because they believe that the animal announces the arrival of an angel to guide and lead the deceased's soul to heaven.

The Taraumara tribe believe that the soul of the dead returns to the family home within a year and spreads disease, kills domestic animals and threatens the lives of the survivors. In order to avoid this curse, a sorcerer talks to the soul, asking it to come and eat meat that has been cooked several days after the death and served in a dish on ox skin.

On November 2, All Souls' Day, it is an annual custom to remember and pray for the deceased, just as they do in other Catholic countries. This day is called *Dia de los Muertos* (Day of the Dead). The *santocalli* at the family home is decorated with flowers, and tamales, mole, sweet bread, beverages, playing cards and other items are offered. The people also go to the graves of their beloved, and following the old Aztec and Mayan tradition, they make a candy in the shape of a skeleton and present it to someone with the recipient's name on its forehead. The skeleton is called *hudas*, which is the Spanish pronunciation of Judas, the disciple who betrayed Jesus. Throughout the day's events, the Mexicans ponder death. Plays with skeleton dolls are also performed in various places in Mexico.

At the pantheon in the city of Guana Juato, more than 200 mummified bodies are lined up along each side of the cave. This is a very unusual site, known as The House of the Dead. The corpses may have become naturally mummified, because it is located at a high altitude.

Among the Amuzgo, living in the lower portion of the Sierra Madre del Sur near the Pacific Ocean, funeral custom is a combination of Catholic and traditional elements. The deceased who have been married are buried with their heads facing west, and single people and children with their heads facing east. The body is intered at a grave yard.

NETHERLANDS ANTILLES

These islands are located in the Carribean Sea, comprising the southern group of Curacao and Bonaire. The majority of the people are of mixed European and Carribean Indian descent and follow the Roman Catholic tradition. For them, funerals are very important and elaborate events.

NICARAGUA

The Republic of Nicaragua is located in the heart of Central America. Honduras lies to the north and Costa Rica to the south. Mountainous areas with primeval forests cover the country, and the humidity and the temperature are very high. Most of the people are native Indians and *mestizos*, a mixture of white and Indian. There are also black people, white people and Native Americans. The majority of the people are Catholic.

In 1979, a revolutionary government was established, but since then the country has not been peaceful. Natural disasters, continuous civil war, and the oil crisis have hindered the country's economic revival and caused much hardship in the lives of the people. However, most seem optimistic and, in general, are friendly and sociable.

When someone dies, the neighbors get together at the family home, hold a wake, and pray with rosaries. The next morning, they attend a funeral mass at the church and bury the body at the cemetery. Most are buried in their coffins. The mourners usually send to the bereaved family flowers or wreaths in the shape of crosses, hearts, circles and so forth.

In the rural areas, some of the traditional customs and beliefs continue. For the Sumu, living in the Mosquitia region in the east, death was formerly believed to have been caused by evil spirits. Shamans are invited at the funeral to drive them away.

PANAMA

The Republic of Panama is located at the junction of North America and South America. Both temperature and humidity are high throughout the year. The humidity (discomfort) index is the highest in Central America. The Panama Canal is a very important waterway connecting the Pacific Ocean with the Atlantic Ocean. The population is composed mainly of Spanish Panamanians and those of native Indian and African descent, but a great diversity of people make Panama their home. Most Panamanians are Catholic.

In cities, like the capital, Panama City, there are private mortuaries of various sizes. When requested by the family, the mortuary obtains permission from the Health Office to bury the body of the deceased. It also arranges the funeral for the family.

At the bereaved family home, the body of the deceased is bathed and placed in a casket. The walls of the living room are covered with a white hanging cloth. The mourners eat and drink, and sometimes they even play dominoes. The wake is usually held in the chapel in the mortuary, instead of the family home. In either case, the bereaved family invites a priest and prays the rosary. The next morning, the body is moved to the church for the funeral mass, then only the male mourners head to the cemetery. If the funeral is for a celebrity, many flowers are offered. Following the hearse, many cars, decorated with flower wreaths, join the procession. It is a magnificent sight.

There are two kinds of burial: in the ground or in a niche. After the burial the family goes home and during a nine-day period of mourning, they pray with rosaries everyday. On the last day, the family goes to the church to attend mass. The family goes to visit the cemetery a year later. Many people visit the grave on All Souls' Day every year. Usually after 18 months, the body is removed and re-buried in a mausoleum. At a public cemetery that was recently built in a new section of Panama City, there are flat tombstones rather than standing ones, which perhaps reflects the influence of the United States.

In Panama, there are also native groups such as the Kuna, Choco, and Gaymi. The Kuna tribe holds a self-governing territory called the San Blas Islands in the Caribbean Sea. In this territory, at the time of someone's death, people call a magician and hold a ceremony called the *Ceremony of the Smoke of Cocoa Beans and Pepper Seeds*. The body is bathed and placed in a hammock. At the funeral, a choir sings songs of mourning. The next morning, the body is carried by two men and placed in a canoe to be carried to the main island, where it is buried in the evening in a graveyard far away from the cities. Once they bury the body, they try to forget about the death.

The Chinese population in Panama have a cemetery that is used exclusively by their community. The bodies are temporarily buried so that they can be buried again in the family's cemetery.

Among the Bugle, living in the easternmost part of Bocas del Toro Province and the westernmost part of northern Veraguas Province, individuals are buried at the graveyard with some of their personal belongings.

PUERTO RICO

Puerto Rico is one of the islands in the Caribbean that line up like stepping stone, between the United States and the countries of Latin America. It is politically and economically dependent on the United States, but the people are more Latin American than American. As a result of the Spanish-American War, it became a territory of the United States, but the people speak mostly Spanish, and Catholicism is the dominant religion.

On the tip of San Juan, the capital of Puerto Rico, is Fort El Moro, which overlooks the city and dates back to the days of Spanish rule. In the hilly city of San Juan, there are towering highrises. The scene is no different from what one would see in a modern city in the United States. However, in the slum areas, there are those who live from day to day depending on the advice of fortune tellers. Many Puerto Ricans believe in the existence of Satan and are afraid of the eyes of the devil, so they make their children wear bracelets to guard them against demonic possession.

When someone dies, the family reports the death to the nearby municipal office with a doctor's medical report. In the cities, there are private mortuaries that take care of all the matters related to the funeral. During the wake, relatives and close friends of the dead gather around the body to pray for the soul's passage into heaven. Throughout the night vigil, people who knew the deceased come and go while a small group of women and men who were particularly close to the dead say the rosary. Candles burn and the prayers last until the dawn of the day,and the body is to be buried.

The funeral is usually held in the family church, and the body is buried in the church cemetery. Following the funeral, the *novenas* (nine consecutive days of prayer) take place in the house of the deceased. In most cases, the body is interred in the family grave. There is no custom of cremation. Later, on All Souls' Day, many visit the grave and bring red and white flowers.

SAINT CHRISTOPHER AND NEVIS

The Federation of Saint Christopher and Nevis consists of the first West Indian islands to be colonized by Britain in 1623 and 1628, respectively. They became independent in 1983. In recent years, due to the beautiful beaches, tourism has replaced the sugar industry, which was nationalized in 1975.

The majority of the people follow Protestantism and are regular church goers. Churches play an extremely important role among the people and serve as the basis for a variety of social activities. When there is a death, the funeral rites are performed at the church that the deceased belonged to, followed by burial at the cemetery nearby.

SAINT LUCIA

Saint Lucia is a mountainous, forested island of extinct volcanoes. It changed hands between British and France 14 times before finally being ceded to Britain in 1814. It became independent in 1979.

Saint Lucia now has a rich, tension-free racial mix of descendants of Africans, Carib Indians and European settlers. The majority of the people follow Roman Catholicism. Despite relaxed attitudes, family life is still important to most Saint Lucians, many of whom are regular churchgoers. Funerals are held at the church to which they belong, followed by burial at the cemeteries nearby.

SAINT VINCENT AND THE GRENADINES

Saint Vincent, a mountainous and volcanic island that boasts luxuriant vegetation, was discovered by Europeans in 1498, and became a British colony in 1783. The majority of the people follow Protestantism, and family life on St. Vincent is heavily influenced by the Anglican Church. Racial tensions are few, and intermarriage has meant that the original communities of African slaves, Europeans and the indigenous Carib Indians can no longer be distinguished.

TRINIDAD AND TOBAGO

The Republic of Trinidad and Tobago, the islands known for their lively, upbeat Calypso songs, is located in the southernmost end of the West Indies. The majority of the people are blacks or Indian, and follow various religions, such as Catholicism and Anglicanism as well as Hinduism.

When someone dies, people hold the funeral according to their own religious customs. The funeral procession is accompanied by a musical band. For the most part, Christians and Muslims are interred in cemeteries; whereas, Hindus are cremated. Funeral, in general, are held at the respective church, mosque or temple, followed by a rite at a cemetery and a feast at the house of the bereaved family.

UNITED STATES OF AMERICA

The United States of America is situated on the North American continent between Canada and Mexico and comprises 48 contiguous states and the outlying states of Alaska and Hawaii. The population, except for the Native Americans, is made up of immigrants from various countries and their descendants. Many of the immigrants, while preserving the traditions of their former lands, have brought unique new modes of living. Although the door to immigration is not as wide open as before, and the country has entered a period of stability, it is easy to imagine that there will be dramatic changes in American society so that the country can adjust to the new era.

With such social changes, increasing secularization and an improvement in the standard of living in this century, funeral customs have changed and the funeral business has prospered. In fact, the boom in the extension and renovation of mortuaries in the United States continued until the 1960s. In 1880, there were only about 5,000 mortuaries, but by 1960 there were 22,000 mortuaries with nearly 50,000 employees. Most of the employees have a bachelor's degree in mortuary science from a college of mortuary science, and are well trained and skilled in preservation of the corpse and carry a technical license granted by their state's Department of Public Health.

Some of the changes involved the elimination of the gloomy funerals, giving them a lighter, more modern image. The image change began with the revision of the language relating to death and funerals: For example, from *mortuary* to *funeral home*, from *undertaker* to *funeral director*, from *dead bady* to *earthly remains*, from *coffin* to *casket*, from *cemetery* to *memorial park*.

Because more people now use funeral homes instead of the home or church to hold a funeral, the ways in which deaths and funerals are handled have also changed. Usually people begin by calling a nearby funeral home when a family member passes away. The morticians rush to the family home, transport the corpse to the mortuary, and embalm the body. Then the corpse is placed in a coffin, which is kept in a room where the mourners can view the deceased.

Mortuaries can help the bereaved family not only in obtaining the death certificate and burial permission, but also in arranging for the casket, the vault and the flowers. The mortuary may also call a priest and make arrangements for the wake, the funeral and the burial service. There are also mortuaries that take care of the family's insurance, inheritance and other family business. They even provide consultation sessions for the family of the deceased.

In the Catholic church, the funeral is, in principle, performed in the church, and churches such as the Episcopal and Lutheran recommend that their members have the funeral at the church, though few now follow such advice. The wake usually takes place a day before the funeral, and there those expressing their condolences can view the deceased and meet with the family. Wakes are held by religious and non-religious people. They are attended by co-workers, acquaintances, distant relatives, neighbors; while people close to the deceased or survivors attend the funeral.

The trend of having the funeral at a funeral home has resulted in keeping people away from the church, which has deprived the church of a position of leadership and eliminated a source of income. Usually, the funeral home combines the pastor's fee with other fees charged to the bereaved family. The mortuary selects the pastor and sets the fee unless the family requests a special arrangement or the church and pastor clearly specify the fees involved.

Moreover, fees paid to mortuaries had been rising along with the cost of other goods. However, since the expenses for the most part applied to the cost of the casket and the vault, people began to question whether or not such expenses were a necessity. In the past, the expenses were not itemized, and neither were they clearly explained in the bill, so they became the target of public criticism. This forced the Federal Trade Commission, which is an advisory committee to the United States Congress, to investigate the issue. In 1982, a bill was passed that required the mortuary companies to give a detailed account of the expenses to the deceased family and to let them choose the services that they desired.

Nonetheless, mortuaries play an important role in assisting with death in the family. They also provide various funerary options, the most popular being burials and cremation. At present, there are approximately 200 crematoriums all over America, and most of them are operated by private cemetery management unions. The crematorium usually has a waiting room for mourners, a committal chamber, a chapel, a crematory chamber, an office, a room where the urn can be selected and a columbarium (niche).

The Cremation Association of North America revealed that as of 1997 Hawaii ranked first in porportion of cremations versus burials: 56 percent were cremated in Hawaii, followed by 54 percent in Alaska. (Americans of Asian ancestry, who make up a large portion of Hawaii's population, tend to cremate their deceased.) Many western states had cremation rates higher than 40 percent, but the southern states have continued to follow the traditional way of burial.

In earlier times, those who advocated cremation were mainly German immigrants, priests of the Free Protestant Church and doctors. In the 1900s, however, cremation societies were established in various locations. In 1913 these societies were unified as the Cremation Society of America. Hugo Erichsen, M.D., the first president of the Cremation Society of America, stated that "every crematist must be a missionary for the cause, and must take every suitable opportunity to spread its gospel, the glad tidings of a more sanitary and more aesthetic method of disposing of our beloved dead."

In addition to religious reasons, there are many other factors involved in why more people choose cremation. These factors involve public health issues, problems of transporting the body to distant cemeteries and finding burial space. Moreover, it is somewhat easier to say farewell to the deceased. There is no worry about contamination from bacteria or that the corpse may rot. It is also less expensive because there is no need for a casket or vault. There is no reason to worry that the grave may be robbed, and it is easy to move the remains. It is also possible to place the ashes inside a building without their being affected by the weather. Some even use the ashes after cremation as fertilizer, or scatter them over a place meaningful to the deceased.

Mortuaries that do not have cremation facilities depend mainly on services such as cosmetic or orthopedic preservation and the sale of vaults as their sources of income. Also, if a corpse must be transported a long distance, it must be properly and legally preserved 24 hours after death. When the corpse is transported by a commercial airline, or when the person has died from an epidemic disease, a tightly sealed vault is required.

The main advantage of a burial is that the emotions evoked in the process of bidding farewell are more natural. The way the body decays in the earth is more natural as well. There are also people who insist on burial for such reasons as the religious belief in the reincarnation of the body.

The following lists the religious groups in the United States and shows how each approaches cremation:

1. Assembly of God (optional)
2. Baptist (optional)
3. Brethren Church (acceptable)
4. Buddhist (approves)
5. Christ Union Church (acceptable)
6. Christian Alliance Church (reluctant)
7. Christian Scientist (acceptable)
8. Church of Christ (acceptable)

 9. Episcopal Church (approves)
10. Evangelical Church (optional)
11. Greek Orthodox Church (disapproves)
12. Hindu (acceptable)
13. Islam (disapproves)
14. Jehovah's Witness (optional)
15. Judaism (disapproves)
16. Lutheran Church (acceptable)
17. Mennonite Church (optional)
18. Missouri Lutheran Church (optional)
19. Mormon Church (reluctant)
20. Nazarene Church (approves)
21. Reformation Church (optional)
22. Roman Catholic Church (disapproves)
23. Salvation Army (acceptable)
24. Seventh Day Adventist (optional)
25. Unitarian Union Church (prefers interment)
26. Union Methodist Church (acceptable)
27. Union Presbyterian Church (acceptable)
28. Wisconsin Evangelical Lutheran (disapproves)

(Data from Dale V. Hardt, *Death*, pp. 122-123.)

Cremation is allowed by 70 percent of the denominations, and 23 percent are against it; 7 percent prefer interment. The increase in the number of deaths made the expansion of areas used for burials unavoidable. Recently, because of regulations requiring urban planning, the Natural Environment Law, and the like, the development and expansion of graveyards within church grounds are prohibited or restricted. As a result, the fee for the use of the plot and the price of tombstones went up, and the use of memorial parks in the suburbs, where the funeral expenses are much lower, has become more popular.

Moreover, in the past, tombstones were very plain and simple, but as larger-scale memorial parks opened in the cities, people began to have expensive, elaborate tombstones erected. The shapes of the tombstones also began to show more variety. Cross-shaped marble or granite tombstones, stones cut into elaborate forms of the cross, simple crosses, coffin-shaped stone tombstones, urn-shaped ones, bible-shaped ones, altars, standing flat stone tombstones, flat stone markers, platform-shaped ones, pinnacle-shaped ones, designs involving garden motifs, ones shaped like a line of pillars, mausoleum type ones, relief type ones, abstract carvings are among the kinds that one can see. Among the tombstones for Protestants, those for individuals and married couples are common, whereas the majority of those for Catholics are for the whole family.

Since the time Hubert Eaton built Forest Lawn Memorial Park in 1917 in Glendale in the suburbs of Los Angeles, memorial parks have been built in the suburbs of various cities in the United States. The vast memorial park is covered with beautiful grass just like a country club. The graveyard is neatly divided like a chess board, and instead of the erect-type tombstone, flat grave markers with individual bronze name plates are placed on the ground, making it easier to take care of the grounds. In some parks in one corner, mausoleums are built, or underground niches are available. These memorial parks have chapels and crematoriums as well. The memorial park management, unassociated with the private mortuaries, takes care of all the business including burial and cremation (traditional mortuaries have also begun this type of management). With the newest facilities and a pleasant environment, the goal of the memorial park is to provide solace to its clients. Even in the United States, with its vast land area, it is hard to obtain space for cemeteries in the city, because of urban population growth. Especially for those cemeteries that are maintained in a nice natural environment, land is difficult to buy and may cost hundreds of thousands of dollars. Among the more popular memorial parks are Woodlawn Memorial Park in New York City, Georgetown Memorial Park, Pinelawn Memorial Park of Long Island, Forest Hills Memorial Park of Los Angeles and Westwood Memorial Park. In the case of privately owned memorial parks, there are some whose ownership can be legally transferred. In such cases, people may even buy a cemetery for investment purposes.

Many of the funeral homes in America are still small and privately owned. As of 1990, there are some 21,300 mortuaries. However, due to difficulties in finding family successors to run the mortuaries, the smaller funeral homes are gradually merging with larger ones. Among larger mortuaries, the largest is Service Corporation International, which has a chain of 551 mortuaries (as of 1989). In the past 10 years, the number of people who made contracts with these kinds of mortuaries has increased. Some 33 percent of the adult population arranged their own funeral, and 10 percent paid their funeral expenses in advance.

Some people want their ashes to be scattered in the sky or at sea after being cremated. In 1965, the scattering of ashes from an airplane became legal in California on the condition that the ashes be scattered at least three miles away from shore. Since that time, this has become popular. Grey Funeral Home in San Francisco in 1972, for example, handled as many as 4,000 cases of burial in the sky that were approved by the Department of Public Health. Also, there are those who wish to donate their body to medical organizations for research or request that it be preserved by being frozen. Such requests can be made by the deceased's family or in a will. Some refuse to have lavish funerals or expensive burials and have private memorial gatherings among close friends and family.

A recent issue of *Newsweek* (March 31, 1997) mentioned that cremation has been on an upswing for the past 10 years and may account for as much as 40 percent of all post-mortem arrangements by 2010. Jack Springer, executive director of the Cremation Association of North America, predicts an eventual rate as high as 60 percent. Driving the trend, he says, is the increased mobility of the population.

Alaska

The state of Alaska, a detached territory, is the northernmost part of the United States. Most of the area of Alaska is barren, and the average temperature for the year is below zero. Nevertheless, the Inuit people have lived there for more than 2,500 years. This cultural zone spreads from the Chekchu peninsula of Siberia as far as Alaska, Canada and Greenland. After 1867 when the United States bought the Alaskan territory from Russia at a cost of $7,200,000, petroleum development began. Many white people moved to the state and settled in the growing population centers of Anchorage and Fairbanks.

When someone dies in Alaska, the death is reported to the local office of government and the death certificate is submitted. Mortuaries in various locations prepare the necessary documents and make the arrangements for the funeral, which is usually held in the chapel of a funeral home. Because the ground in the cemetery is frozen for much of the year, the corpse is often kept in a columbarium in the mortuary and then buried after the snow has melted. Recently, however, the number of people who choose cremation has increased.

The Inuit people reside in the coastal areas of the northernmost part of Alaska. Usually, 200 to 300 people organize and form a community without any chief or other central figure of authority. In the case of the Kopar Inuit, a female corpse is kept for three days in the family home, whereas a male corpse is kept for four days. The corpse is then removed to a distant burial site. They dig a deep hole and bury the corpse facing toward the sun. The hole is then filled with soil, and stones are spread over the ground. The people believe that there is a spirit of death, so sometimes they ask a shaman to pray for them so that they may escape its curse.

Hawaii

Hawaii, known as "the bridge over the Pacific Ocean," became the fiftieth state of the United States of America on March 12, 1959. The state prospers as an important link between East and West, and is, with its mild climate, one of the best resort locations in the world. There is a diverse multi-ethnic population of whites, Japanese, Chinese, Filipino, Korean and native Hawaiians on the major islands, which include Oahu, where the state capital, Honolulu, is located, Kauai, Molokai, Maui and Hawaii.

When someone dies, the death is reported to the proper government office and a death certificate is submitted. On each of the islands there are private mortuary companies, which are operated in the same way as their counterparts on the mainland. The funeral service is usually arranged by a mortuary. Rarely are funeral services held in a church chapel. Mortuaries have brochures with pictures of ministers from different religious groups so that the deceased's family may choose the one they prefer. In most cases, the mortuary will call the designated minister to officiate at the funeral, which is held in the evening at the mortuary. The mortuary chapel is designed to accomodate separate religious services. For instance, for a Buddhist funeral, an image of Amitabha Buddha is placed on the inner altar, which can be closed so that when a cross is placed in front of it, the room changes into a Christian chapel. By replacing the cross with the Star of David, the chapel can be used for Jewish funerals. The mortuary usually has a room in which the caskets are displayed, a crematory chamber, a columbarium, a dining hall, and a memorial park.

A corpse that is delivered to the mortuary is placed on a table in a room for treatment. Then one of the employees who is licensed in preservative techniques removes the blood from the body and injects a red antiseptic solution into the arteries, and if necessary the deceased's face and limbs are also adjusted. Then the body is prepared for viewing by the mourners. Even for Buddhists or Protestants who are cremated right after the funeral, families will often not hesitate to buy ornate coffins and will request for preservative treatment of the body.

Recently, the formality in funerals has declined in Hawaii, as in other places in the United States. The mourners dress rather casually for funerals–for example, some wear Aloha shirts. Also, the number of families who decline the offering of flowers from the mourners has been increasing.

When a funeral ends, a police escort usually leads the mourners to the place of burial, as a procession of cars follows the hearse. It used to be that each of the ethnic groups—the Japanese, Chinese and Caucasians—had separate cemeteries, but in the newly built memorial parks, there is no such segregation. More people buy, according to their taste or budget, a corner of a columbarium or a section of the cemetery that is for sale. On the island of Oahu, there are several cemeteries of this type. One of them is the Valley of the Temples Memorial Park and Mortuary. At the center of the park is a temple that is an exact replica of the Byodoin Temple at Uji in Kyoto, Japan. Mililani Memorial Park is also famous. In the past, the operation of the cemeteries and funerals was conducted only by churches and temples, but after World War II, funeral homes and the memorial park business took over the job. As a result, the financial foundation of religious groups was greatly affected. Churches and temples became only places for memorial services, regular memorial services, weddings and Sunday services.

The native Hawaiians have their own traditional customs that are based on the belief that the corpse is the source of defilement. Although relatives were allowed to stay in their home with the body, it was taboo for friends and neighbors to enter the house with the body or risk defilement, and because of their contact with the body, even the family was considered defiled. The family was not allowed to touch another person during this state of defilement. Only a priest could remove the defilement through a ceremony called *huikala*. However, after the ceremony, it was not uncommon that the lover of the deceased would unearth his or her bones, place them in a pillow, and sleep with them, even though the dead body was considered defiled. This custom seemed to be a sign that although the two lovers were separated by death, their love was still alive. Today, however, even the Hawaiians have adopted the Christian practice of burial and abandoned their old customs.

The image of death itself has changed. In the past, it was something that was sacred and feared. Today, however, it seems that, as the French sociologist Roger Caillois noted in his book *L'homme et le Sacre*, the denial of the sacred nature of death has already begun to be established in the minds of the people. Especially due to the phenomenon of urban sprawl, more people live in residential areas, and as a result, Americans who prefer efficiency and progressiveness now tend to do business without ever leaving their cars. For restaurants, movie theaters, banks, churches, and even funeral sites, the style of the drive-in or drive-through is now becoming common. For example, in a funeral site designed by a mortuary called Hershel Thorton in Atlanta, Georgia, the main building has huge glass windows on both sides, so that mourners can bid farewell to the deceased without leaving their cars. Perhaps one of these days, we will see people paying their final respects to the deceased by simply viewing the body by means of television.

Today it is rare for one to die at home tended to by family members and friends. Most of the elderly die alone in a hospital or a home for the aged. In many cases, their spirits are already dead before their bodies, and their worries and fears are not understood by anyone. After a while the elderly person meets death and the body is removed to a chamber in a mortuary. Only after the corpse's face is nicely made-up and preserved can the family and other mourners view the body.

In the United States, the miserable reality of death has come to be viewed as something to be avoided. No matter what the cause of death may have been, it is always approached in the same way. Whether the death was the result of age, disease or unnatural causes, it was regarded as an unfortunate accidental occurrence, and without considering the meaning of death, an attractive and pleasant funeral service is conducted. Then the deceased's body is interred in a memorial park, usually one with a nice view. This kind of "culture of immortality" may be the result of the combination of the concept of resurrection promulgated by the church and its priests and the funeral home, which as a business finds it advantageous to extol the merits of such a concept. We must realize, however, that no matter how much we would like to avoid the reality of death, we cannot escape it.

In an effort to oppose such a trend, movements to accept death as a reality emerged during the 1960s to the 1970s among thoughtful people. The new trends included the Jesus movement, which seemed to revive the Puritan spirit in the early history of pioneers in America, a theological argument about the "death of God," and an admiration for Asian religions. Thanatology became popular, and it was even adopted in high school and college textbooks.

The eminent American psychologist James Leuba conducted a survey in 1916, where he found that 60 percent of a thousand randomly selected American scientists did not believe in God, and he predicted that such disbelief would increase as education spread. In 1996, a similar survey was conducted by Edward J. Larson and Larry Witham; the result was that about 40 percent of American scientists still believe in a personal God and an afterlife. In both surveys, roughly 45 percent disbelieved and 15 percent were doubters (agnostic).

According to a commentary in the April 1997 issue of the scientific journal *Nature*:

In the intervening years religious belief has become more diverse. But, to the extent that both surveys are accurate readings, traditional Western theism has not lost its place among U.S. scientists, despite their intellectual preoccupation with material reality. But, it should not be forgotten that Leuba's finding of widespread disbelief among U.S. scientists was astounding in its day. And today, even more than in 1916, more scientists have no use for God or an afterlife.

Today, the average American still believes in heaven (according to the survey by Yankelovich Partners Inc. for *Time* and CNN on March 11-12, 1997, 81 percent of respondents believe in the existence of heaven).

Moreover, in recent years, death and funerals have become a pressing issue of increasing concern. Nonetheless, as Freud said, people are not willing to recognize their mortality, and they unconsciously wish for eternal life. Among the more individualistic and practical, some insist that such practices as formal funerals, viewing an artificially made-up corpse, and the use of tombstones are outdated and have no value in modern society. They consider these simply as relics of the past, something old-fashioned and meaningless. It is not hard to imagine that people will someday create their own type of homemade funerals without the help of churches and mortuaries. However, since death is always with us in this world, we must somehow find a way to deal with it.

In the United States, there are several memorials for those who have died fighting for the country. Arlington National Cemetery is the American national burial ground and patriotic shrine in Virginia, on the Potomac River directly opposite Washington D.C. It occupies an area of more than 500 acres and is generally semicircular in shape. The cemetery of the Friends of the Dead, an organization which takes care of the ashes of unknown soldiers, with their seemingly endless lines of plain stones is organized in the manner of the national cemeteries in the United States. The grave of former President John F. Kennedy with an eternal flame burning is situated in this cemetery.

By the end of World War II, several hundred temporary cemeteries had been established by the American Graves Registration Service of the United States Army. During the years 1947 to 1954, the Service, complying with the expressed wishes of the next of kin and by authority of law, repatriated the remains of some 172,000 soldiers. The remainder were given final interment in permanent military cemeteries on foreign soil, in private cemeteries overseas, and in national cemeteries in Honolulu, Sitka, Alaska and Puerto Rico. Fourteen sites in foreign countries were selected as permanent cemeteries in 1947 by the Secretary of the Army and the American Battle Monuments Commission. Their locations are as follows:

In Belgium, Ardennes (Neupre) and Henri-Chapple; in England, Cambridge; in France, Brittany (St. James), Epinal, Lorraine (St. Avold), St. Laurent-sur-Mer and Rhone Draguignan; in Italy, Florence and Nettuno; in Luxembourg, Luxembourg City; in Philippines, Makati; and in Tunisia, Carthage. The American Battle Monuments Commission was created by a congressional act in March 1923 to erect and maintain memorials in the United States and foreign countries where the U.S. Armed Forces have served since April 6, 1917, and to control the design and provide regulations for the erection of monument markers and memorials in foreign countries for other U.S. citizens and public or private organizations.

CHAPTER 8

South America

ARGENTINA

The Republic of Argentina is located on the southernmost tip of South America. People of Italian and Spanish descent make up the majority of the people. It is said that Argentina is the most Europeanized country in Central and South America. The national religion is Catholicism, and the influence of the church over politics, the economy and even society in general is significant.

When someone dies, the family obtains a doctor's medical certificate and reports the death to the Registro Civil. The family initiates the arrangements for the funeral, but the mortuary for the most part takes care of the details. The wake is held at the family home on the night of the death or the following night. The body is transported to the cemetery either by a flower car or hearse in the style of a procession, and then, after the funeral in the chapel, it is buried.

There is only one crematorium, at the Chakarita Cemetery in the northwestern part of Buenos Aires. However, cremation is seldom performed, and it is possible only when it is desired by the deceased's will or the family. Recently, more people are requesting cremation. Also there are more standardized cemeteries in which the height of the tombstones is restricted to 80 centimeters. In this cemetery, big mausoleum-style marble tombstones are erected for the whole family. There are even huge tombstones, which are the size of houses. Probably because about 10 percent of the population lives in the capital, there are 23 other cemeteries in Buenos Aires. Older cemeteries usually have sections divided according to race, religion and nationality.

The columbarium in the Chakarita Cemetery is unique and very interesting. The surface ground is flat, and plants and flowers are planted on it. The underground is made into two stories, and the place is sectioned by shelves, and on each of the doors, the name, number and the date of death are carved. Flower vases are attached to the doors.

Funerals for the rich or high-ranking officials are elaborate and grand. Memorial services are held on the fiftieth day and on the anniversary of the funeral every year. Usually the family goes to the graveyard with flowers before or after All Souls' Day. If they are remembering the death of a parent, they go to visit the graveyard on Father's Day or Mother's Day.

At the center of Buenos Aires is the Recoleta Cemetery where wealthy citizens and heroes who fought for freedom are buried. The magnificent mausoleums are eye-catching.

In some parts of the country, the old customs still remain. For example, a child's death should not be lamented. Children are supposed to become angels, but if people cry and shed tears, the tears wet the angel's wings and the child cannot fly up to heaven.

When someone dies among the traditional Tehuelche people living in the Patagonia region, the body is placed on a hilltop and a cairn of stones is built over it. Among the Maka Indians living in the Gran Chaco of Argentina, Bolivia and Paraguay, death is never attributed to natural causes. Funerary rites include stoning and drubbing the corpse in the belief that harm will then revert to the evil-doer who caused the person's demise.

When someone dies among the Mataco Indians, he or she is buried with a jug of water, because the deceased is supposed to initiate a long journey and must do so without disturbing or molesting the living. Among the Lengua Indians, when someone died, the person's property was also burned, so that it could accompany him or her to the afterworld.

BOLIVIA

The Republic of Bolivia is an inland country in South America. One-fourth of its land area is the high plateaus of the Andes Mountains. Forests and plains spread out in a wide area as the basin of the Amazon River. The population consists mainly of *mestizos*, a mixture of Spanish and native Indians, and the majority of the people are Catholic. The customs and manners, however, are blended with native religious beliefs, handed down from the days of the Incan civilization. Some people also worship various magical deities.

When someone dies in Bolivia, the death is reported to the Registro Civil with a doctor's medical certificate, but the body is handled for the most part by the mortuary. Generally, the funeral is held at the family home. After the body is buried, a memorial service is held in the church.

Among the Siriono, death is feared and so are the evil spirits connected with it, so that a complex traditional funerary ritual involves a series of preventive measures prior to expiring, mourning, placing the body on a mortuary platform, recovering the bones and readjusting after a death.

BRAZIL

The Federal Republic of Brazil is the largest country in South America. A large percentage of Brazil's population is white, but there are also over 600,000 Japanese immigrants as well as Brazilian Indians.

Brazil is a Roman Catholic country. In most places, even in the remote colonial areas, one can find images of Christ and the Virgin Mary. People light candles and pray every morning and evening. There are, however, also people who believe in the African deities and spirits, such as *Umbanda* and *Condomble*, and are afraid of the curses of Satan.

In Sao Paulo, there are 22 public cemeteries and 17 private cemeteries, the largest being the Villa Formoza, where one and a half million corpses are buried. At present about 100 bodies are cremated a month, and the number is increasing.

When a foreigner dies, the family or a friend reports the death to a local Registro de Obido and submits a doctor's medical certificate. At this time, two witnesses are required to bring the deceased's identification, a record of his possessions and the bereaved family's names. Then the site of burial and the time it takes to obtain a death certificate before the burial are reported. Foreigners can be cremated in the crematorium of Biralhina San Petro Cemetery in Sao Paulo.

Among the Japanese Brazilians, there are many followers of Buddhism or new religions. A Buddhist priest (sent from Japan to do missionary work) goes to pray at the death bed and the wake. The priest also conducts the funeral and goes to the cemetery to recite a *sutra* when the body is buried. The wake for a Buddhist is usually held at the family home with assistance from a private or public mortuary. The funeral is also usually held at the home, but occasionally it is held in the chapel of the hospital or the mortuary. In general, the body is buried within 24 to 36 hours after the death.

The Catholic funeral is relatively simple. The priest comes to the wake and funeral and prays, but he usually does not join the funeral procession or burial. Mourners who are not closely associated with the deceased also come to the procession. On the road when the hearse is passing, people stop and take off their hats. In the country, stores often close as a way to offer their condolences.

Requiem mass is held at the church seven days after the burial. The body is placed in concrete and then is kept on an underground shelf, and four to five years later, it is taken out and moved into a columbarium. On November 2, All Souls' Day, people go to the cemetery.

In the case of an accidental death, a doctor performs an autopsy in the presence of an inspector at the school of Legal Medicine. After that, the body is returned to the family, but if the family is overseas, the body must be embalmed first. And then such documents as a permit to transport the body, a certificate for embalming, and a death certificate issued by the Brazilian government office must be obtained. The coffin must be closed securely in the presence of an official from the consulate.

Cemeteries can be found everywhere, but most of them are privately operated. There are some smaller cemeteries in the rural areas that are operated by the community. The largest cemetery in Brazil is the San Juan Baptista Cemetery in the center of Rio de Janeiro. The cemetery is surrounded by mountains, is enclosed by a long wall, and has a total area of about 2,000 square meters. Mausoleum-type tombstones are not common here. The marble and granite pavement is lined with images of angels and Greek goddesses.

Among the Apalai Indians living on the border of Surinam, serious illness and death are believed to be the result of the actions of malevolent beings, shamans, spirits or supernatural beings. The Apalai traditionally buried their dead in the home or abandoned a shaman's corpse in the forest. The village had to be abandoned after many deaths occurred or upon the death of a chief or a shaman. Among the Apiaka living in the northern part of Mato Grosso, widows or widowers formerly remained lying in hammocks over the graves of their spouses. Their faces were painted black and their hair was cropped. However, these customs have recently diminished.

CHILE

The Republic of Chile stretches along the western coast of South America. The northern part of Chile is a desert, and the southern part is cold. Therefore, most of the country's population is concentrated in the capital of Santiago, which is located in the middle of the country. The Araucanian Indians, who are native to Chile, used to live throughout the country, but their numbers have gradually decreased. Today in the southern areas there are only about 200,000 Araucanians. The majority of the people today are *mestizo*, a mixture of Spanish and native people, who speak a localized form of Spanish, and are mostly Catholic. However, there is freedom of religion, so recently a number of people who are Protestant, Greek Orthodox, Jewish and Muslim have come to Chile from Europe.

When there is a death in Chile, the family must obtain a death certificate from a doctor or hospital and report to the Registro Civil. When there is an accidental or otherwise unnatural death on the outskirts of Santiago, the body is transported to the morgue. In the urban areas funeral arrangements are often taken care of by the mortuary, but the funeral is usually held at the home or the church of the bereaved family, and the mourners go to the cemetery to bury the body.

In Santiago, there is an old cemetery called Cemeterio General, where the corpses of the past presidents of Chile are buried in the mausoleums. Also there is a Jewish cemetery, which is rather secluded by a wall and is not open to the public. Recently privately run cemeteries such as Parque del Recuerdo and Cemeterio Pargue STGO have been established in the suburbs.

For cremation, the family must submit an application at the Office of Sanitation. Permission will be given the next day. In Santiago, there is a crematorium in the Cemeterio General on La Paz Avenue.

In the towns of Chile there are small shrines on the street corners with statues of the Virgin Mary. Flowers are generally placed as an offering at these shrines. In the cemeteries in the urban areas, European-style tombstones are commonly seen, but in the rural or remote areas simple crosses are much more common.

Easter Island is situated in the South Pacific Ocean. In the past, the deceased was placed on the Ahu platform and left to decompose. The bones were then buried in the Ahu vault. The funeral service involved a lavish feast with singing and dancing. Today, Roman Catholic practices have replaced the traditional ones, although the latter survived into the 20th century. The body is now displayed in the home, followed by the church rite and burial in a coffin in a public cemetery. A simple wooden cross is usually erected on top of the grave.

COLOMBIA

The Republic of Colombia is located at the northern end of South America. The Pacific Ocean is to the west and the Caribbean Sea to the north. It is connected to Central America by the isthmus of Panama. Columbia was originally the land of the Incas, and the natives centering around the Chipecha tribe inhabited the land when it was discovered by Alfonso de Ojeda, who accompanied Columbus on his third voyage in 1499. At that time Spain began to colonize Colombia. The people's movement to resist the Spanish rulers and to fight for independence became very active, and on August 7, 1819, they finally obtained independence after Simon Bolivar's troops defeated the Spanish in the Boyaka War. The majority of the people are a mixture of Spanish and native people, but there are also whites, blacks and native people. Freedom of religion is accepted, but most people are followers of Catholicism, which is considered the national religion.

When someone dies in the capital, Bogota, the death is reported to the Registro Civil. In most cases, the mortuary is asked to help the family to arrange the funeral. Usually the wake is held at the mortuary and the funeral is held the next day at the church. The body is then buried in the cemetery. Mourners customarily offer arranged flowers and wreathes. Close relatives and friends go to the cemetery with the family. There is no custom of cremation. Once the body is buried, it is impossible to open the grave and move the body for at least three to five years after the death.

Among the Cubeo living in the Amazon region, traditionally funeral services were associated with a complex ritual that has now been abandoned. Today, when a person dies he or she is buried near the center of the house, together with his or her belongings used in daily life. Many still believe that when one dies, the body disintegrates in the underworld and the spirit returns to its ancestral home.

ECUADOR

The Republic of Ecuador is located in the Andes mountains of South America. More than half of the population are *mestizo*, a mixture of Spanish and native Indian. There are other Indians, Spaniards and *mulattos*, who are of African and Caucasian ancestry.

In Article 141 of the Constitution, repromulgated in 1972, religious freedom is clearly mentioned. However, Catholicism dominates over all other religions and is treated as if it were the national religion.

When someone dies in the urban area, the mortuary usually takes care of the funeral arrangements for the family. However, in the remote area like Otavaro, which is 70 miles from the capital of Quito, the old traditions remain. When someone dies, the family buys a casket and cross for the grave from a dealer. If the deceased is a child, the coffin is white, whereas for an adult, the coffin is painted orange, deep red and other colors. The bereaved family gives the body a hot bath and then wraps it in a white cotton cloth. After the body is placed in the coffin, some food is placed at the head of the coffin, and flowers and young rosemary stems are placed at the foot of the coffin. On the day after the wake, the body is carried to the cemetery. The procession is accompanied by a musical band playing dirges.

The cemetery is divided by a high wall into a section for whites and another for blacks. There is a stand for the cross, and the coffin is placed near it and then opened. The mourners light candles; then the older women call out with emotion saying, "We are friends. I am glad we lived together by sharing our hardships and our joys." The sad songs harmonize with their sobbing voices. Then the coffin is closed and placed into the ground facing south. While a prayer is read, holy water is sprinkled over the coffin, which is then covered with dirt. A cross bearing the person's name, the date of birth and other information is placed on the mound. In front of the stand, boiled Irish potatoes and corn are offered. Finally, all of the mourners make a big circle and proceed around the graveyard. In many parts of the country, people generally go to the cemetery on All Souls' Day, November 2.

The Jivaro tribe, which inhabits the mountainous regions, were once known for headhunting. The Jivaro used to attack other tribes and kill them, and, as a symbol of their victory, they took their enemies' heads home with them. The heads were boiled and dehydrated. It was the custom to hang the heads around one's neck when there was a feast or festival. When the person who owned the heads died, the heads were buried with the deceased as his possessions.

However, the heads were occasionally sold by merchants in the city. This custom is now prohibited by law.

The Embera living in the northern part of Ecuador bury their dead in shaft tombs with a lateral room located under their dwellings. Bodies are wrapped in bark cloth or bamboo matting. At the wake, female relatives sing songs of lament that proclaim the deceased's virtues as well as the faults that caused his or her death. Nowadays, the corpses are buried in cemeteries.

FALKLAND ISLANDS

Located in the South Atlantic, there are two islands, East Falkland and West Falkland. There was the Falklands War between Argentina and Great Britain in 1982, and the islands are now governed by the British government. The majority of the people follow the Christian tradition.

FRENCH GUIANA

Sandwiched between Brazil and Surinam on the northeast coast of South America, French Guiana is the only remaining South American colony. The majority of the people are of mixed European-African descent, who follow the Roman Catholic tradition.

GUYANA

The Cooperative Republic of Guyana, known as "the land of water," is located on the Atlantic coast of the northern part of South America. The coastal area is a plain, but to the south there is a forest zone that occupies nearly three-quarters of the total land area. For many years, Guyana has accepted immigrants. Therefore, although it is in South America, half of the country's population is Indian. Next in number is the black population. The official language is English, but because there are many Indians, Hindi is widely used. Hinduism is second in popularity to Protestantism, so cremation is common.

The outskirts of Georgetown, the capital, is infamous for being the place where a mass suicide took place. In November 1978, led by Jim Jones, the founder of a new fanatical religion called "The People's Temple," 914 people took their lives here. A week after their deaths, the bodies were embalmed and sent to the Dover Air Force base by the United States Air Force, so that the families could identify the remains. Later, the bodies of Jim Jones and some unidentified followers were cremated.

Among the Akawaio Indians living along the Guyana-Venezuela border, sudden death is attributed to sorcery (*edodo*), whereas slow death reflects a curse of evil being. The body, in a hammock, is interred in a space between two sheets of tree bark, the head of the grave being faced toward the sunrise. The family leaves the house for three months, and a series of deaths of important people in a village may lead to the complete abandonment of a village.

Among the Waiwai living in the tropical forests on the border with Brazil, death is explained as soul loss caused by spirits, witchcraft, disease, or neglect of taboos. The personal belongings, and the house of the deceased are destroyed by his or her spouse to avoid contact with residues of the deceased's soul.

PARAGUAY

The Republic of Paraguay is a landlocked country in South America. It is divided into east and west by the Paraguay River, which flows through the center of the country. The eastern part of Paraguay is hilly land covered with forests; the western is a flat monotonous plain. The majority of the people are a mixture of Spanish and the native Guarani. There are also Europeans and Asians. The official language is Spanish. There are many Catholics, and the festival *Fiesta de San Blas* is very popular. At the festival, everyone, regardless of sex, age or religion, celebrates the resurrection of the saints.

If someone dies a natural death in Paraguay, the family reports the death to the Registro Civil and then, with a doctor's medical certificate and a burial permit, requests the mortuary to take care of all the funeral arrangements. In the rural areas a report is made only to a judge.

The family bathes the corpse and places it in the coffin. Candles and crosses are placed on the head of the coffin at the wake. The following morning, the body is carried to the church in a hearse and buried after the funeral. White flowers are preferred and people present many flower wreaths for the funeral. The family members wear black mourning clothes. Some people invite a priest to a chapel at the cemetery to hold the funeral there.

In Paraguay, where the disparity between rich and poor is great, the casket of a rich person is usually placed in a mausoleum, whereas most of the deceased are kept in an underground grave or niche. The bones are sometimes removed and placed in other graves after a period of about five years. The Spanish people prefer to be buried in graves that are above the ground, but the Russians, Germans and Jewish people prefer underground graves.

At one time, there was no custom of cremation in Paraguay, so when the family specifically requested it, the body was sent to Argentina. Recently however, in the public cemetery in Asuncion City, a crematorium has been built and cremation is becoming more popular. Now, mortuaries with modern American style facilities have been provided.

Among the Ache, living in the eastern part of Paraguay, a hut was traditionally built on the ground where the deceased was buried. If an important person died, small children were offered as sacrifices and placed in the same grave. Among the Toba, in the southeast, death was considered unnatural and the result of human or nonhuman actions that caused illness. The dead were thought to have belonged to the nonhuman realm and were thus feared. Customarily, the deceased is buried in a grave with all his or her belongings.

The destruction of personal property is meant to keep the dead away.

PERU

The Republic of Peru is located on the Pacific coast of central South America. Although Peru is located in the tropics, because of the Humboldt current, temperatures are moderate. In the Andes Mountains there is even an occasional snowfall. The population consists of a mixture of Spanish with the native Quechua whose ancestors developed the Incan civilization. The people speak Spanish and Quechua.

Peru, together with Mexico, was once the base for the Spanish colonization of South America and has a history of terrible religious suppression. Because the Catholic missionaries had a very important role in colonization, Peruvians who were not Christians were brought to court and tried as criminals. As a result, the majority of the native people, the descendants of those who were oppressed, are now Catholics. In the coastal areas, especially around the capital, Lima, the people live a Western or European style life. The Christians in Lima used to be buried in the underground graveyard of San Francisco Church. It is said that 600,000 to 700,000 bodies are buried there.

In the urban areas, a death is usually reported to the Registro Civil with a doctor's medical certificate, as is done in other countries. The mortuary takes care of the necessary arrangements for the family. The wake is held at the family home, from which they go to the cemetery. In normal cases, except in the case of a death resulting from an epidemic, a very simple funeral is held by the grave and the body is buried.

The largest cemetery in Lima is in District 10 in the northeastern part of the city and is divided into two sections: new and old. In the old section, there are graves of renowned people such as former presidents.

In the remote or rural areas, funerals are held according to the local traditions and customs. In the mountainous areas, the women who come to pay their last respects to the deceased wail very loudly and stay with the body throughout the night. Their derby hats are charms which protect them from disease and from possession by bad spirits, so they keep them on most of the time. The colors of the hats differ depending on the tribe. For example, the Agmara wear black hats and the Quechua wear white ones. They are very religious. There are animal decorations and crosses to ward off evil placed on the roofs of most of the houses in the city of Cuzco. The mourning period is usually more than a year. The Cholas still mourn the deaths of the Incas and wear black clothes even now.

Among the Amuesha living in the high central jungle of Peru, there was a simple ceremony connected with the burial. Nowadays, there is a wake with the burial the next day.

SURINAME

The Republic of Suriname is located on the Atlantic coast of South America between Guyana and French Guiana. It is a country with a multi-ethnic population, such as immigrant Indians, Indonesians, and the *mulattos*, who are a mixture of Surinameans and blacks. They speak Dutch. Because Suriname was once a Dutch colony, many immigrants were brought there as laborers from Indonesia, which was also a Dutch colony.

Hindus and Muslims coexist with Christians and Jews. In Suriname, each ethnic group keeps its own religious customs, which is unusual in South America. It is a very successful country in the production of bauxite, but there are also many fishermen and farmers.

When someone dies, the funeral is taken care of by the relatives except in the city of Paramaribo. Because it is hot all year round, the body must be buried quickly. As for the funeral, each ethnic group holds it according to their traditional customs. Except for the Catholic ones, graveyards are very simple. Native South American Indians live in the mountainous area close to the Brazilian border and continue to preserve their own funeral customs.

Among the Saramaca, living along the Suriname River, the dead play an active role in the lives of the living. A death calls for complex rituals that last about a year, culminating in the final passage of the deceased to the status of ancestor. These rites include divination with the coffin (to consult the sprit of the deceased) by carrying it on the heads of two men, feasts for the ancestors, all-night festive performances, and the telling of folktales.

URUGUAY

The Republic of Uruguay lies on the Atlantic coast between Argentina and Brazil. It is located on hilly lands at the mouth of the Plata River. Spanish, Italians and other Caucasians represent 90 percent of the population. Most are Catholic, but the church and state are completely separate, and religious freedom is guaranteed to the extent that Christmas is called "Family Day" and Easter is called "Tourist Week." Among the South American countries, Uruguay is the most secular.

When someones dies, the death is reported to the Registro Civil with a medical certificate from a doctor. Also, it is common practice for the family to ask the mortuary for its services and assistance. Then, the funeral director is requested to send to the home of the bereaved family all the necessary equipment and supplies for laying out the body, including the casket. When the dead lie in state, the funeral director supplies a large crucifix and candle stands as accessories. The wake is usually held at the family home, and the body is buried in a public cemetery. The graveyards in Uruguay are for the most part rented out. In the case of Catholics, a memorial mass is held at the church within a week after the burial.

The typical Uruguayan cemetery contains burial chapels owned by rich families. In some of these the caskets are grouped and not placed in crypts or niches. In other family chapels, the caskets are placed in wall niches. The bodies of the poor are not placed in monuments or niches above the ground, but are buried in the earth in wooden coffins. At the appointed time the procession leaves the home for the church with the mouners following the hearse in cars or in buses. The officiating priest or minister joins the procession and at the graveside reads the committal service.

It is likely that Uruguyans of German, Russian and Jewish descent will use earth burial, while those of Spanish and Slavic descent will bury their dead in niches and pantheons. The Italians are divided in their practice.

VENEZUELA

Venezuela, located on the northern coast of the South American continent, was once a poor agricultural country but since becoming an oil-producing country, it has transformed itself into a modern nation, the nucleus of which is Caracas, the capital. The name Venezuela refers to Venice in Italy. When the early immigrants first saw the land, they said, "This place is just like Venice, the land of water." This is said to be the origin of its name.

The majority of the people are a mixture of Spanish and black people or native Indians, and most are Catholic. The official language is Spanish.

In the inner part of Venezuela, there are native people who live in a very simple way. For example, when one dies among the Yanomami people, living in remote areas, the corpse is burned immediately after death. Afterward, a feast is held in which the remaining bones are ground into a power and mixed into a soup made of plantains, then eaten by close relatives. The Yanomami believe that this communal act symbolizes the continuation of their life and frees the soul of their beloved.

When someone dies in the urban areas, the family usually has a mortuary take care of all the business relating to the funeral for the family, from reporting the death and obtaining the medical certificate to the burial. When the family home is large, the funeral may be held there, but usually the chapel of the mortuary is used. The funeral must be held between 10 A.M. and 4 P.M., and the body must be buried within 24 hours after the confirmation of the death. If the death was caused by a contagious disease, the body is buried right away.

Venezuela is a Catholic country, so cremation is restricted by law. When a request is made concerning the removal of a body in a grave by a foreign family, it is possible to take it out of the country if more than five years have passed since the burial. When the body is transferred soon after death, it must be treated with resin within 72 hours after death before being transported.

Among the Panare, living along the Orinoco River, death occurs when the soul leaves the body. The body is buried, but it is believed that the soul becomes a dangerous spirit. During the funeral ceremony, it is invited to dance with the living for one last time and then dispatched back to the spirit world. Among the Pume, living in southwestern Venezuela, death is a sorrowful event, but also transcendent because it signifies that the spirit will join those of previously deceased relatives.

Epilogue

Nowadays, in various countries throughout the world, many different funeral customs have been inherited as the basic culture from the past. There is no predicting how they will be transformed from now on, but it is not difficult to assume that, following modern trends, they will develop in the direction of uniformity and coordination, in keeping with changes in the sociopolitical structure and progress within the information industry, both of which constitute and influence popular culture. The reason for this is that in the funeral customs prevalent in the industrialized and urban areas, regardless of the cultural or religious heritage they may retain, surprisingly common features and similarities can be seen. That is to say that in these areas, the employees of the professional and specialized public offices, the medical centers and the undertakers' offices have come to stand proxy for the bereaved families and are able to swiftly and efficiently attend to the formalities of the funeral. People constantly strive for a more pleasant life for themselves; families have become nuclear families and as a result of the weakening of their feeling of solidarity with the local community, they are alienating and isolating themselves from it. The traditional customs that have hitherto been practiced continue to be simplified, and sometimes under the pressure of commercialism they are becoming mere formalities. Such a tendency is particularly noticeable in highly modernized countries.

At the present time, little space is available for cemeteries, at least in some of the urban areas, and traditional cemeteries will likely continue to cope by adding wings to mausoleums or columbaria (a wall of niches for cremated remains) or by stacking the remains or by scattering the ashes at specified places which are legally permitted. People's options go far beyond that and are multiplying almost daily. Adventurous descendants can opt to have bits of their "cremains" encased in molten glass objects d'art or placed in flat glass"skipping stones."

Recently, the Houston-based Celestic Inc. launched human ashes into space at a cost of $4,800 per body. The ashes, secured in a sealed vial, accompanied a mission to send Spain's first satellite into orbit via Pegasus rocket launched over the Canary Islands. The ashes will remain in the earth's orbit for anywhere between 18 months to 10 years before gravitiy pulls them back into the atmosphere, where they will burn up like a shooting star. Moreover, one Japanese company wanted to use lunar land for burial plots, and once this was publicized many inquiries poured in from those who desire to do so.

A recent issue of *Newsweek* (March 31,1997, international edition) says that a space flight may offer a leg up on the journey to heaven, but many of us will always want at least some memorial to ourselves here on earth. Eleanor Weinel, Associate Professor of Architecture at the University of Oklahoma has studied cemeteries extensively and believes they will endure in some form. "What's important is a place for the memory," she says. "So maybe we'll find new ways of creating that without the idea of physical burial." Cyberspace is one candidate. The Internet is already rife with memorial Web pages, offering pictures, stories, poems–even music–in tribute to the departed.

In view of the deplorable situation regarding attitudes toward death and afterlife, a number of intellectuals in Europe and America, including Jeffrey Gorer of England, the author of *The Pornography of Death*, and Philip Aries of France, author of *Western Attitudes towards Death*, are concerned about the development of these attitudes in the future, since they feel that by ignoring death, people are ignoring life, and their books serve as a warning in this respect.

Nowadays, it seems that most people are concerned only with living as long as possible, and we often tend to spend our time idly. Nevertheless, no matter how long advances in medical science may prolong our lives, sooner or later death is sure to come. As an old poem states: "I thought death was a matter which only concerned others, but it's unbearable that I myself should die." But it is no use being flurried when we confront the moment of death. At such a time if we can think that we have lived such a life that we can peacefully smile at it, we may say we are happy. In connection with this, if we would be able to die surrounded by our loved ones, who lament our passing and who will cherish our memory for future generations, it may be said that there can be no greater favor for a human being. However, if we were to die with no one to comfort us on our death bed and without our understanding what we have lived for, then I wonder for what purpose we can die. I am convinced that it is never meaningless for us to reexamine our view of life and death and the way funeral customs should be by comparing them with those of other countries.

Thus far, the great religious traditions have given us meaning and significance to life by framing death within a larger picture of eternity and destiny through the idea of salvation. However, in recent years, these are being replaced by the increasingly secular nature of contemporary society. Ritual has come to be seen as something which can stand alone and apart from traditional religion, as a basic human and social behavior with the power to comfort and encourage individuals during difficult periods of life. Thus, gradually churches have been replaced by hospitals and funeral homes, theology by ecology, priests by doctors and counselors, the soul by the body, and heaven by earth. Seeing these tendencies, in *Death and Bereavement Across Cultures,* Pittu Laungani and Bill Young wrote:

Most Western societies have witnessed a decline in the status of established religion. At a psychological level this has resulted in diminishing beliefs in an afterlife, rebirth, and heaven and hell. This, along with the dissolution of the extended family and community networks, has meant that the beliefs and practices, as well as the institutional structures which would have supported the bereaved are now often unavailable or inadequate. In addition, the socio-political process of humanization and secularization shifted our attention away from the destiny of the deceased towards the fate of the bereft (pp. 220-221).

Regarding the incidents involving the Aum Shinrikyo Cult Religion, Japanese critic, Osamu Hashimoto wrote in his book, *I Am Not Afraid of Any Religion*: "religion is a kind of ideology which had once governed humankind before modern rationalism had been introduced. Therefore, what we have now in the name of religion is nothing but a legacy which is already dead or is dying. Afterlife is also a fiction which is made up by humankind." The Zen scholar D. T. Suzuki, on the contrary, said, "it would be nice to have a belief that an afterlife exists, because frail humans that we are, with this concept we could die at ease." Moreover, it is the fact that in the past millennium, our predecessors have lived with some kind of thought of life beyond death, and their next-of kin, relatives or friends have observed funerary rites and erected markers for the memory of their loved ones.

From the cloning of the sheep Dolly, it is clear that a new age of discovery is at hand. Cloning, the manipulating of a cell from an animal so that it grows into the exact duplicate of that animal, is a result of modern biotechnology. And the research has not stopped with animals in the field. In 1993, embryologists at George Washington University cloned human embryos. The February 1997 issue of *Nature,* that published the paper on "Dolly," added in its editorial: "human cloning would be possible within ten years." If realized, I believe that this would mean a commodification of human life and a morally unjustifiable intrusion against the dignity of our humanity. Until such a time should come, funeral rites and customs will perhaps continue to provide us with the opportunity to reflect upon ourselves and upon the nature of life itself. A medieval Japanese Haiku poet, Issa, composed the following heartfelt poem shortly after the death of his only daughter: *The World of dew is a world of dew, yet even so, yet even so...*

As this earth is becoming more and more congested with so many people, the last haven for survival may be the unspoiled Antarctica. However, even in this southernmost part of the world, we can already find a huge iron cross standing on the coast of Paradise Bay in the Antarctic peninsula, which was built in memory of those who died in Antarctic expeditions. Also, a memorial tablet in honor of those who died in the Arctic Ocean was erected on the Franz Josef Land in Russia, the northernmost part of the earth.

A few years ago, at the Bishop Museum in Honolulu, Hawaii, I noticed a grave in the courtyard. The epitaph read: *In Memory of Man (2,000,000 B.C. to A.D. 2030), who once dominated the Earth, destroyed it with his wastes, his poisons, and his own numbers.* Unfortunately, this grave was removed some time ago and is no longer there. Perhaps the last human being to escape from our polluted earth will have lived somewhere on a deserted Pacific island, like Robinson Crusoe, who might erect another epitaph: "*In memory of Humankind, once existed on this Earth, but, because of foolishness, extinct forever.*" I would like to dedicate this book as a record to those who witness what we have done on this earth. Until then, whether or not our footprints will remain on this earth, we should tread our path together.

Selected Bibliography

Aiken, Lewis R. *Dying, Death, and Bereavement*. Boston: Allyn and Bacon, 1985.

Albery, Nicholas, ed. *The Natural Death Handbook*. London: Natural Death Centre, 1993.

Aries, Philippe. *The Hour of Our Death*. Translated by Helen Weaver. New York: Alfred A. Knopf, 1981.

———. *Western Attitudes Towards Death*. Translated by Patricia M. Ranum. Balimore: Johns Hopkins University Press, 1974.

Baring, Andrew. *Family of Man*. London: Marshall Cavendish, 1976.

Becker, Carl B. *Breaking the Circle*. Carbondale and Edwardsville: Southern Illinois University Press, 1993.

Barret, David B., ed. *World Christian Encyclopedia*. Oxford: Oxford University Press, 1983.

Bechert, Heinz, ed. *The World of Buddhism*. London: Thames and Hudson, 1991.

Bendann, E. *Death Customs*. London: Dawson of Pall, 1969.

Block, Maurice, ed. *Death and Regeneration of Life*. Cambridge: Cambridge University Press, 1982.

Bowen, John R. *Muslims through Discourse*. Princeton, NJ: Princeton University Press, 1993.

Bowker, John. *The Meaning of Death*. Cambridge: Cambridge University Press, 1991.

———, ed. *The Oxford Dictionary of World Religions*. Oxford: Oxford University Press, 1997.

Brown, Alan, ed. *Festivals of World Religions*. London: Longman, 1986.

Brown, Stephen F., et al. *World Religions*. 8 volumes. New York: Facts on File, 1991.

Burenhult, Goran, ed., *Traditional People Today*. New York: HarperCollins Publishers, 1994.

Catedra, Maria. *This World, Other Worlds*. Chicago: The University of Chicago Press, 1992.

Chadwick, Henry and G. R. Evans. *Atlas of the Christian Church*. Oxford: Phaidon Press, 1990.

Chidester, David. *Religions of South Africa*. London: Routledge, 1992.

Comstock, W. Richard. *Religion and Man* (Japanese edition). New York: Harper & Row, 1972.

Curl, James S. *A Celebration of Death*. London: Comstable and Company, 1980.

Crystal, David, ed. *The Cambridge Factfinder*. Cambridge: Cambridge University Press, 1997.

Davidson, Art. *Endangered People*. New York: Sierra Club Books, 1993.

Davis, Douglas J. *Death, Ritual and Belief*. London: Cassell, 1997.

Davis, Russell. *The Law of Burial, Cremation and Exhumation*. London: Shaw and Sons, 1982.

Doi, Takuji, et al. *Summary on the Funeral Customs in Japan* (in Japanese). 5 volumes. Tokyo: Meicho Shuppan, 1979.

Eliade, Mircea, ed. *The Encyclopedia of Religion*. 16 volumes. New York: Macmillan, 1987. Also, its compendium, *World Religioms*, 1998.

Esposito, John L., ed. *The Oxford Encyclopedia of Modern Islamic World*. 4 volumes; Oxford: Oxford University Press, 1995.

Faruqi and Sopher, ed. *Historical Atlas of the Religions of the World*. New York: Macmillan, 1974.

Feifel, Herman. *New Meanings of Death*. New York: McGraw-Hill Inc., 1977.

Fisher, Mary Pat, *Living Religions*. London: I.B. Tauris Publishers, 1997.

Fujii, Masao, ed., *Encyclopedia of Funeral Rituals* (in Japanese). Tokyo: Kamakura Shinsho, 1980.

Georges, Eliane. *Voyage de la Mort*. Paris: Berger-Levraut, 1982.

Gorer, Geoffrey. *Death, Grief and Meaning in Contemporary Britain*. London: Creset Press, 1965.

Grainger, Roger. *The Social Symbolism of Grief and Mourning*. Jessica Kingsley: London and Philadelphia, 1998.

Grollman, Earl A. *Concerning Death*. Boston: Beacon Press, 1974.

Habenstein and Lamers. *Funeral Customs the World Over*. Milwaukee, WI: Bulfin Printers, Inc., 1974.

Haga, Noboru. *The History of Funeral Custom* (in Japanese). Tokyo: Yuzankaku, 1970.

Hamilton, Malcolm B. *The Socioloy of Religion*. London: Routledge, 1995.

Hara, Hiroko. *The Hare Indians* (in Japanese). Tokyo: Heibonsha, 1991.

Hardt, Dale. *Death*. Englewood Cliffs: Prentice-Hall, Inc., 1979.

Hinton, John. *Dying*. Harmondsworth: Penguin Books Ltd., 1967.

Holm, Jean and John Bowker, eds. *Rites of Passage*. London: Pinter Publishers, 1994.

Holy, Ladislav. *Religion and Custom in a Muslim Society*. Cambridge: Cambridge University Press, 1991.

Hood, Ralph W., et al. *The Psychology of Religion*. New York: The Guilford Press, 1996.

Huntington, Richard and Peter Metcalf. *Celebrations of Death*. Cambridge: Cambridge University Press, 1979.

Irion, Paul E. *The Funeral, Vestige or Value?* Nashville, TN: Parthenon Press, 1966.

Jankelevich, Vladimir. *La Mort*. Paris: Flammarion, 1966.

Jones, Constance. *R. I. P.* New York: Harper Collins Publishers, 1997.

Kastenbaum, Robert. *Encyclopedia of Death*. New York: Avon Books, 1989.

Kertzer, David. *Ritual, Politics, and Power*. New Haven: Yale University Press, 1988.

Kightly, Charles. *The Customs and Ceremonies of Britain*. London: Thames and Hudson, 1986.

King, Victor. *The Peoples of Borneo*. Oxford: Blackwell Publishers, 1993.

Kitagawa, Joseph, ed. *The Religious Traditions of Asia*. New York: Macmillan, 1987.

Kligmann, Gail. *The Wedding of the Dead*. Berkeley: University of California Press, 1988.

Krist, Gustav. *Alone through the Forbidden Land*. Cambridge: Ian Faulkner, 1992.

Kuroiwa, Toru. *Affluent British* (in Japanese). Tokyo: Chuo Koronsha, 1984.

Levinson, David, ed. *The Encyclopedia of World Cultures*. 10 volumes. Boston: G. K. Hall, 1993.

Levinson, David. *Religion*. Santa Barbara: ABC-CLIO, 1996.

Lewis, James R. *Encyclopedia of Afterlife Belief and Phenomena*. Detroit: Gale Research, 1994.

MacGaffey, Wyatt. *Religion and Society in Central Africa*. Chicago: University of Chicago Press, 1986.

Matsunami, Kodo. *Funeral Customs in the World* (in Japanese). Tokyo: Shinchosha, 1991.

Mayer, Tony. *La Vie Anglaise*. Paris: Presses Universitaires de France, 1959.

Melton, Gordon. *The Dictionary of American Religions*. Detroit, MI: Gale Research Inc., 1987.

Miller, Sukie. *After Death*. Simon & Schuster: New York, 1997.

Minority Rights Group, ed. *World Directory of Minorities*. London: Longman Group UK Ltd., 1990.

Mori, Kenji. *The Sociology of Burial and Funeral Customs* (in Japanese). Tokyo: Kodansha, 1993.

Noss, David. *A Dictinary of World Religions*. New York: Macmillan College Publishing Co., 1994.

Iona Opie and others. *A Dictionary of Superstitions*. Oxford: Oxford University Press, 1992.

Obayashi, Hiroshi, ed. *Death and Afterlife*. New York: Praeger Publishers, 1992.

Parkes, Collin M. et. al. *Death and Bereavement across Cultures*. London: Routledge, 1997.

Parry, Jonathan. *Death in Baranas*. Cambridge: Cambridge University Press, 1994.

Polson and Marshall. *The Disposal of the Dead*. London: The English Universities Press, 1975.

Puckle, Bertram S. *Funeral Customs*. London: T. Werner Laurie Ltd., 1926.

Sabata, Toyoyuki. *The Culture of Cremation* (in Japanese). Tokyo: Shinchosha, 1990.

Sabatier, Robert. *Le Dictionnaire de la Mort*. Paris: Editions Albin Michel, 1967.

Saito, Tadashi. *The Study on the Funeral and Burial Customs in East Asia* (in Japanese). Tokyo: Daiichi Shobo, 1987.

Shneidman, Edwin S., ed. *Death: Current Perspectives*. Palo Alto, CA: Mayfield Publishing Co., 1984.

Rippen, Andres. *Muslims*. 2 volumes. London: Routledge, 1990.

Smith, Donald K. *Why Not Cremation*. Philadelphia, PA: Dorrance & Co., 1970.

Snelling, John. *The Buddhist Handbook*. London: Century Hutchinson, 1987.

Sutherland, Stewart, et al. *The World's Religions*. New York: Routledge, 1988.

Tamamuro, Taisei. *Funeral Buddhism* (in Japanese). Tokyo: Daihorinkaku, 1976.

Tanase, Joji. *Primitive Forms of the Idea of the Other World in Greater Oceania* (in Japanese). South-eastern Asia Study series 1. Kyoto: University of Kyoto, 1966.

Thomas, Louis-Vincent. *Rites de la Mort*. Paris: Fayard, 1985.

Van Gennep, Arnold. *The Rites of Passage*. Translated by Vizadom and Caffee. London: Routledge and Kegan Paul, 1965.

Vovelle, Michel. *La Mort et l'Occident de 1300 A nos jours*. Paris: Gallimard Traditions, 1981.

———. *L'heure du Grand Passage*. Paris: Decouvertes Gallimard Traditions, 1993.

Wakamatsu, Minoru, et al. *Ceremonies in Korea* (in Japanese). Tokyo: Korai Shorin, 1986.

Warner, W. Lloyd. *The Family of God*. New Haven: Yale University Press, 1961.

Watson, James et al. *Death Ritual in Late Imperial and Modern China*. Berkeley: University of California Press, 1988.

Weenolsen, Patricia. *The Art of Dying*. New York: Baror International Inc., 1996.

Wells, Kenneth E. *Thai Buddhism*. Bangkok: Surivahun Publishers, 1975.

Wilcox, Sandra Galdieri and Marilyn Sutton. *Understanding Death and Dying*. Sherman Oaks, CA: Alfred Publishing Co., 1981.

Wilkins, Robert. *The Fireside Book of Death*. London: A.M. Hearth and Company, Ltd., 1990.

Ziegler, Jean. *Les Vivants et les Morts*. Paris: Le Seuil, 1975.

Index of Country and Territory Names

About the Author

KODO MATSUNAMI is Professor of International Cultural Studies at Ueno Gakuen University of Japan. He is the Director of the University Library and Kinryuji Searchlight Center.

ISBN 0-313-30443-2

90000>

EAN

9 780313 304439

HARDCOVER BAR CODE